T0074734

UNDERSTANDING INTERACTIVE DIGITAL NARRATIVE

This remarkably clearly written and timely critical evaluation of core issues in the study and application of interactive digital narrative (IDN) untangles the range of theories and arguments that have developed around IDN over the past three decades.

Looking back over the past 30 years of theorizing around interactivity, storytelling, and the digital across the fields of game design/game studies, media studies, and narratology, as well as interactive documentary and other emerging forms, this text offers important and insightful correctives to common misunderstandings that pervade the field. This book also changes the perspective on IDN by introducing a comprehensive conceptual framework influenced by cybernetics and cognitive narratology, addressing limitations of perspectives originally developed for legacy media forms. Applying its framework, the book analyzes successful works and lays out concrete design advice, providing instructors, students, and practitioners with a more precise and specific understanding of IDN.

This will be essential reading for courses in interactive narrative, interactive storytelling, and game writing, as well as digital media more generally.

Hartmut Koenitz is an associate professor at Södertörn University in Stockholm, a visiting researcher at the University of Amsterdam, and a visiting research fellow at Trinity College Dublin. He has published over 60 scholarly publications including the co-edited volume *Interactive Digital Narrative: History, Theory and Practice* (Routledge 2015). Koenitz is the president of ARDIN, the Association for Research in Digital Interactive Narratives (https://ardin.online). He is also the creator of the Advanced Stories Authoring and Presentation System authoring tool (ASAPS), which has been used to create more than 150 works, and a visual artist whose works have been shown in Atlanta, Paris, Istanbul, Seoul, Copenhagen, and Porto.

UNDERSTANDING INTERACTIVE DIGITAL NARRATIVE

Immersive Expressions for a Complex Time

Hartmut Koenitz

Routledge
Taylor & Francis Group
LONDON AND NEW YORK

Designed cover image: Mirjam Palosaari Eladhari

First published 2023
by Routledge
4 Park Square, Milton Park, Abingdon, Oxon OX14 4RN

and by Routledge
605 Third Avenue, New York, NY 10158

Routledge is an imprint of the Taylor & Francis Group, an informa business

British Library Cataloguing-in-Publication Data
A catalogue record for this book is available from the British Library

Library of Congress Cataloging-in-Publication Data
Names: Koenitz, Hartmut, author.
Title: Understanding interactive digital narrative : immersive expressions for a complex time / Hartmut Koenitz.
Description: Abingdon, Oxon ; New York, NY : Routledge, 2023. |
Includes index. | Identifiers: LCCN 2022047695 (print) |
LCCN 2022047696 (ebook) | ISBN 9780367617592 (hardback) |
ISBN 9780367617585 (paperback) | ISBN 9781003106425 (ebook)
Subjects: LCSH: Narration (Rhetoric) | Digital storytelling. |
Interactive multimedia. | Storytelling in mass media.
Classification: LCC P96.N35 K64 2023 (print) | LCC P96.N35 (ebook) |
DDC 808.036–dc23/eng/20221213
LC record available at https://lccn.loc.gov/2022047695
LC ebook record available at https://lccn.loc.gov/2022047696

ISBN: 978-0-367-61759-2 (hbk)
ISBN: 978-0-367-61758-5 (pbk)
ISBN: 978-1-003-10642-5 (ebk)

DOI: 10.4324/9781003106425

Typeset in Bembo
by Newgen Publishing UK

CONTENTS

FIGURES

Every effort has been made to trace and contact copyright holders, but this has not been possible in every case. The publishers would be pleased to hear from any copyright holders not acknowledged here so that this may be amended at the earliest opportunity.

FOREWORD

As a university student I was fascinated by both narrative and computers, but for a long time I saw these two areas as separate. It was during the work on my masters' thesis that I first encountered the notion of 'interactive narrative' and I was hooked immediately. This is where the journey started that has led to this book. The work on Interactive Digital Narrative, as a researcher, teacher, and artist has been incredibly rewarding ever since. Through it, I have met many fascinating and inspiring colleagues and students, it has taken me to exciting new places, and it has empowered my own artistic expressions. In addition, the topic provides intriguing and ongoing intellectual challenges, opportunities for research, collaboration, and expressive works.

The story of this book reaches back almost a decade ago. It is a statement to not giving up and seeing the project through, in spite of initial rejections and difficult circumstances. I am saying this so that others know that it is possible to go on and deliver in the end, even if it takes a considerable amount of time. I wish my parents could have seen this book, but both died while I was writing it. My life has undergone many changes and I am no longer entirely the same as I was when I started this project – as it should be. During the past couple of years, the book took over my life in the sense that every bit of the scarce available free time went into it. This book has been written everywhere, many times in motion, on planes, busses, commuter trains, dictated in cars (Hey Siri…), in airport lounges, and in places ranging from Atlanta to Amsterdam, Berlin, Stockholm, Stuttgart, Tokyo, Seoul, Melbourne, New York City, Los Angeles, San Francisco, Riga, Tallinn, Gdańsk, Torino, Sardinia, Corsica, Reunion, Sicily, and many more. This means to say that traveling inspires me.

Colleagues are the other form of inspiration I thrive on. There are so many I need to thank for their help in making this book a reality. First of all, I want to thank Janet Murray for her unwavering support, encouragement, great discussions, and feedback. Without Janet none of it would have happened, both for me on a personal level, and for the academic field. Then, I want to thank my academic alter ego, sparring partner, and wonderful critic, Mirjam Eladhari, who cheered me on, inspired me and kept me on course over the past couple of years. There is nothing better to keep you on track than honest criticism by a competent colleague who wants you to succeed. Mirjam also provided the wonderful cover art. Equally, I want to thank Mads Haahr, who patiently provided a steady stream of comments and suggestions which have considerably improved the book. There are so many more people I need to thank: my fellow INDCOR (https://INDCOR.eu) scholars – and the COST association for granting the action – especially Jonathan Barbara, Mattia Bellini, Péter Makai, Frank Nack, and Feng Zhu for reading my chapters and providing insightful and constructive feedback. I also want to thank Agnes Bakk, Josh Fisher, Lissa Holloway-Attaway, Sandy Louchart, Kris Lund, Greta Olson, Maria Reyes, Rebecca Rouse, and Claudia Silva for many fruitful discussions. I learned much about evaluation from Christian Roth and much about teaching and design from Teun Dubbelman. And I learned about perspectives different from the global north from Evaristo Abreu, Murefu Barasa, Deglaucy Jorge Teixeira, Maria Reyes, and Claudia Silva, about feminist perspectives from Celia Pearce and queer perspectives from Rebecca Rouse. Roger Altizer, Lindsay Grace, Nick Montfort, Annakaisa Kultima, Scott Rettberg and Stella Wisdom were also great conversation partners. Finally, I would like to acknowledge my ever-patient and supportive collaborators at Routledge, Natalie Foster and Kelly O'Brien. There are many more I have not mentioned, for which I apologize. It takes a village to write a book. Now go on and read it!

Part 1

INTRODUCTION

Characteristics and challenges of interactive digital narrative[1]

What is interactive digital narrative?

Narrative has a central role in communication and knowledge transfer as well as individual and societal sense-making. Consequently, humans have used new communication technologies for narrative, applying their potential to expand the space of narrative expression. The digital medium provides such an opportunity by means of interactive digital narrative. What is interactive digital narrative? Most people, when asked, will not have an answer to this question. The purpose of this book is to change that situation and provide readers with an understanding of this novel means of narrative and its potential as a tool for communication and expression in the 21st century. This is also an opportune discussion at a time when 'immersive media' and the 'metaverse' have become buzzwords. We need to consider how to use these types of infrastructure in the best way possible, taking into account what we have learned from the use of digital platforms so far. Fundamentally, interactive digital narrative describes narrative expressions in the digital medium[2] that change due to input from an audience. I will refer to such works as IDN when I mean the overarching category and IDNs when I mean individual works. There are different forms of IDN and the type of input and the extent of the change can vary considerably among them. For example, in an interactive documentary, the audience might choose between different perspectives, while in a narrative-focused video game, the actions of the audience can determine both the course and the eventual outcome. An augmented reality IDN may invite its audience to explore a historical overlay to a real space and thus to learn more about past events, while a virtual reality (VR) experience can take us to spaces foreign to our normal reality. Journalistic IDN may enable us to explore vast amounts of data and see the effect of different perspectives, while artistic IDN installations can challenge the conventional understanding of a given topic. IDN is therefore a combination

DOI: 10.4324/9781003106425-1

of digital technology and narrative expression that can be used in different ways and support different multimodal (text, image, video, audio, haptic) manifestations, similar to the way the printing press enabled different forms such as the short story, novel and newspaper article. Conceptually, IDN is a cross-cutting perspective which provides a shared framing for expressive forms in the digital medium which combine narrative and interactivity.

Book overview

This book is divided into five parts. In part one, I will introduce the topic and discuss the potential of IDN, its history so far and the challenges for understanding IDN. Then I will discuss aspects necessary to enable further development, chiefly among them is the need for a specific conceptual framework and a specific approach to design. These topics will be extended upon in later parts. In part two, I address in more detail the considerable challenges IDN has been facing due to *narrative fundamentalism* and *narrative indifference*. To overcome these challenges, I introduce a specific theoretical framework in part three, the *system, process, and product (SPP) model*. In part four, I focus on IDN design, first by discussing challenges and common misconceptions and then by describing elements of IDN and by detailing the IDN design process. The final part considers current and future opportunities and provides an outlook on work necessary for the further development of IDN. This introduction will now continue with a discussion of the essential characteristics of IDN, namely interactivity, dynamic system, and the changed roles of audience and creator.

Characteristics of IDN

As interactivity is a foundational aspect of IDN, it is necessary to consider the term in more detail. Provisionally, we can define interactivity as the ability of computational artifacts to react to input and sustain an engagement over a non-trivial amount of time. However, engagement with any mediated experience results in cognitive activity and can thus be seen as a form of interactivity. When we read J.R.R. Tolkien's *The Lord of the Rings* (Tolkien, 2009), we imagine how the characters and the landscape look and we speculate about the characters' motivations and hidden agendas and how the narrative will continue. Narrative scholars have considered this form of interactivity since Louise M Rosenblatt's groundbreaking study *Literature as Exploration* (1938), who writes:

> The word exploration is designed to suggest primarily that the experience of literature, far from being for the reader a passive process of absorption, is a form of intense personal activity. The reader counts for at least as much as the book or poem itself; he responds to some of its aspects and not others; he finds it refreshing and stimulating, or barren and unrewarding.
>
> *Rosenblatt, 1938*

Rosenblatt's book precedes later work in the same vein from the 1960s onward, for example Roland Barthes' understanding of the "writerly" properties of literary texts (Barthes, 1975) – essentially how such works can be open to interpretation and multiple meanings – and his famous pronouncement of the "death of the author" (Barthes, 1967), alerting us to the important role of the audience when it comes to narrative comprehension and sense-making. Similarly, Umberto Eco described many 20th century literary texts and artworks as not having a central point of view and thus being open to interpretation in *Open Work* (1989, first published in 1962). In addition, reader-response theory (e.g., Iser, 1979) describes interactive aspects in the act of reading. Yet, this 'interactivity of speculation' cannot change the artifact and is thus "safe but impotent" (Aarseth, 1997). For better distinction, I will refer to this aspect as *interactivity 1*. In contrast, the interactivity of the digital medium is one of planning and execution, characterized by an engagement in which we consider our options, formulate plans, and eventually execute them. We make plans when we ponder which path to take (e.g., in an augmented reality experience), what perspective to choose (e.g., in an interactive documentary), what to take with us (e.g., in an adventure game we might pick a sword or a bucket), or which character to talk to (e.g., in a role-playing game). And if we can actually execute one of these plans and consequently see their effects on the artifact, we encounter the type of interactivity that distinguishes the digital medium from the static manifestations of most other mediated forms. I will refer to this type of interactivity as *interactivity 2*. While *interactivity 1* of interpretation and speculation is always present, with regard to IDN, the focus is on *interactivity 2* of planning and execution.

Dynamic systems, interactors, and system builders

The next question we need to ask is what *interactivity 2* means in terms of the IDN artifact. *Interactivity 2* is the result of a fundamental shift – from static object to *dynamic system*. Static narrative objects such as the novel or movie become dynamic only through interpretation by readers and viewers. In contrast, with IDN, audiences encounter a dynamic system they can influence and, in some instances, even change to a considerable degree; for example, by adding their own content for others to see. In that sense, IDN engenders a *double dynamic* (of both interpretation and impact on the system) in contrast to the single dynamic of static narrative objects. Two more key aspects follow from dynamic system and *interactivity 2* – changed roles for both audiences and creators. With IDN, audiences are no longer just readers or viewers, they take on the role of "interactors" (Murray, 1997) or participants, who make decisions and thus play an active part in the shaping of their own experience within the frame of possible actions afforded by the respective work. With *interactors*, there is no longer Coleridge's willing "suspension of disbelief" (Coleridge, 1894), but an "active creation of belief" as Murray has explained (Murray, 1997). Consequently, the role of creators also changes – IDN creators need to make room for the different role of interactor, for a more shared responsibility, where they no longer determine the final, fixed shape of the narrative object.

Instead, IDN creators produce a dynamic system with opportunities for decision-making and sometimes co-creation by interactors – they are no longer literary authors or film directors, they are *system builders*. This change is not only a pragmatic one, it also requires a change in perspective. IDN system builders need to adopt an attitude of 'I will sit back and watch with amazement what the interactor will do with my creation.' Especially for creators who are used to having full control in creating narrative objects, this change can be difficult.

In summary, *Interactivity 2* of planning and execution, the nature of the IDN artifact as a dynamic system, the audience as interactors and the creators of IDN as systems builders – these characteristics set IDN apart from earlier narrative forms.

Narrative in IDN

What remains unchanged however, is the focus on narrative. What is narrative and how can it be interactive? While I will tackle this question in depth in part three of this book, I want to start by providing an initial definition. I take narrative as a sequence of events purposefully put together in an artifact to be recognized by a "forgiving, flexible cognitive frame for constructing, communicating, and reconstructing mentally projected worlds" (Herman, 2002). This definition of narrative from David Herman's book *Story Logic* recognizes narrative as a function of our brain, and no longer of any particular artifact. This cognitive frame can be evoked by many different manifestations and is thus not tied to traditional literary, cinematic, or dramatic forms.

What about non-digital forms?

In this volume, I will concentrate on digital forms. Certainly, interactive narratives existed in non-digital forms for a long time. Call-and-response in oral storytelling has a history which most likely predates written accounts, and board games (which can have characteristics of interactive narrative) can be found among the remains of ancient civilizations. Military planning simulations like the Prussian army's 19th century wargames, interactive forms of theater and live-action role-playing games (LARP) are more recent variants. The challenge of understanding non-digital interactive forms in the same manner lies in the difference of the artifact. IDN works in their various forms provide us with a digital, procedural work for analysis, which is not available for other interactive manifestations. There are certainly ways to understand non-digital interactive forms from the perspective of performance studies, but to include them in a treatment of IDN carries too much risk of compromising the focus on specificity. This does not mean any disregard for such forms and although I think much can be learned from them, this discussion is beyond the scope of this book.

Conversely, I want to make clear that the focus on the digital does not mean the absence of analog elements. An augmented reality IDN necessarily includes the analog world around us and many 1980s text adventures included 'feelies' (e.g., the ones published by Infocom such as *Deadline* (Blank, 1982)) – printed maps and codes as well as figurines that enhanced the experience with embodied analog elements. The criteria for treating such works as IDN is the presence of a digital system.

A definition of IDN

Based on the characteristics of IDN I have described so far, I can now define interactive digital narrative as follows:

> Interactive digital narrative is a narrative expression in various forms, implemented as a multimodal computational system with optional analog elements and experienced through a participatory process in which interactors have a non-trivial influence on progress, perspective, content, and/or outcome.

The term 'expression' describes an artifact which carries meaning in such a way that it invites sense-making and further meaning-making by an audience. Here, I take 'meaning-making' as creation/encoding and 'sense-making' as reception/decoding[3]. 'Various forms' describe the fact that IDN can manifest in different current and future ways. Current forms include interactive documentaries, narrative-focused video games, extended reality works (AR/VR/MR), installation pieces, journalistic interactives, interactive films, and so on. In the foreseeable future, experiences driven by a brain-computer interface could become more common and additional forms of IDN are certain to emerge.

A focus on specificity

In this book, I will emphasize the specificity of IDN to better understand characteristics such as *interactivity 2*, the double dynamic, and the systemic nature of the artifact as well as the changed role of interactor and system builder. This volume therefore has a clear position in the discourse on a long-contested topic – the question of the ontological status of IDN, of *what* IDN actually is.

When it comes to the conceptual understanding of interactive digital forms, there is a fundamental dichotomy. On the one hand, there is what can be understood as the 'continuation school' (e.g., Jay Bolter, Richard Grusin, Astrid Ensslin, and Souvik Mukherjee), which takes digital interactive works including IDN as the continuation of earlier forms (Bolter & Grusin, 2000). Scholars in this camp apply and adapt existing analytical frameworks (Ensslin, 2014; Mukherjee, 2015). On the other hand, there is the 'specificity school' (e.g., Brenda Laurel, Celia Pearce, Pamela Jennings, and Janet Murray) – scholars that emphasize the opportunity for novel forms of expressions based on the material differences and specific characteristics of the digital computational medium. The latter group of scholars challenge and rethink established theoretical and practical approaches (Jennings,

1996; Laurel, 1986; Murray, 1997; Pearce, 1994). This book continues this line of thinking, taking as its basic premise that interactive digital narrative is a specific form of mediated expression. The focus on specificity means to leave adaptive and derivative perspectives behind and to no longer treat IDN as versions of something else. Interactive digital narratives are neither interactive forms of novels or films nor are they simply transmedial additions to a core conventional narrative. In addition, IDN works are also not simply video games with an added frame narrative for contextual or ornamental reasons. I will address theoretical questions and practical issues from this foundational perspective on specificity.

An expressive form for the 21st century

What makes IDN such an exciting means of expression is the connection it provides between narrative as a fundamental means of human communication and the opportunities provided by the digital interactive medium. However, IDN are much more than just a creative opportunity – it has the potential to express aspects of 21st century reality in all its complexity and multi-perspectivity in novel and convincing ways. To understand this opportunity, we need to first consider the context of our postmodern reality.

The crisis of representation in democracies

Jean-François Lyotard identified the "postmodern condition" (Lyotard, 1984) as a crisis. His analysis centered on the insight that traditional "grand narratives" of nation, church, professions, and so forth no longer capture the complexity of contemporary reality and the multiplicity of perspectives. This development is embedded in concepts such as *amalgam, dispositif,* and *heterotopia* – terms to describe multiplicity, indeterminacy, and the parallel existence of seemingly exclusive perspectives, for example official LGBTQ+ rights and politically or religiously motivated rejections of such rights.

While the postmodern perspective is a liberation from overbearing and outdated norms and perspectives, the absence of such norms can also be confusing as we lack the means to make the complex contemporary situation accessible and comprehensible. Lyotard has expressed this issue by calling postmodernity a "crisis of representation." (Lyotard, 1984)

We can see the rise of populism with its simplifying narratives as a reaction to this crisis – as a way to escape the complexity of reality and seek shelter in an unrealistic space, a negative, delusionary heterotopia. As this escapist refuge from reality is under constant threat from the actual world, there is considerable effort necessary to uphold it, including the creation of conspiracy theories and assumed enemies. The vicious and violent behavior from groups subscribing to such simplistic narratives come from this perspective, from the effort to uphold something that is un-real and incapable of representing actual reality.

IDN as representations of postmodern reality

Narrative has always played a major part in the representation of the world around us, either in the form of fictional treatments or as non-fiction reports. Indeed, narrative is so central to human communication and sense-making that the term "homo narrans" (the narrating human) has been proposed (Fisher, 1984; Ranke, 1967) to describe our species. Conversely, narrative is a crucial component for the creation of personal identities (Ricoeur, 1991) and a means to construct reality (Bruner, 1991) as well as cultural cohesion (Bruner, 2010). When we put these two aspects together – the centrality of narrative as a means to understand ourselves and the world around us, as well as the crisis of traditional narrative in representing the complex postmodern reality – then we see the need for novel types of narratives. Or, in the words of a report for the Wilson Center[4], "complexity requires new narratives" (Rejeski, Chaplin, & Olson, 2015). This is the significance of IDN as "new narrative forms" embodying a transformed "narrative function" (Ricœur, 1984) to represent postmodern reality and help us reflect, communicate, and understand its complexity. In this way, IDN can also contribute to the further development of democratic societies.

There is already a considerable amount of IDN works that serve as examples in this regard, and I will discuss them throughout the book, starting with an historical overview in the next section. Conversely, it is clear that there is still much more to try out and learn. This is what this book is about – to advance the knowledge about IDN and provide a foundation for further development.

A short history of interactive digital narrative

The history of IDN can be traced back six decades, since early interactive digital narratives can be found in the 1960s, for example Grime's 1961 story generator (Ryan, 2017), and Weizenbaum's famous artificial intelligence (AI) experiment *Eliza* (Weizenbaum, 1966). Starting in 1976[5], text adventure games (Crowther, 1976) became a dominant category for a number of years, before graphics on personal computers ushered in the era of graphical adventure games. In parallel, hypertext fiction works, starting in the late 1980s (e.g., *Afternoon, A Story* (Joyce, 1987)), explored the potential of a form where pieces of text (lexias) are connected through hyperlinks, a tradition that continues until today (cf. Rettberg, 2018). With the introduction of CD-ROM storage media as standard equipment, higher fidelity graphics in games became the norm, for example in the highly successful puzzle adventure game *Myst* (Cyan, 1993), shortly to be followed by full motion video games (FMV) (e.g., *The 7th Guest* (Trilobyte, 1993), *Phantasmagoria* (Sierra On-Line, 1995)), which combine graphics with varied live-action video content. These ambitious productions sometimes featured Hollywood stars and required considerable budgets as many versions of the narrative trajectory had to be shot in order to accommodate the audience's choices. High production costs were the Achilles' heel of FMV and they mostly disappeared in the second half of the 1990s with the advent of cheaper and more reactive 3D graphics epitomized by games like *Doom* (ID Software, 1993). It was during this period when the narrative-focused meta-genre of adventure games seemed in sharp decline, causing pundits in the trade press to wonder whether adventure games were dead. An overlooked masterpiece of narrative-focused games, *The Last Express* (Smoking Car Productions, 1997) can be seen as a victim of the circumstances of this period, but also because its production method – rotoscoping real-life video – was more costly than creating 3D graphics. However, narrative-focused video games were very much alive with 3D games increasingly incorporating narrative aspects in titles like *Half-Life* (Valve, 1998), *Bioshock* (2K Games, 2007), *Mass Effect* (Electronic Arts, 2007), *The Last of Us* (Naughty Dog, 2014), and many others. Telltale Games' considerable success with titles such as *The Walking Dead* (Telltale Games, 2012) and *The Wolf Among Us* (Telltale Games, 2013) brought narrative games even further into the limelight, while *Dear Esther* (The Chinese Room, 2008) and other first-person experience games (FPE) like *Gone Home* (The Fullbright Company, 2013) and *Firewatch* (Campo Santo, 2016) provided room for the exploration of trauma and other deeply meaningful events. Examples of IDN exploring novel narrative means include cross-session memory in *Save the Date* (Cornell, 2013), the relationship narrative expressed through interactivity in *Florence* (Mountains, 2018), or the deeply unsettling VR experience in *A Breathtaking Journey* (Kors, Ferri, Van der Spek, Ketel, & Schouten, 2016) concerned with the plight of refugees attempting to enter the European Union. These works can be described as a narrative avant-garde, as I have argued earlier (Koenitz, 2017). The use of AI functions to preserve the testimony of a holocaust survivor in the form of an installation piece that can reply to questions from an audience (Traum et al., 2015) is yet another example. Accordingly, there is a split in the practice of IDN design – bold experiments in the vein of the above examples and traditionalistic productions stuck in a mindset of cinematic representation, exemplified in the use of long cinematic cut-scenes in big-budget productions like *Unchartered 4: A Thief's End* (Naughty Dog, 2016) or *The Last of Us 2* (Naughty Dog, 2020).

Another variety of IDN, interactive film (Hales, 2015), can be traced back to *Kinoautomat*, a showpiece originally made for the Czechoslovakian pavilion at the 1967 Montréal world fair. Already, this early experiment revealed the particular challenges to this form. While video games were built on the platform of the digital computer which included input devices as a standard, the canonical platforms for film presentation, the cinema and increasingly the home TV set, lacked any form of input. Consequently, *Kinoautomat* included a custom cinema installation, with buttons for voting at every seat. The alternative, distribution of interactive films on personal computers, was initially hampered by low resolution and frame rate as well as high storage demands. Experiments with a backchannel for interaction on TV sets were fractured and only ever reached critical mass in select markets, most prominently the BBC's 'red button' system (Ursu et al., 2008). Interactive movie and TV works finally reached an international mass audience with the increasing availability of broadband internet. It is for this reason that streaming provider Netflix'

Bandersnatch (2019) is an important milestone, as it exposed large audiences to inter-active video for the first time (cf. Roth & Koenitz, 2019). Interactive documen-taries, sometimes called i-Docs (Aston, Gaudenzi, & Rose, 2017), have a tradition reaching back to the 1980s and Glorianna Davenport's experiments in representing issues connected to urban development in New Orleans (Davenport, 1987).

Challenges for understanding IDN

As the short historical overview shows, there is a rich variety of different types of IDN, spanning several decades. Yet, the understanding of these kinds of works is still underdeveloped. In order to improve this situation, it is necessary to first acknowledge what kind of obstacles are in the way of understanding IDN and what conceptual tensions exist. Most broadly, as I have described previously (Koenitz, 2021), there is a tension between continuity and specificity, between perspectives that frame IDN as a continuation of long-established analytical and professional practices and the ones that emphasize specific characteristics and the opportunities for novel narrative expressions.

In the following sections, I will describe various obstacles for understanding IDN – many originating with the continuity perspective – as challenges for research, practice, and future development. I will start with two general issues, the status of IDN as a challenge to conventional notions of narrative and the 'add-on' perspective toward interactivity.

IDN challenges normalized eurocentric notions of narrative

For many of us, the concept of IDN is difficult to understand when we first encounter it. One reason for this situation is the prevalence of fixed, static narrative forms we are surrounded by from a very early age, especially in westernized soci-eties. In this setting, non-interactive narrative forms are dominant and become normalized in the education system as well as in public discourse. Consequently, it is a considerable challenge to imagine narratives that differ from this 'norm' in important ways. Learning to understand IDN means to firstly overcome this deeply rooted, but limited comprehension of narrative as a Eurocentric, non-interactive, and literary form mostly created by white men. This is the reason why, when I give a talk about IDN, I start by explaining that a large variety of different kinds of narrative forms and structures exist in different cultural settings. What we may take as universally valid when it comes to narrative is in reality dependent on the dom-inant culture surrounding us. Even such seemingly essential aspects as the 'tension arc', the notion of 'climax,' and the need for conflict are Eurocentric constructs and many narrative forms exist worldwide that do not use these aspects. A concrete example is the Japanese form of Kishōtenketsu, a four-part structure (ki – intro-duction, shō – development, ten – twist, ketsu – conclusion) which substitutes a surprise element (the twist) for conflict-based, tension build-up (see Koenitz, Di Pastena, Jansen, de Lint, & Moss, 2018 for some additional examples debunking the myth of universal narrative models). I will discuss this aspect and its effects on understanding IDN in more detail in part two of this book under the heading "Narrative Fundamentalism."

For now, it is important to realize that our conventional notion of narrative – of what it is and what it can do – is limited due to the influence of the dominant culture surrounding us, along with the associated educational system. Understanding IDN starts by overcoming the limitations of conventional and normalized perspectives in order to gain an extended comprehension of narrative. To reach this goal we need to re-evaluate and often unlearn widely held notions and particular conceptions of narrative, an effort which is worthwhile for gaining access to the expressive potential of interactive forms of narration in the digital medium. This is the journey on which this book takes its readers.

Interactivity is not an 'add-on feature'

The next important step in understanding IDN is in overcoming what I call 'add-on' perspectives. This particular difficulty originates partly from the term 'interactive digital narrative' itself, as the compound connecting interactivity and narrative can lead to a misunderstanding that takes interactivity as an 'add-on feature' for conventional narrative projects – a practice I call *interactivization*. Yet, interactivity is not an add-on feature, it is a fundamental aspect that needs to be considered from the start of a project and not as an afterthought – as an opportunity to re-purpose existing material. Equally, IDN works are also not simply video games with an added narrative, even though, unfortunately, many examples of narrative as an add-on feature to games exist. Here, we see the other side of this particular tension field: *narrativization* is how we can understand the practice of adding narrative elements to games for purely ornamental or contextual reasons. Even in recent years, ads in professional internet forums can be found in which game writers are sought for the practice of adding a narrative layer as the final finishing touch to an otherwise complete game. This practice is not what IDN is about either. Interactivization and narrativization projects more often than not result in disappointing works with a negative impact on the reputation of IDN. Most importantly, these 'add-on practices' fail to make full use of the expressive potential of IDN. If we want to properly understand the characteristics and potential of IDN, we need to consider interactive digital narrative as its own specific expression and associated practice with unique characteristics and opportunities. These aspects need to be at the core of IDN design and analysis.

This also means that there needs to be a conscious choice for IDN, backed by well-considered reasons in order to create meaningful and convincing works. This volume provides many arguments for IDN, but it is also clear on limitations. Embracing IDN does not mean to lose sight of the more conventional forms of narration, but to enhance our palette of narrative expressions. To help make the decision for or against IDN in a concrete project, I will provide a questionnaire in the design part of this book to serve as a starting point.

Challenges for IDN in research and higher education

Despite more than three decades of research (taking Marie Anne Buckles' (1985) PhD thesis as a starting point), several overarching issues persist in the scholarly realm, which I have discussed previously in a paper with Mirjam Eladhari, as "Challenges for IDN Research and Education" (Koenitz & Eladhari, 2019). We identified five major challenges, which we connected to specific metaphors. First, we described the inability to progress as long as specific frameworks are missing and consequently the same discussions are repeated about the nature and status of IDN in foreign contexts (as literature or games, or in a transmedial context). We likened this situation to the endless loop of the movie *Groundhog Day* in which Bill Murray has to repeat the same day again and again until he transforms into a better version of himself. The "Babylonian Confusion" describes the lack of a shared vocabulary in the field. This issue originates with the interdisciplinary nature of IDN research and practice, since a range of very different fields and disciplines – from computer sciences to media/communication studies and humanities-based approaches – are involved in the study and production of IDN, each using different conceptual models and vocabulary, rooted in a particular history. Conversely, the same IDN artifact and its various aspects might be described quite differently from each of these vantage points. It is therefore a considerable challenge to avoid misunderstandings, identify common ground, and enable a productive cross-disciplinary dialogue.

Other essential issues are the "amnesia" of the missing institutional memory of the field, the absence of established benchmarks ("No Yardstick"), and the over-production of uncoordinated and quickly abandoned tools ("Sisyphonian[6] Tool Production"). In the next sections, I will describe several theoretical and practical challenges in more detail.

The limitations of understanding IDN as 'texts'

A specific perspective on interactive digital narrative runs counter to one of the most potent paradigms in the humanities – the conviction that narrative transcends different media and can be analyzed as 'text' (in the semiotic meaning of the word as an assemblage of signs) independently of its actual mediated form. According to this school of thought – building on work by Saussure (1959) and connected to influential scholars such as Barthes (1975; 1977) and Derrida (1976) – the framework of writing and reading as well as the method of 'textual analysis' always applies, regardless how much the analyzed phenomenon diverges from the original literary and other print-based manifestations we might commonly associate with the notion of text. Through the influence of poststructuralism and its rejection of stable meanings, "text" has essentially become to mean any kind of mediated expression in a specific cultural context, even though Barthes originally used the term (in contrast to "work") only for manifestations which were particularly open to interpretation as he did not think that all kinds of manifestations or even all kinds of literary texts were open to interpretation (Barthes, 1986). This development has enabled the use of textual analysis for almost any meditated phenomena; for example, clothing can then be seen as a 'text'. Yet, in this process, the notion of 'text' has lost categorial precision. Consequently, taking IDN artifacts as 'texts' means to work on a level of abstraction that obscures the specific qualities of this expression.

Conversely, the paradigm of text as a semiotic category of analysis takes all creation of mediated artifacts as *writing* and all consumption of such works as *reading*. This means there is a principled issue when creation is system building and consumption is no longer just *interactivity 1* of interpretation and speculation, but also *interactivity 2* of planning and execution. This question is one of granularity and precision. Certainly, if we take 'text' as an abstract concept – as 'meaning carried by signs' – almost anything can be seen as a text. Yet, the problem arises when we want to understand how the creation, gestalt of the artifact and experience of an IDN differ from that of a book or movie. When we take both experiences as reading, we either fail to see the differences between *interactivity 1* and *2*, or, if we detect a difference but do not have an appropriate category, we extend the meaning of 'reading' to a point where it becomes vague and loses analytical precision. The same is true for writing. If we take *writing* to also mean *system building*, we cannot understand the specific opportunities and challenges of creating interactive digital experiences, such as IDN.

In 1997, Espen Aarseth introduced the notion of "cybertext" (Aarseth, 1997) – a compound of cybernetics and text – in order to describe novel phenomena not fully covered by traditional notions of media artifacts. Yet, this move does not heal the underlying issue of media agnosticism, which becomes manifest when Aarseth extends the notion of "cybertextual machines" to paper-based literary experiments that lack essential qualities of cybernetic systems, especially a feedback loop. The media-agnostic perspective inherent in the concept of "text" results in what Liv Hausken has rightfully branded as "media blindness" (Hausken, 2004), expanding on N. Kathrine Hayles' earlier call (Hayles, 2002) for analytical perspectives that recognize the importance of the respective mediated layer of representation.

The restrictive lens of literature

In 1991, Jay Bolter positioned hypertext fiction as a way to overcome limitations of the printed book and thus – maybe unwittingly – defined this variety of IDN in relation to print literature and not on its own merits:

> [...] the printed book as an ideal has been challenged by poststructuralist and postmodern theorists for decades, and now the computer provides a medium in which that theoretical challenge can be realized in practice
>
> *Bolter, 1991*

Similarly, Robert Coover positioned hypertext fiction as the "end of books" over-coming "the tyranny of the [printed] line" (Coover, 1992).

There are considerable issues when IDN is framed as a form of literature and thereby frameworks created for studying literature are applied to non-literary artefacts. What can be gained from such a move is scholarly recognition in fields such as literature studies and the humanities, as well as access to established ana-lytical frameworks. However, we also inherit the limitations of a foreign framing and the conceptual baggage that comes with it – basic assumptions which do not apply to IDN, including that of a static artifact, of the role of the audience as readers restricted to *interactivity 1* of speculation, and of creators as authors. Certainly, we can identify a commonality here, since both print literature and IDN are narrative expressions, but otherwise the differences are significant – as I have already shown for interactivity, the nature of the artifact, and the roles of audiences and creators. The danger of a shared analytical framing is in misconstruing one of the involved phe-nomena as a variant of the other, and in ignoring the latter's specific characteristics. In other words, applying a literary framing to IDN is akin to saying that a movie is like the novel and therefore analytical frameworks for printed works will directly apply to film, essentially ignoring the characteristics of moving images, sound, and the absence of printed pages. In this regard, David Bordwell's thoughts on the pri-macy of language are significant.

> If language sets the agenda for all narrative, then we ought to expect all media to follow along. So in a film the analyst will look for equivalents of first-person point of view, or something analogous to the voice of a literary narrator. But if we think that language is on the same footing as other media, a vehicle for some but not all more fundamental narrative capacities, then we might not expect to find exact parallels between literary devices and filmic ones. Different media might activate distinct domains of storytelling. Perhaps, that is, filmic point of view might be quite different from literary point of view, and there may be no cinematic equivalent of a verbal narrator.
>
> *Bordwell 2007*

In addition, terms often lose their original categorial precision as a part of the adap-tation process. Aarseth alerts us to exactly that danger.

> Do theoretical concepts such as "story," "fiction," "character," "narration" or "rhetoric" remain meaningful when transposed to a new field, [or are they] blinding us to the empirical differences and effectively puncturing our chances of producing theoretical innovation?
>
> *Aarseth, 2012*

We need to be aware that instruments of inquiry are not neutral – they are created to detect and understand aspects of its original objects. When applied to analyze different objects, they will only allow us to see whichever characteristics are similar, but they will be unable to detect features that are outside of their original scope. The instrument used for the analysis determines the result, as we can learn from the example of the wave/particle dualism of light in physics. This scientific field debated the status of light for a considerable time – whether the phenomenon should be understood as a waveform or as composed of light particles. Many experiments were conducted to prove either hypothesis – yet the results confusingly seemed to verify both. Even more puzzling was the fact that careful investigations of these contradicting results were unable to find faults in the respective setups. Eventually, the scientific field realized the influence of the instrument of measurement in determining the result. Light can be variously detected as particles or waves depending on whether a given experiment uses an instrument to measure waves or particles. Similarly, outside of the natural sciences, feminist scholars and academics working on postcolonial studies have alerted us to the patriarchal and colonial biases underlying many analytical frameworks and the ways in which these affect and limit the results obtained by using them. Accordingly, applying a framework built for studying literature to non-literary artefacts will frame phenomena such as IDN as a form of literature and essentially detect their 'literariness' and the engagement with them as a form of reading, and will be limited in its ability to provide insights into what is novel and specific about these objects. A particular issue will be ontological categories originally meant to describe print literature which would need to be either extended or replaced to cover *interactivity 2*, interactors, and dynamic systems. A framing of IDN as literature is therefore problematic and acts as an obstacle toward a better understanding of IDN. I will expand on this perspective in part two of this book.

Narrative as an expendable function in video games

In video game studies, even the existence of IDN in the form of narrative-focused games was questioned when Jesper Juul started the so-called 'ludology vs. narratology debate' (which I will discuss in more detail in section two of this volume) by pronouncing games not to be a narrative medium (Juul, 1999). Additionally, Aarseth framed IDN (in the guise of "interactive narratives") in the academic context as a scheme by scholars in the humanities to take over game studies.

> Underlying the drive to reform games as "interactive narratives," as they are sometimes called, lies a complex web of motives, from economic ("games need narratives to become better products"), elitist and eschatological ("games are a base, low-cultural form; let's try to escape the humble origins and achieve 'literary' qualities"), to *academic colonialism ("computer games are narratives, we only need to redefine narratives in such a way that these new narrative forms are included")*. [my emphasis]
>
> *Aarseth, 2004*

Later, Juul (2005) described narrative as ornamental, as serving a function in providing context that is dispensable once a player has been thoroughly introduced to a given game. While these positions are from an early period of game studies, they had a profound impact that persists even today. Certainly, conceptualization of games have advanced considerably and the usage of narrative as an element is no longer contested, but the theoretical understanding of narrative in games stayed underdeveloped and non-interactive theoretical perspective originating in literary studies remained influential in both theory (Ip, 2011a; 2011b; Ensslin, 2014; Mukherjee, 2015; 2016) and practice. It is telling that many game developers consider 'cinematics' – non-interactive video 'cut scenes' – as the standard way to convey narrative in games.

Transmedia perspectives: the core outside of IDN

Transmedia perspectives are also not sufficient when it comes to the understanding of specific aspects of IDN, especially in the "franchise" (Phillips, 2012) variety (sometimes referred to 'west coast' transmedia[7]), which starts with the assumption of a 'core narrative' realized as conventional and non-interactive forms of narration. Consequently, such perspectives locate IDN works on the fringes, marking them as dependent and derivative to the core, original narrative object. Henri Jenkins' proposed narrative modes for IDN (Jenkins, 2004) are a concrete example of this problem, as he considers the role of IDN in terms of enhancing existing conventional narrative products like the *Star Wars* movies. Certainly, IDN can be used in the capacity Jenkins is describing, but if we want to understand IDN's specific characteristics and potential, we need to move beyond perspectives which are concerned with extensions to existing franchises.

These issues – the limitations of frameworks originating with literary, game-focused or transmedia perspectives – are the reason for theoretical innovation, for a specific perspective that takes interactive digital narrative as the core object in order to help us understand its characteristics, potential, and challenges. This is the topic of the third part of this book, where I will introduce a specific framework for IDN – the SPP model.

Making IDNs: the creative practice of IDN design

Another kind of challenge is in the creation of IDN, as this practice requires a particular and wide-ranging combination of knowledge and skill sets. These include a conceptual understanding of interactive digital narrative and a good grasp of the possibilities of digital technology – what we can understand as the craft of IDN design, an aspect I will focus on in part four of this book – as well as artistic sensibility. This list of prerequisites might seem daunting, but it is actually not that different overall to what is needed for a writing a book or producing a movie. In both of these latter cases, conceptual framings and production workflows have become so well established that we have almost forgotten how much effort and time it took to develop them in the first place. If we take Miguel de Cervantes' *Don Quixote* (1605) as the first European novel, then it took a century and a half of development after Johannes Gutenberg's intervention of the printing press with moveable type (the earlier Chinese printing presses did not have moveable type) for this form to be established. This means the technical aspects of turning handwritten manuscripts into printed books, of editing, typesetting, and usage of presses for production runs was already well understood. Equally, distribution networks had been set up to sell production runs of printed matter in different places. If we see the creation of books as comparatively low-tech today, it is because its technical aspects are so well understood and implemented that they appear to be frictionless. Yet, it took a long time to arrive at this stage and the latest largescale innovation push happened not that long ago in the form of the desktop publishing (DTP)-revolution of the 1980s that digitized printing and all but eliminated the profession of the typesetter.

In comparison, the development of film production starting in the late 19th century happened much faster on the backdrop of accelerated technical development. What we can learn from the establishment of film is that many puzzle pieces had to be in place for this medium to become successful, including the development of the cinema theater as a place for commercial distribution of moving images, continuous improvements in camera optics, lights, film stock, and studio technology, as well as the establishment of production workflows.

If we see IDN in this context, we are faced with a somewhat perplexing situation. As I have already mentioned, the practice of creating IDN can be traced back to the 1960s (cf. Ryan, 2017; Weizenbaum, 1966). The text adventure, as a more developed form, appeared in 1976 (Crowther, 1976). This means we are looking at six decades since the first experiments and well over four decades of continuous practice. At the same time, academic research into these expressive forms can be traced back more than 30 years. Consequently, we can expect to look at a developed field of practice and research. Yet, this is not the case and as recently as 2016 Rebecca Rouse likened the status of the field to that of early film, as an unsettled practice, a "media of attraction" (Rouse, 2016). Rouse's argument certainly has merit when we consider how quickly in contrast film outgrew the 'attraction status' and became both a widely recognized form and an established production workflow after only a couple of decades.

However, there is also an important difference between film and IDN in this regard, as the latter is a cross-cutting perspective applicable to different manifestations. Some variants of IDN, for example, forms of narrative-focused video games as well as interactive documentaries, can be seen as quite well established. In addition, the lack of full recognition of IDN as a field for research and practice has made it difficult to acknowledge and celebrate the considerable achievements in the form of award-winning narrative games, interactive documentaries, and many other variants. At the same time, the continuous development of digital technology will arguably make IDN a form that will have variants in the attraction stage for the foreseeable future, which means the professional practice will keep evolving concurrently.

The theory-practice divide

Another unfortunate reality of the creative practice of IDN (and other forms of narrative expressions for that matter) is the divide between theory and practice. There are exceptions, especially in communities concerned with hypertext and interactive fictions, yet overall, a considerable gap exists. One reason for this situation is the ongoing alienation of narrative theory from practice. While narrative theory increasingly questioned the existence of identifiable structures and stable meanings through structuralism (e.g., by introducing the distinction between fabula and syuzhet, essentially the narrative as an imagined construct and its concrete realization for example as the novel) and post-structuralism (rejecting the notion of stable structures and binary pairs for descriptions as well as emphasizing the need for deconstruction), many narrative practitioners searched for clear and universal guidelines. There are many good reasons for the developments on the academic side as scholars became aware of the limitations inherent in seemingly stable structures and meanings. Yet, when academics abandoned these apparent 'ground truths' of understanding narrative, they also lost a means to communicate with practitioners. Scholars so far have been unable to come up with a new pragmatic paradigm directly applicable in the practice of journalists, scriptwriters or game designers. From the outside, what can be observed is that concepts deemed problematic and outdated in the scholarly realm like the 'three act structure' or the 'hero's journey' are still the backbone of professional training and practice worldwide – I will discuss these issues in more detail in part two of the book. It is high time to engage this chasm and develop approaches that bring practice and scholarly understanding more in line with each other. I have written this volume as a contribution toward this goal, based on my own experiences as a scholar and practitioner. In my work, I see the combination of practice and theory as essential and therefore I have implemented the first version of my theoretical framework in the authoring tool ASAPS (Koenitz & Chen, 2012), which has been used for more than 150 IDN projects.

Fragmentation

Fragmentation is another issue that particularly applies to the practice of creating IDN. Here, the demarcation lines are defined by particular output: video games, interactive documentaries, artistic installation pieces, journalistic interactives, VR projects, and so forth. While academics have maintained some measure of dialogue across disciplinary boundaries, the same cannot be said for the professional sphere. For example, the creators of interactive documentaries rarely, if ever, draw any connection to interactive fiction projects or narrative-focused video games[8] and the two groups, segregated for all intents and purposes, meet in documentary film festivals and games conferences, respectively. One consequence of this fragmentation is that approaches toward conceptualization and design of IDN are being perpetually reinvented instead of shared and further developed. There is a definite lack of a shared understanding, of an awareness of other forms of IDN. In addition, even within the same type of practice, there seems to be little to no memory of earlier attempts – another version of the amnesia in the field. This ahistorical disposition is, for example, visible in contemporary approaches towards virtual reality (VR) which discuss this technology as a novelty and thus ignore the knowledge gathered in the previous wave of VR in the 1990s (e.g., Mine, 2003). The cross-cutting framing of IDN is an opportunity to break open these silos and connect the different strands of interactive digital narratives.

Strategies to overcome the challenges for IDN

IDN has come a long way since the 1960s. Yet, much more should be done to further develop the field. Concretely, we can start by addressing the five major challenges of the endless circle of *Groundhog Day* due the lack specific frameworks, the Babylonian confusion due to the lack of shared vocabulary, the 'amnesia' of the missing memory of the field, the absence of established benchmarks ('no yardstick') and the overproduction of authoring tools ('Sisyphean tool production').

This book mainly addresses the first issue of the need for specific frameworks. It also provides precise vocabulary as a contribution to addressing the second issue. Ultimately, the issue of vocabulary needs to be a communal effort and I am happy to report that such a project is underway in the form of a community-authored *Encyclopedia for Interactive Digital Narrative* organized by the members of the COST Action network INDCOR (https://indcor.eu) which I will co-edit with Mirjam Eladhari, Sandy Louchart, and Frank Nack, to be published by Routledge (for a description of the project see (Koenitz, Eladhari, Louchart, & Nack, 2020)). Equally, the remaining three issues require communal efforts, for which an academic discipline would provide the ideal framing.

The question of a discipline for IDN study and design

At this time, in 2022, there is no specific academic department focused on interactive narrative study and design at an institute of higher education. However, considerable progress has been made over the course of the past three decades (see (Koenitz, 2018)). Foundational approaches and specific terminology exist, developed in Murray's seminal work *Hamlet on the Holodeck* (Murray, 1997), but also in the earlier work of Brenda Laurel (Laurel, 1986; 1993), Celia Pearce (Pearce, 1994), and Pamela Jennings (Jennings, 1996). There is a flagship conference – International Conference for Interactive Digital Storytelling (ICIDS) – which is in its second decade, as well as a successful sister conference which ventures into novel territory (Zip-Scene, since 2019). A professional association exists since 2018 in the form of ARDIN, the Association for Research in Digital Interactive Narratives (https://ardin.online) and a number of scholars active in the field have reached tenure and full professor status. Their PhD students continue to drive research in a thriving area.

In the same context, I have also considered the status of the discipline by using criteria which have been established to understand the status of research fields such as robotics (McKerrow, 1986) and women's studies (Buker, 2003). Similar to women's studies, IDN study and design would be a multidiscipline attracting researchers and students from a variety of fields connected by a shared interest. A further result of this evaluation was the insight that IDN research and study is mostly missing full degree programs to be considered a discipline. The masters' program Digital and Interactive Storytelling Lab at the university of Westminster in the UK is a first example in this regard. Additional programs exist, including for game writing in the UK, Sweden, and the US as well as the minor in interactive narrative design at HKU Utrecht, which I helped to create and which now continues under the leadership of Christian Roth.

In terms of positioning within academic disciplines, IDN study and design would be a combination of computation, design, and humanities that would realize the promise of what digital humanities could be, connecting the critical and creative perspectives of the humanities with a deep understanding of the creative opportunities and limitations of computation. This perspective contrasts favorably with the unfortunately widespread practice of digital humanities as 'humanities methods + computation as an auxiliary service for data processing' with little regard for the potential or inner workings of computation.

I will consider additional aspects in regard to the development of the field in the final section of this book, including in the areas of education and criticism.

Specific terminology

The need for terminological precision is an important aspect I will emphasize throughout this book. To address it, I will introduce specific terms to be used throughout this volume. This does not mean that I deem other terminology necessarily deficient, nor that I am unaware of possible alterative choices. However, making such decisions explicit is a crucial step toward an improved discourse in theory and practice since many terms associated with the topic of IDN are vague and have multiple meanings depending on the context. As already mentioned, this is the "Babylonian confusion" I diagnosed together with Eladhari (Koenitz & Eladhari, 2019) as one of the particular challenges of the field. For example, *storytelling* can mean the activity of communicating a narrative between humans in general, but in the contexts of journalism and public relations it can also be interpreted as a specific manner, in the sense of adding 'human interest' aspects and emotions to an otherwise factual narrative, to make an article more appealing to a general audience. A similar use of the term exists in educational settings, where storytelling is understood as a particular way of conveying facts in an accessible manner. Additionally, storytelling might sometimes be used to describe only oral means of conveying narratives.

The main reason I usually avoid the term in my work[9] and why I instead use the term 'interactive digital narrative', or IDN in short, is that storytelling also implies a storyteller, which is a problematic proposition in an interactive context. As Marie Laure Ryan reminds us (2004), there is no narrator in the sense of classical narratology in video games and other forms of IDN, and no storyteller recounting past events in a fixed sequence to an audience of narratees. Instead, the audience as interactors shape (and in some instances co-create) the experience through their actions with the material provided by a narrative architect (Jenkins, 2004). Consequently, as Teun Dubbelman explains, the "classical definition of narrative as recounting (i.e., story-telling) becomes problematic or even inapplicable" (Dubbelman, 2016) to IDN.

What follows are short definitions of additional vocabulary. Throughout the book, I will introduce additional terms, especially in part three, which is concerned with the SPP framework. For now, the following terms are important.

> **Interactivity:** as already discussed earlier in this part, I consider 'interactivity 2', the ability to make plans and execute them as foundational for IDN. Yet, 'interactivity 1', active imagination and speculation is always present. In the remainder of the book, I use interactivity to mean 'interactivity 2'.
>
> **Interactor:** to describe the function of audience members as participants, I adopt Murray's (Murray, 1997) usage of 'interactor'. 'User' and 'player' are closely related terms, but they do not convey the active participatory nature in the same way. 'Player' is also strongly connected to games and therefore does not fit non-game forms of IDN.
>
> **Creator:** to emphasize a distinction with literary authors, I use creator, system builder, and narrative architect (Jenkins, 2004) in this volume.
>
> **Multi-linear:** IDN are often described as 'non-linear'. The word means "Not denoting, involving, or arranged in a straight line." Or "not linear, sequential, or straightforward; random."[10]. In the context of narrative, the term is used to describe works in which the parts are arranged not in a direct temporal, spatial, or causal order. For example, we might see the heroine waking up and watch them going to work, but what they had for breakfast is presented only later. What complicates the notion is the fact that – baring the invention of a time machine – all our experiences, including of so-called 'non-linear narratives' are time-forward and hence linear. Therefore, the term 'non-linear' creates a disconnect between presentation and experience – we can have a non-linear representation, but no non-linear experience. Or, in other words, we experience a non-linear representation in a linear manner. The addition of interactivity does not fundamentally change this aspect, as the decisions and consequences are still experienced in a time-forward, linear fashion and result in a linear narrative. In order to avoid this confusion, Murray refers in her writing to IDN as "multi-linear" (Murray, 1997) and I will continue in this vein.
>
> **IDN type:** this describes the main purpose of an IDN work as explained in part four. An IDN type can be realized in different forms, for example, an IDN type of *parallel perspectives* as an IDN form of *narrative-focused video game* or an *interactive documentary*.

Summary

In the introduction, I discussed what interactive digital narrative is and described its specific characteristics in terms of 'interactivity 2' of planning and execution, enabled by *dynamic systems* where audiences are *interactors* and creators are *system builders*. I positioned IDN as a narrative expression for the 21st century and provided a short history of its development. This part of the book continued with an outline of challenges for IDN in terms of general conceptualization, research, and creation and ended with an overview of strategies to overcome them – aspects that will be expanded in later parts of this volume.

Notes

1 Some of the material in this part has been previously published as "Continuity or Specificity: Interactive Digital Narrative and Other Interactive Forms as Continuation or new Beginning" in Mendes da Silva, B. & Neves Carrega, J. M. (Eds.) The Forking Paths – Interactive Film and Media, Faro, 2021, used with permission.

2 I take 'medium' to mean the technical basis, where for example print literature and comics are different forms facilitated by the medium of print.

3 There is no consensus about the differentiation between meaning-making and sense-making in the literature. For my understanding, I take Bruner's perspective of narrative as the activity of making sense of experiences and cognition (Bruner, 1991) as a starting point, and have also considered more recent contributions from several fields ((Bijlsma, Schaap, & de Bruijn, 2016; Floridi, 2018; Salvatore, 2019).

4 The Woodrow Wilson International Center for Scholars (short Wilson Center) is a US non-partisan think tank and research center concerned with public policy: www.wilsoncenter.org/

5 By some accounts in 1975.

6 More correct would have been "Sisyphean," an insight I thank Peter Makai for.

7 "Franchise"/'west coast' transmedia is the practice of extending central narratives such as the Star Wars movies with additional products such as novels and video games. In contrast, "native"/'east coast' transmedia refers to projects which are conceptualized as transmedial right from the beginning (Phillips, 2012).

8 Amsterdam-based production company submarine (https://submarinechannel.com) might be a notable exception.

9 An exception is Koenitz, 2016 where the editors insisted on the term 'interactive storytelling'.

10 Both definitions are according to Lexico.com, a collaboration between dictionary.com and Oxford University Press.

References

2K Games. (2007). BioShock. Novato, California, U.S.: 2K Games.

Aarseth, E. J. (1997). *Cybertext*. JHU Press.

Aarseth, E. J. (2004). Genre Trouble. In N. Wardrip-Fruin & P. Harrigan (Eds.), *First Person: New Media as Story, Performance, and Game*. Cambridge, MA: MIT Press. Retrieved from www. electronicbookreview.com/thread/firstperson/vigilant

Aarseth, E. J. (2012). A Narrative Theory of Games (pp. 1–5). Presented at the Foundations of Digital Games 2015. http://doi.org/978-1-4503-1333-9/12/05

Aston, J., Gaudenzi, S., & Rose, M. (2017). *I-Docs: The Evolving Practices of Interactive Documentary*. Columbia University Press.

Barthes, R. (1967). The Death of the Author. Aspen. Retrieved from www.ubu.com/aspen/aspen5and6/threeEssays.html#barthes

Barthes, R. (1975). *S/Z*. (R. Miller, Trans.). New York, NY: Hill and Wang.

Barthes, R. (1977). *Image, Music, Text*. New York, NY: Hill and Wang.

Barthes, R. (1986). From Work to Text. In *The Rustle of Language* (pp. 56–68). New York City: Hill and Wang.

Bijlsma, N., Schaap, H., & de Bruijn, E. (2016). Students' Meaning-Making and Sense-Making of Vocational Knowledge in Dutch Senior Secondary Vocational Education. *Journal of Vocational Education & Training*, 1–17. http://doi.org/10.1080/13636820.2016.1213763

Blank, M. (1982). Deadline. Cambridge, MA: Infocom.

Bolter, J. D. (1991). *Writing Space: The Computer, Hypertext, and the History of Writing*. Lawrence Erlbaum Associates.

Bolter, J. D., & Grusin, R. (2000). *Remediation: Understanding New Media*. Cambridge, MA: MIT Press.

Bordwell, D. (2007). *Poetics of Cinema*. New York: Routledge.

Bruner, J. (1991). The Narrative Construction of Reality. *Critical Inquiry*, 18(1), 1–21. http://doi.org/10.1086/448619

Bruner, J. (2010). Narrative, Culture, and Mind. In D. Schiffrin, A. De Fina, & A. Nylund (Eds.), *Telling Stories* (pp. 45–49). Washington, DC: Georgetown University Press.

Buckles, M. A. (1985). Interactive Fiction: The Computer Storygame "Adventure." University of California, San Diego. Retrieved from https://search.proquest.com/docview/303372594/

Buker, E. (2003). Is Women's Studies a Disciplinary or an Interdisciplinary Field of Inquiry? *NWSA Journal*, 15(1), 73–93. http://doi.org/10.2307/4316945

Campo Santo. (2016). Firewatch. Portland, OR: Panic.

Coleridge, S. T. (1894). *Biographia Literaria; Or, Biographical Sketches of My Literary Life and Opinions; and Two Lay Sermons*. London: George Bell and Sons.

Coover, R. (1992). The End of Books. *New York Times Literary Review*. NYC, NY: New York Times Book Review. Retrieved from www.nytimes.com/books/98/09/27/specials/coover-end.html

Cornell, C. (2013). Save the Date. Paper Dino Software.

Crowther, W. (1976). Adventure [Video game]. Self-published.

Cyan. (1993). Myst. Eurgene, Oregon: Broderbund.

Davenport, G. (1987). New Orleans in Transition, 1983–1986: The Interactive Delivery of a Cinematic Case Study. Presented at the International Congress for Design Planning and Theory, Education Group Conference, Boston, MA.

de Saussure, F. (1959). *Course in General Linguistics*. (W. Baskin, Trans.). New York City: The Philosophical Society.

Derrida, J. (1976). *Of Grammatology*. Baltimore: Johns Hopkins University Press.

Dubbelman, T. (2016). Narrative Game Mechanics. In F. Nack & A. S. Gordon (Eds.), *Interactive Storytelling 9th International Conference on Interactive Digital Storytelling, ICIDS 2016* (pp. 39–50). Springer International Publishing. http://doi.org/10.1007/978-3-319-48279-8_4

Eco, U. (1989). The Open Work. (A. Cancogni, Trans.). Cambridge, MA: Harvard University Press.

Electronic Arts. (2007). Mass Effect [Video game]. Edmonton: Electronic Arts.

Ensslin, A. (2014). Literary Gaming, 1–217.

Floridi, L. (2018). Semantic Capital: Its Nature, Value, and Curation. *Philosophy & Technology*, 31(4), 481–497.

Fisher, W. R. (1984). Narration as a Human Communication Paradigm: The Case of Public Moral Argument. *Communications Monographs*, 51(1), 1–22.

Hales, C. (2015). Interactive Cinema in the Digital Age. In H. Koenitz, G. Ferri, M. Haahr, & T. I. Sezen (Eds.), *Interactive Digital Narrative* (pp. 36–50). New York: Routledge.

Hausken, L. (2004). Coda. In *Narrative Across Media* (pp. 391–403). University of Nebraska Press.

Hayles, N. K. (2002). *Writing Machines*. Cambridge, MA: MIT Press.

Herman, D. (2002). *Story Logic*. Lincoln, NE: University of Nebraska Press.

ID Software. (1993). Doom [Video game]. ID Software.

Ip, B. (2011a). Narrative Structures in Computer and Video Games: Part 1: Context, Definitions, and Initial Findings. *Games and Culture*, 6(2), 103–134. http://doi.org/10.1177/1555412010364982

Ip, B. (2011b). Narrative Structures in Computer and Video Games: Part 2: Emotions, Structures, and Archetypes. *Games and Culture*, 6(3), 203–244. http://doi.org/10.1177/1555412010364984

Iser, W. (1979). *The Act of Reading*. The Johns Hopkins University Press.

Jenkins, H. (2004). Game Design as Narrative Architecture. In N. Wardrip-Fruin & P. Harrigan (Eds.), *First Person: New Media as Story, Performance, and Game*. Cambridge, MA: MIT Press. Retrieved from www.electronicbookreview.com/thread/firstperson/lazzi-fair

Jennings, P. (1996). Narrative Structures for New Media. *Leonardo*, 29(5), 345–350.

Joyce, M. (1987). Afternoon, A Story. Eastgate.

Juul, J. (1999). *A Clash between Game and Narrative*. Danish Literature.

Juul, J. (2005). *Half-Real*. Cambridge, MA: MIT Press.

Koenitz, H. (2016). Interactive Storytelling Paradigms and Representations: A Humanities-Based Perspective. In *Handbook of Digital Games and Entertainment Technologies* (pp. 1–15). Singapore: Springer Singapore.

Koenitz, H. (2017). Beyond "Walking Simulators" – Games as the Narrative Avant-Garde (pp. 1–3). Presented at the DIGRA 2017, Melbourne, AUS. Retrieved from http://digra2017.com/static/Extended%20Abstracts/149_DIGRA2017_Koenitz_Walking_Simulators.pdf

Koenitz, H. (2018). Thoughts on a Discipline for the Study of Interactive Digital Narratives. In R. Rouse, H. Koenitz, & M. Haahr (Eds.), *Interactive Storytelling: 11th International Conference for Interactive Digital Storytelling, ICIDS 2018* (pp. 36–49). Cham: The 3rd International Conference for Interactive Digital Storytelling. Retrieved from https://doi.org/10.1007/978-3-030-04028-4_3

Koenitz, H. (2021). Continuity or Specificity: Interactive Digital Narrative and Other Interactive Forms as Continuation or new Beginning. In B. M. da Silva & J. M. N. Carrega (Eds.), *The Forking Paths* (pp. 67–77).

Koenitz, H., & Chen, K. J. (2012). Genres, Structures and Strategies in Interactive Digital Narratives – Analyzing a Body of Works Created in ASAPS. In D. Oyarzun, F. Peinado, R. M. Young, A. Elizalde, & G. Méndez (Eds.), *Interactive Storytelling: 5th International Conference, ICIDS 2012, San Sebastián, Spain*, November 12–15, 2012. Proceedings (Vol. 7648, pp. 84–95). Berlin, Heidelberg: Springer. http://doi.org/10.1007/978-3-642-34851-8_8

Koenitz, H., Di Pastena, A., Jansen, D., de Lint, B., & Moss, A. (2018). The Myth of "Universal" Narrative Models. In R. Rouse, H. Koenitz, & M. Haahr (Eds.), *Interactive Storytelling: 11th International Conference for Interactive Digital Storytelling, ICIDS 2018* (pp. 107–120).

Cham: The 3rd International Conference for Interactive Digital Storytelling. Retrieved from https://doi.org/10.1007/978-3-030-04028-4_8

Koenitz, H., & Eladhari, M. P. (2019). Challenges of IDN Research and Teaching. In R. E. Cardona-Rivera, A. Sullivan, & R. M. Young (Eds.), *Interactive Storytelling: 12th International Conference on Interactive Digital Storytelling, ICIDS 2019* (Vol. 11869, pp. 26–39). Cham: Springer Nature. http://doi.org/10.1007/978-3-030-33894-7_4

Koenitz, H., Eladhari, M. P., Louchart, S., & Nack, F. (2020). INDCOR white paper 1: A Shared Vocabulary for IDN (Interactive Digital Narratives). arXiv.org (Vol. cs.MM).

Kors, M. J. L., Ferri, G., Van der Spek, E. D., Ketel, C., & Schouten, B. A. M. (2016). A Breathtaking Journey. On the Design of an Empathy-Arousing Mixed-Reality Game. (2nd ed., pp. 91–104). Presented at the ChiPlay 2018, New York, NY, USA: ACM. http://doi.org/10.1145/2967934.2968110

Laurel, B. (1986). *Toward the Design of a Computer-Based Interactive Fantasy System*. Ohio State University.

Laurel, B. (1993). *Computers as Theatre (2nd ed.)*. Boston, MA: Addison-Wesley.

Lyotard, J. F. (1984). *The Postmodern Condition*. Minneapolis: University of Minnesota Press.

McKerrow, P. J. (1986). Robotics, an Academic Discipline? *Robotics*, 2(3), 267–274. http://doi.org/10.1016/0167-8493(86)90035-5

Mine, M. (2003). Towards Virtual Reality for the Masses: 10 Years of Research at Disney's VR Studio, 1–9.

Mountains. (2018). Florence. Annapurna Interactive.

Mukherjee, S. (2015). *Video Games and Storytelling*. Springer. http://doi.org/10.1007/978-1-137-52505-5

Mukherjee, S. (2016). Videogames as "Minor Literature": Reading Videogame Stories through Paratexts. *Gramma Journal of Theory and Criticism*, 60–75.

Murray, J. H. (1997). *Hamlet on the Holodeck: The Future of Narrative in Cyberspace*. New York: Free Press.

Naughty Dog. (2014). The Last of Us [Video game]. Tokyo: Sony Computer Entertainment.

Naughty Dog. (2016). Unchartered 4: A Thief's End. Tokyo: Sony Computer Entertainment.

Naughty Dog. (2020). The Last of Us 2. Tokyo: Sony Entertainment.

Pearce, C. (1994). The Ins & Outs of Non-Linear Storytelling. *SIGGRAPH Comput. Graph.*, 28(2), 100–101. http://doi.org/10.1145/178951.178956

Phillips, A. (2012). *A Creator's Guide to Transmedia Storytelling: How to Captivate and Engage Audiences across Multiple Platforms*. McGraw-Hill Education.

Ranke, K. (1967). Kategorienprobleme der Volksprosa. *Fabula*, 9(1-3), 4–12. http://doi.org/10.1515/fabl.1967.9.1-3.4

Rejeski, D., Chaplin, H., & Olson, R. (2015). *Addressing Complexity with Playable Models*. Wilson Center.

Rettberg, S. (2018). *Electronic Literature*. John Wiley & Sons.

Ricœur, P. (1984). *Time and Narrative*, Vol. 2. Chicago: University of Chicago Press.

Ricœur, P. (1991). Narrative Identity. *Philosophy Today*, 35(1), 73–81. http://doi.org/10.5840/philtoday199135136

Roth, C., & Koenitz, H. (2019). Bandersnatch, Yea or Nay - Reception and User Experience of an Interactive Digital Narrative Video (pp. 247–254). *Proceedings of the 2019 ACM International Conference on Interactive Experiences for TV and Online Video*, New York, NY, USA: ACM. http://doi.org/10.1145/3317697.3325124

Rosenblatt, L. M. (1938). *Literature as Exploration* (pp. 1–366). New York: D. Appleton-Century Company.

Rouse, R. (2016). Media of Attraction - A Media Archeology Approach to Panoramas, Kinematography, Mixed Reality and Beyond. The 11th International Conference for Interactive Digital Storytelling.

Ryan, J. (2017). Grimes' Fairy Tales: A 1960s Story Generator. In N. Nunes, I. Oakley, & V. Nisi (Eds.), (Vol. 10690, pp. 89–103). Cham: Springer International Publishing. http://doi.org/10.1007/978-3-319-71027-3_8

Ryan, M. L. (2004). *Narrative across Media: The Languages of Storytelling*. Lincoln, NE: University of Nebraska Press.

Salvatore, S. (2019). Beyond the Meaning Given. The Meaning as Explanandum. *Integrative Psychological and Behavioral Science*, *53*, 632–643. http://doi.org/10.1007/s12 124-019-9472-z

Sierra On-Line. (1995). Phantasmagoria. Los Angeles: Sierra On-Line.

Smoking Car Productions. (1997). The Last Express. Eugene, OR: Broderbund.

Telltale Games. (2012). The Walking Dead. San Rafael: Telltale Games.

Telltale Games. (2013). The Wolf Among Us. Telltale Games.

The Chinese Room. (2008). Dear Esther. Portsmouth, UK: The Chinese Room.

The Fullbright Company. (2013). Gone Home. Portland, OR: The Fullbright Company.

Traum, D., Jones, A., Hays, K., Maio, H., Alexander, O., Artstein, R., et al. (2015). New Dimensions in Testimony: Digitally Preserving a Holocaust Survivor's Interactive Storytelling. In H. Schoenau-Fog, L. E. Bruni, S. Louchart, & S. Baceviciute (Eds.), *Interactive Storytelling 8th International Conference on Interactive Digital Storytelling, ICIDS 2015* (pp. 269–281). Cham: Springer. http://doi.org/https://doi.org/10.1007/978-3-319-27036-4_26

Trilobyte. (1993). The 7th Guest. London, UK: Virgin Interactive Entertainment.

Ursu, M. F., Kegel, I. C., Williams, D., Thomas, M., Mayer, H., Zsombori, V., et al. (2008). ShapeShifting TV: Interactive Screen Media Narratives. *Multimedia Systems*, 14(2), 115–132. http://doi.org/10.1007/s00530-008-0119-z

Valve. (1998). Half-Life. Oakhurst, CA: Sierra Studios.

Weizenbaum, J. (1966). Eliza — a Computer Program for the Study of Natural Language Communication Between Man and Machine. *Communications of the ACM*, 9(1), 36–45. http://doi.org/10.1145/365153.365168

Part 2

CONCEPTUAL CHALLENGES FOR IDN

Assessing narrative fundamentalism and narrative indifference

Considerable resistance exists against the very notion of interactive digital narratives, to the point that some practitioners and scholars question if IDN are even possible. In this part, I explore these voices and critically reflect on the assumptions they are based on. I will identify *narrative fundamentalism* – a restrictive view that privileges specific forms of narrative – as a common foundation for arguments against IDN. Its concrete manifestations exist in academic and professional discourse as I will demonstrate by analyzing the persistent myth of universal story structures and the ludology v narratology debate in game studies. In particular, narrative fundamentalism engenders a theoretical/conceptual imperialism which ignores the specificity of IDN in both analysis and design. Conversely, identifying narrative fundamentalist elements helps to separate ideology from foundational issues in IDN and thus allows us to focus on the latter.

At the end of this part, I will draw attention to a related and equally important issue – *narrative indifference* – the tendency to use terms in the semantic field around narrative (e.g., narrative, story, storytelling, storyworld) without providing a definition. Narrative indifference subjects the concrete meaning of terms to personal interpretation and thus prevents the proper assessment and application of a given contribution.

What is *narrative fundamentalism*?

Narrative fundamentalism describes a restricted understanding of narrative, built on a totalizing, colonialist view that takes specific forms – mainly the written tradition leading to the 19th century European novel and Hollywood-style cinema – as representing the entirety of narrative expressions. This perspective ignores many long-established forms of narrative originating outside of Europe but also oral European forms (e.g., Norse sagas) and 20th-century developments such as

DOI: 10.4324/9781003106425-2

postmodern literature. Moreover, narrative fundamentalism is a lens through which novel forms such as interactive digital narrative are either seen as impossible or as deficient manifestations that should rather aspire to be actual novels or movies.

Narrative fundamentalism persists because a dominant cultural form of narrative is impressed on its audience from a very early age on, as I have discussed in the introduction. In the western tradition, this process starts with the bedtime stories many of our parents read to us – and is later reinforced throughout primary school and high school. The problem here is certainly not with the bedtime stories themselves, but that they represent the start of a process that, over time and almost subconsciously, turns a specific type of narrative into what is seen as being a standard model for all narratives. This mechanism is not limited to linear western forms – the dominant structure and content of narrative depends on context and differs between cultures. In inter-cultural communication, this is a known effect – for example, for people who grew up in a Japanese cultural setting with its own dominant narrative structure, a conscious switch to the dominant western narrative structure is considered a key factor to enable successful communication in the US and other western countries (Kopp, 2013).

Yet, through westernized school systems around the world and the global reach of western literature and movies, Eurocentric narratives have reached a dominant status in many places outside of its originating culture. Many of us, schooled in a western-style education system, learn about narrative only by reading literature. The model we take from these examples is further reinforced when we are taught to reflect on narrative in written accounts that follow the same linear form. We can see this as a closed circuit that organizes and normalizes both the production and reception of narratives. Other forms of narratives, for example different varieties of oral storytelling (African, Australian Aboriginal, Norse, Serbian storytelling, etc.) or non-European written forms (e.g., those based on the Japanese Kishōtenketsu structure) are, at best, marginalized but more often simply ignored in western education systems and the respective dominant cultural discourse.

The result is a severely restricted conception of narrative that has become normalized and is deeply ingrained – to such a degree that we might easily mistake the dominant model for a universal one. This mechanism is deeply problematic. We should consider the political and cultural implications of this restricted understanding of narrative and its ignorance of non-European, non-literary (and often non-male) forms in much the same way that in the 20th century we started to question the patriarchic marginalization (and often complete absence) of women and minority voices by means of feminism (de Beauvoir, 2014, orig. French version 1949), post-colonialism (Spivak, 1988), queer theory (Watson, 2005), intersectionality (Crenshaw, 2017), and critical race theory (Delgado & Stefancic, 2017). In this regard, narrative fundamentalism is an aspect of marginalization that so far has been mostly overlooked. Just as we do no longer accept a white cisgender male perspective as the only legitimate one, we need to stop privileging a specific form of western linear narrative. This means we need to recognize the reality that many alternative forms of narrative exist and start teaching these in our kindergartens and schools. Indeed, Roland Barthes and Lionel Duisit begin their investigation of the phenomena of narrative by reminding us that "there are countless forms of narrative in the world" (Barthes & Duisit, 1975) before enumerating many of the existing varieties:

> Among the vehicles of narrative are articulated language, whether oral or written, pictures still or moving, gestures, and an ordered mixture of all those substances. Narrative is present in myth, legend, fables, tales, short stories, epics, history, tragedy, *drame* [suspense drama], comedy, pantomime, paintings (in Santa Ursula by Carpaccio, for instance), stained-glass windows, movies, local news, conversations.
>
> *ibid*

Yet, more than four decades later, Barthes & Duisit's inclusive and expansive understanding of narrative still has not become the norm in school education and public discourse. Instead, considerably more restricted perspectives abound, representing a widespread – and often undetected – narrative fundamentalism.

The 'myth' of the story arc

Narrative fundamentalism incorporates specific structural models, which are taken as universal. The most prominent example is the myth of the universal story arc, the idea that narrative in general can be described in the form of rising action, climax, and falling action. Indeed, the concept is frequently referred to in the context of interactive digital narrative, for example by game designer and scholar Tracey Fullerton, who writes about the universal "dramatic arc" in her practice-oriented book *Game Design Workshop*.

> [...] the tension in a story gets worse before it gets better, resulting in a classic dramatic arc [...]. This arc is the backbone of all dramatic media, including games
>
> *Fullerton, Swain, & Hoffman, 2008*

In the more than a dozen years since Fullerton wrote these words, little has changed, as we can for example see in a 2017 interview for the influential online games industry magazine *Gamasutra (now Gamedeveloper)*, in which game designer Tariq Mukhttar references the "8 Point Story Arc methodology" – from Nigel Watt's book on how to write a novel (Watt, 2010) – as a major influence on his level design:

> Midway through development I employed the '8 Point Story Arc' methodology to test how well the narrative plays out. It forced me to make some big changes to the level design.
>
> *LeRay, 2017*

Fullerton, an internationally renowned game scholar/developer from the US and Mukhttar, an independent developer from the Arabian Peninsula, certainly represent very different areas of the overall landscape of developers and scholars. It is therefore even more remarkable how both take the universal applicability of the specific structural concept of the story arc/dramatic arc as a given. Such is the dominance of this concept, that Mukhttar does not seem at all to reflect on the fact that Watt's recipes are created for an entirely different narrative medium – print literature. He is certainly not alone with this perspective. Indeed, Jesse Schell, another influential game designer/scholar, denounces any attempt to question the fundamentalist dogma of universal 'mechanics of storytelling', in his book *The Art of Game Design: a Book of Lenses* (Schell, 2008). "The idea that the mechanics of traditional storytelling, which are innate to the human ability to communicate, are somehow nullified by interactivity is absurd." (Schell, 2008). Schell's remark is certainly in line with Mukhttar's application of literary structure and thus representative of a discourse that remains unchanged to this day. And given the dominant notion of universality, it is not surprising that Schell does not seem to consider that the mechanics he writes about represent only a specific Eurocentric tradition and not a universal one. Around the world, different cultures have developed very different narrative mechanics and structures. For example, cyclical, multi-climactic forms exist in some African oral traditions (cf. Scheub, 1985; Finnegan, 2012), while the Japanese Kishotenketsu structure substitutes a surprise element for conflict-based tension built-up that is prevalent in many Eurocentric narrative forms. The 'story arc' concept with introduction, raising action, climax and falling action is therefore not a universal structure of narration, but only one specific manifestation. To look for alternatives that are potentially a better fit for interactive forms is therefore a logical step and not preposterous as Schell suggests. Indeed, as early as 1996, Pamela Jennings advocated for the consideration of African oral narrative structures in this regard:

> Aristotle's *Poetics* is an inadequate narrative model for the creation of computer interactive art [...] it is to non-Western cultures that one should look for narrative structures that fit the sophistication of Western new technologies. The theories and processes of African oral literature provide the groundwork for such a narrative model.
>
> *Jennings, 1996, p. 347*

Jennings especially addresses Brenda Laurel's Neo-Aristotelian model (a later interpretation of Aristotelian *Poetics*) in her influential book *Computers as Theater* (Laurel, 1991). It is tempting to cast this perspective as an early recognition of the perils and limitations of narrative fundamentalism. However, in Jennings' perspective also lures the danger of a different fundamentalism: simply substituting the dominant Eurocentric model for one based on African oral storytelling means to exchange one limited framing for another. Instead, we should broaden our perspective and realize that many alternative structures exist. In addition, we need to be open to the possibility of novel models, specific to interactive forms. As Murray puts it in *Inventing the Medium*: "The digital designer is more often inventing something for which there is no standard model, like word processing in the age of the typewriter, or video games in the age of pinball." (Murray, 2011). Interestingly, this kind of innovation is not at odds with narratology, as Seymour Chatman points out: "literary theory [...] should assume that definitions are to be made, not discovered" (Chatman, 1980). This insight might be the ultimate counter-argument against any attempt at narrative fundamentalism – when it comes to narrative, definitions are created, imagined from an outside position and then applied for the analysis of artefacts, they are not innate and discovered in the sense of the discovery of a law of physics, or of a new messenger element in cell biology.

To illustrate this point, my investigation into the "story arc" concept continues. Even if we no longer uphold the claim to universal applicability, the term still appears to represent a long tradition in western narration, seemingly dating back to Aristotle. However, upon closer examination, this connection is tenuous at best. The *Poetics,* Aristotle's perspective on the formal aspects of tragedy, includes a requirement for a sequential order of beginning, middle, and end as well as "proper magnitude." While he considers the narrative logic and aspects of the content in detail, Aristotle offers no comments on the shape of the structure beyond a remark on two aspects – complication and unraveling – essentially the parts before a 'turning point' and after. Yet, there is no mention of a story arc, or about the placement of the turning point. The term 'story arc' is absent from the *Poetics* and so is the word 'tension.'[1] Only with considerable goodwill can Aristotle's division into two parts separated by a turning point be seen as a predecessor to the 'story arc' concept.

Furthermore, the claim of universal applicability of narrative structures is certainly not supported by Aristotle's written account. The primary focus in the *Poetics* is the tragedy, a specific form of stage play, which Aristotle clearly distinguishes from other dramatic manifestations such as comedy and non-dramatic, written, epic forms (lesser manifestations not worthy of special attention, according to Aristotle). On this basis, Aristotle expressively rejects the possibility of transferring narrative structures across media:

> Again, the poet should remember what has been often said, and not make an epic structure into a tragedy – by an epic structure I mean one with a multiplicity of plots
>
> *Aristotle, translated by S H Butcher, 1902*

At this point, it should be clear that the mythical universal story arc does not begin with Aristotle and that such a concept is in direct disagreement with the positions stated in the *Poetics*.

Where does the seemingly universal concept originate, then? The *Oxford English Dictionary* points to literary criticism as the origin of the term. It chronicles a first appearance in 1962 of the related term "dramatic arc" and points to the first proper occurrence as "arc of story" in 1978:

> orig. Literary Criticism. The principal plot or narrative development of a literary or dramatic work considered in outline form. Now also: spec. (freq. in story arc) a background plot or ongoing storyline in a serial narrative (esp. a television series), within which self-contained episodes are set; an episode or number of episodes which develop such a background story.
>
> 1962 F. N. Mennemeier in P. Demetz Brecht 148 There is no 'great dramatic arc' in *Mother Courage*... In Brecht's play there is an artfully static structure which carefully balances individual scenes against each other.
>
> 1978 G. Stewart in ELH 45 483 In the proliferated death scenes of *Bleak House*, Dickens brings death as never before into the pages that intervene between the implied oblivion before and after the arc of story, the unvoiced voids of narrative.
>
> *OED Online, n.d.*

The 'story arc' is therefore a problematic concept in several ways – not only does it lack universal applicability; its origins are also not actually within Aristotle's *Poetics*, but with literary criticism in the latter part of the 20th century. As media scholar Peter Lunenfeld has it:

> The term 'story arc' is used primarily by non-scholar production and fan communities as a way to reduce narrative analysis to a ritualised movement broadly appropriating the structure of Freytag's triangle.
>
> *Lunenfeld, 2010*

What Lunenfeld points out, is that the idea of a visual representation of narrative structure can be traced back to Gustav Freytag, a 19th century German playwright and theatre critic who published an influential book on the art of drama (Freytag, 1863). In that volume, Freytag uses a pyramid shape to explain the ascending and descending tension before and after the climax of drama. Like Aristotle, Freytag is quite clear on the limited scope of his analysis (classical Greek drama, Shakespeare, and the German 'classics') and does not make any claims toward universal applicability. It is the restricting perspective of narrative fundamentalism (Lunenfeld's "ritualized movement") that has engendered this reframing.

The 'myth' of the monomyth

Besides the 'universal story arc,' a second structure with seemingly universal applicability for narrative exists; Joseph's Campbell's 'monomyth,' first conceptualized in *The Hero with a Thousand Faces* (Campbell, 1949) where he deduced a universal "hero's journey" structure from the study of hero myth narratives across a number of cultures:

WHETHER WE LISTEN with aloof amusement to the dreamlike mumbo jumbo of some red-eyed witch doctor of the Congo, or read with cultivated rapture thin translations from the sonnets of the mystic Lao-tse; now and again crack the hard nutshell of an argument of Aquinas, or catch suddenly the shining meaning of a bizarre Eskimo fairy tale: *it will always be the one, shape-shifting yet marvelously constant story that we find*, together with a challengingly persistent suggestion of more remaining to be experienced than will be known or told.

ibid [my emphasis]

Campbell identified 17 phases divided into three parts (departure, initiation, return). The latter division invites alignment with the phases in the mono-climactic 'universal story arc' and thus the two structures are frequently collapsed, especially in books on screenwriting. In particular, Syd Field (1979) has popularized this approach. Campbell's hero story gained particular notoriety in film production and beyond when George Lucas credited him for his influence on the original *Star Wars* trilogy films. However, his influence is also noticeable in more recent books on the topic (e.g., Vogler, 2007; Yorke, 2014).

However, in his attempt to find similarities, Campbell creates a framework that privileges similarities while ignoring difference and specificity. Scholars from various disciplines, including mythology and feminist studies have criticized this approach as ethnocentric and as privileging the patriarchal view (Dundes, 1984; Murdock, 1990). In addition, Campbell's categories have been described as too vague and simplistic to be actually useful. For example, folklore scholar Alan Dundes points out that:

Campbell does not really know what a myth is, and he does not really distinguish it from folktale and legend, two genres that provide most of the illustrative examples in his popular *Hero with a Thousand Faces* [...]. His illustrative examples include Little Red Riding Hood and the Porcupine subtype of Star Husband, neither of which any folklorist would dream of classifying as a myth.

Dundes, 2005 [Dundes' emphasis]

Dundes sees Campbell's 'monomyth' as feeding into the idea that "all peoples share the same stories." Dundes' judgment of this "popular fantasy" needs no interpretation: "This is clearly an example of wishful thinking." (Dundes, 2005) Finally, Dundes addresses the claim of universality: "on the universality issue, the empirical facts suggest otherwise. There is not one single myth that is universal." (ibid)

These critical perspectives point to the same ideological underpinnings I have identified earlier – namely a restricted view on what is actually a larger space of manifestations and the declaration of universal validity of what is actually a specific approach. Therefore, the concept of the monomyth as a universally applicable narrative structure is another manifestation of narrative fundamentalism.

Debunking the 'myths' of story arc and monomyth

Narrative fundamentalism does not stop at the abstract assumption that all narrative adheres to a dominant western example. Instead, this problematic perspective also perpetuates a seemingly universal structural model of narrative by means of the 'story arc' and the 'monomyth.' Yet, the universality of this structure is a 'myth' by itself – a claim that does not stand the test of proper academic scrutiny. Narrative is a phenomenon that cuts across cultures and traditions, yet its manifestations are as diverse as their underlying cultures and languages. We should therefore be suspicious of attempts to find 'universal truths' regarding narrative on anything but very abstract categories (and then we need to be aware of the high level of abstraction).

An important lesson from this enquiry is the realization that the concept of 'universal structures' still exerts considerable influence on authors of practice-orientated books and creators of narrative works. Many creators welcome the seemingly clear guidelines they provide, which appear even more compelling through their perceived status of 'universality.' These concepts have become deeply ingrained and take considerable effort to overcome. As narrative game designer Wolfgang Walk has it, "This is the story of a long and serious error for which I plead guilty and which I would like to cite as an example that we cannot accept anything as proven in our art form. It's about the monomyth as a narrative paradigm in computer games." (Walk, 2018).

This is the reason why this investigation into theoretical-conceptual aspects of narrative has considerable bearing on the practice. Consequently, work on narrative models is an essential aspect in order to improve the design of interactive digital narratives.

Recognizing narrative fundamentalism

I will end this section with some suggestions on how to recognize narrative fundamentalism. This might not always be an easy task, as the effects of this deeply ingrained and normalized perspective can sometimes be subtle and thus difficult to identify. However, its more obvious variants share an easily recognizable characteristic – the overgeneralization of particular forms and narrative structures. This means either, or both, of these two aspects are present.

> The subject is 'narrative', 'story', 'storytelling', or 'fiction' but concrete examples are only taken from (non-avant-garde) print literature or cinema. In most cases, this also means a restriction to Eurocentric forms.

And/or:

> A specific narrative structure, sequence, or collection of 'plot types' is presented as 'universal', or 'innate to human communication'.

These two analytical lenses can be used to identify narrative fundamentalism on a basic level. Underlying motivations and particular effects could then be discussed as a next step. The following section uses these lenses as a basis to recognize narrative fundamentalism in the field of games studies.

Narrative fundamentalism in games studies

Since the late 20th century, video games have become an important cultural expression that has long outgrown its original niche status. The economic impact of today's video games industry is at least comparable to its film-producing counterpart and by some accounts has already outgrown movies.[2] Simultaneously, artists and independent developers have embraced games as a form to explore the human condition, just as other mediated expressions earlier. Today, games address many societal and personal concerns including:

- Adolescence/coming of age – *The Path* (Tale of Tales, 2009), *Gone Home* (The Fullbright Company, 2013), (*Life is Strange* (Dontnod Entertainment, 2015)
- Adult soul-searching – *Firewatch* (Campo Santo, 2016)
- Aging – *The Graveyard* (Tale of Tales, 2008)
- Cancer – *That Dragon, Cancer* (Green & Larson, 2014)
- Depression – *Depression Quest* (Quinn & Lindsey, 2013)
- Difficult decisions of soldiers in action (*Spec Ops: The Line* (Yager Development, 2012)
- Ethics of advanced AI – *Detroit: Become Human* (Quantic Dream, 2018)
- Existence in a totalitarian regime – *Papers, Please* (Pope, 2013)
- Family relations – *The Novelist* (Hudson, 2013)
- Genocide – *Darfur is Dying* (Ruiz, 2006)
- Inner world affected by an outside civil war – *Sunset* (Tale of Tales, 2015)
- Love and death – *Dear Esther* (The Chinese Room, 2008), *To the Moon* (Freebird Games, 2011), *Brothers, A Tale of Two Sons* (Starbreeze Studios, 2013), *Spiritfarer* (Thunder Lotus Games, 2020)

These works are examples of the growing body of narrative-focused games, which occupy an important place in the overall space of IDN. At the same time, developments in game studies/game design and related fields (e.g., human–computer interaction (HCI) and research on game interfaces) can also be important contributions to the understanding of interactive digital narratives.

The 'ludology vs. narratology debate'

I want to start this section by making clear that I am aware that this academic debate has been described as either historic and increasingly overcome (e.g., Campagna, 2018; Vargas-Iglesias & Navarrete-Cardero, 2019,: Núñez-Pacheco & Phillip, 2021) or as something that should essentially be ignored (Apperly, 2019). Conversely, many recent papers and books see value in discussing aspects of the debate, frequently taking it as a starting point for further investigations. An example in this regard is an article by Frans Mäyrä (2020), where he takes the debate as a crucial element for reflecting on a central conflict in game studies between formalist, "purist" tendencies and those more aware of the surrounding culture and politics. Further examples discuss genre theory (Voorhees, 2019) or the anti-feminist and anti-political stance of early game studies (Phillips, 2020). While the debate itself might be historic by now, its ongoing impact is undeniable. If we want to understand games and IDN, we need to critically reflect our history in order to comprehend our trajectory and to avoid repeating earlier mistakes.

In the context of this volume, there are three important reasons why I give the discussion of this topic considerable space. First, the issues which came up in the debate have only been addressed partly while some remain unresolved. Second, several problematic arguments, framings, and other long-term consequences persist until today and are now often uncritically taken as historic fact. The third reason is to draw attention to the effects the debate had on IDN research, essentially closing the door on such work within game studies and relegating scholars interested in both topics to the margins.

To address the first issue, I will unpack the different layers of argumentation. To address the second, I will undertake a critical examination of the development of the debate and reflect on the arguments themselves. To address the third issue, I will propose an inclusive approach which takes games studies and IDN studies as sibling disciplines.

The "ludology vs. narratology" debate (Aarseth, 2001; 2004a; Eskelinen, 2001; Frasca, 1999; 2003; Jenkins, 2004; Juul, 1999a; 2001; 2005; Murray, 2004; 2005) is an academic discussion that exerts considerable influence on the conception of interactive digital narrative in games studies, game design, and related areas. It consists of a number of loosely related arguments, lumped together under one heading. This multiplicity in arguments makes the debate a difficult topic. Later attempts to redefine the debate – or rather, to create a reading of the debate that is favorable to its instigators (Aarseth, 2012; 2014a) – have only added to the confusion. It is therefore beneficial to start with an overview of the different arguments and subtopics.

- Games are not a narrative medium – this is Jesper Juul's original argument (Juul, 1999b) and can be seen as the start of the 'hot phase' of the debate.
  - Games and narrative (in the guise of 'fiction') are a dichotomy and the two can only be combined with considerable difficulty. In the best case, narratives provide auxiliary functions for games, but often they are purely ornamental. This is Juul's later position, most prominently in his book *Half-Real* (Juul, 2005).
- Narratology is inadequate as a framework to analyze games – this is Gonzalo Frasca's original argument (Frasca, 1999), the creator of the term ludology.
- There is a 'takeover attempt' by the humanities to prevent games studies from existing and uphold existing analytical frameworks as the only valid ones – the

origin of this argument is more difficult to pin down, but seems to be Espen Arseth's addition, building on an argument first made in *Cybertext* about "theoretical imperialism" (Aarseth, 1997).

• Janet Murray and Henry Jenkins are the leading narratologists and their work exemplifies a misunderstanding of games as narratives – this framing is first used by Markku Eskelinen (2001) and later becomes a stable of the debate.

• Interactive Narratives/Interactive Storytelling is a strategy to reform games as narratives – This is an argument introduced by Aarseth (Aarseth, 2004a) and later repeated in *Half Real* by Jesper Juul (2005).

In the following section I will investigate these claims in detail. Here is a summary of the results in short form:

1. No. Games can be used for narrative, just not in the same way as the novel or movie. The rejection of narrative is based on a fundamentalist view.
    1.1. No. Thinking in terms of a game-narrative dichotomy more often than not creates unsatisfactory works. Almost all good examples of games as interactive digital narratives overcome the binary distinction and instead focus on creating rewarding narrative experiences in which interactivity plays a key role (and are thus different from the kind of narrative found in the novel or movie). Again, this position is based on a fundamentalist view of narrative.
2. Yes, however ... given its basis in the analysis of print literature and its long-standing disregard for media specificity, narratology in its current form does not provide analytical tools that can fully understand works that are procedural and participatory. However, it is equally important to acknowledge developments in post-classical narratology and their implications for an expanded and more inclusive understanding of narrative. I will further extend this aspect in part three.
3. Yes. There are definitely tendencies in the humanities to understand existing frameworks as universal and superior, even without any evidence provided to support this perspective. I will show an example of such a perspective later in this part. The dogma of media-agnosticism – a tendency in some academic fields to disregard media-specific aspects – has a considerable impact on this issue.
    3.1. No. Neither Murray nor Jenkins are narratologists – nor are they enemies of game studies (Frasca already said this 2003, but was mostly ignored (Frasca, 2003)). Instead, both created academic programs that acknowledge and emphasize the specific qualities of the digital medium.
    3.2. No. Interactive narratives are novel forms of narrative driven by the interest in expressions not possible (or very difficult to realize) with a book, movie, or TV broadcast. Interactive narrative studies are best seen as a sister discipline to games studies.

A brief overview of the "ludology vs. narratology debate"

In 1999, Jesper Juul proclaimed "the computer game is simply not a narrative medium." (Juul, 1999a) In the same year, Gonzalo Frasca proposed the term "ludology" to mean the "discipline that studies game and play activities" (Frasca, 1999). In the same publication, Frasca also emphasized the need for ludology in contrast to narratological analysis. Later, additional scholars – most importantly Aarseth and Eskelinen – joined Juul and Frasca in a movement to establish video games studies. These so-called "ludologists" positioned both narrative and narrative analysis as the opposing side against which the new discipline was to be established. They alleged that without this move, video games were in danger of being misunderstood as narratives and narrative analysis would colonize the understanding of video games.

In the debate, Murray and Jenkins became favorite targets of Aarseth, Eskelinen, and Juul. In Murray's case it was her interpretation of *Tetris* as a narrative (Murray calls *Tetris* a "symbolic drama") representing the onslaught of tasks in contemporary society ("[an] enactment of the overtasked lives of Americans in the 1990s") in *Hamlet on the Holodeck* (Murray, 1997) as well as her 2004 perspective on "game-story" (Murray, 2004) that provided particular points of reference for their critique. In the case of Jenkins, it was his understanding of transmedia narratives and of video game design as "narrative architecture" (Jenkins, 2004) that served as targets. A considerable amount of the debate occurred in discussions at academic conferences (cf. Aarseth's description of such an argument as reported by Jenkins (Aarseth, 2014a)). For posterity, it is most visible in the dialogic form of *First Person* (Wardrip-Fruin & Harrigan, 2004) – for example, Eskelinen's response (2004) to Jenkins (2004) or Aarseth's (2004b) response to Murray's article (Murray, 2004).

Murray attempted to put an end to the debate in a 2005 Keynote for the Digital Games Research Association (DIGRA) Conference ("The last word on ludology vs. narratology in game studies" (Murray, 2005)). In the same year, Juul's book *Half Real* (Juul, 2005) was published and perceived by some as the end of the debate. However, later publications (Aarseth, 2012; Bogost, 2017; Calleja, 2013; 2015; Eskelinen, 2012a; Kapell, 2015; Ryan, 2006; 2009; Simons, 2007) clearly show that the debate continued, albeit with reduced intensity. In the following sections, I will identify and discuss different topics within the debate, starting with the question of narrative vs. narratology.

Mixed categories: narrative vs. narratology vs. interactive narrative

One particularly problematic aspect of the narratology vs. ludology debate is that both "narrative" in general and the academic discipline of "narratology" are addressed in the debate, and oftentimes these different categories are intertwined. Yet, it is important to properly distinguish between narrative (an ontological entity) and narratology (a set of methods to analyze narrative). Juul's early provocative argument is not directed at narratology, but against narrative per se: "the computer game is simply not a narrative medium" (Juul, 1999a). While Juul moderates his stance two years later (Juul, 2001), Markku Eskelinen's 2001 description of the "Gaming Situation" again positions video games against narrative. "If I throw a ball at you I don't expect you to drop it and wait until it starts telling stories." (Eskelinen, 2001) Conversely, Aarseth combines the two aspects in the beginning of his essay "Genre Trouble."

> Currently in game and digital culture studies, a controversy rages over the relevance of narratology for game aesthetics. One side argues that computer games are media for telling stories, while the opposing side claims that stories and games are different structures that are in effect doing opposite things.
> *Aarseth, 2004a*

Aarseth here merges two different aspects without proper discussion. The claim that video games can be used for narrative is not automatically coupled with the assertion that narratology (especially in its contemporary form) should be used to understand games in general or game aesthetics in particular.

In contrast, extending Murray's and Jenkin's arguments, I position IDN as a space for novel and experimental forms of narrative, some of which share characteristics with games. Thus, IDN is neither a continuation of print literature with other means, nor simply a merger of narrative and interaction. For these novel and experimental forms of narrative, existing narratology, derived mostly from the analysis of print-based literature, has little concern. IDN studies and video game studies should thus be 'sisters in arms' since both address limitations in traditional conceptions of mediated experiences. Instead, to the ludologists, any mention of "interactive narratives" is an expression of an ideological movement to "reform games" (Aarseth, 2004a) driven by "narrativistic colonialism" (ibid). Yet, someone speaking about "interactive narrative" is not − as Aarseth alleges − arguing that video games would be better if they were more like stories, nor that narratology provides the tools for a privileged understanding of games. The reason for this misunderstanding is narrative fundamentalism − Aarseth conceives of narrative only in a traditional, Eurocentric sense, as the literary novel and the movie, as is evident in his article:

> *Novels* are very good at relating the inner lives of characters (*films* perhaps less so); games are awful at that, or, wisely, they don't even try. We might say that, unlike *literature*, games are not about the Other, they are about the Self.
> *Aarseth, 2004a [My emphases]*

Arseth's game/narrative dichotomy becomes especially suspect when compared to his own work seven years earlier in *Cybertext*: "hypertexts, adventure games, and so forth are not texts the way the average literary work is a text." (Aarseth, 1997) Here, Aarseth clearly acknowledges the different status of interactive narrative vs. traditional literary forms. We need to wonder why Aarseth so strongly insists on separating games from narratives in 2004 when he himself described adventure games as novel narrative forms seven years earlier?

Some games are interactive narratives

Even Aarseth admits that some games – adventure games, in his mind – are narratives. However, he portrays this category of games as a failed attempt – a type of game that simply does not live up to the expectations of good games, for example in the case of *Myst* (Cyan, 1993): "the gameplay was boring and derivative, with the same linear structure that was introduced by the first adventure game 16 years earlier. Nice video graphics, shame about the game." (Aarseth, 2004a) Yet, *Myst* had considerable success with audiences, as it was the best-selling video game between 1993 and 2002 (when it was overtaken by *The Sims* (Wright, 2000)). The mostly positive critical reception of the game[3] – including an article in the New York Times that takes *Myst* as evidence of games maturing into an art form (Rothstein, 1994) – paints a picture very different to Aarseth's assessment. In addition, the other games criticized by Aarseth in the same essay, *Half-Life* (Valve, 1998) and *Deus Ex* (Ion Storm, 2000) also enjoyed considerable critical and commercial success. The same examples can thus also be seen as testimony for the success of IDN in video game form, and alert us to the limitations of Aarseth's ludological perspective.

The problematic status of narratology in the debate

Another troubling aspect of the so-called ludology vs. narratology debate is the near absence of actual narratological positions or scholars from this discipline on the supposed 'narratology' side, a fact already pointed out by Frasca in 2003 (Frasca, 2003). Neither Murray nor Jenkins (the ludologists' self-selected 'opponents') are narrative theorists by training (Murray's PhD is in English literature, Jenkins' is in communications). The only scholar from the field of narratology to engage in the debate was Marie-Laure Ryan. Also publishing in the inaugural issue of *Games Studies* (Ryan, 2001), in which several of the seminal ludology papers appeared, Ryan clearly acknowledges limitations in existing narratological analysis when it comes to games. As a remedy, she proposes an additional modality – besides the diegetic (literature) and the mimetic (theatre) – to address these limitations. Yet, her proposal for a new modality in narratology was not discussed further in the debate.

In retrospect, it becomes clear that the ludologists ignored important contemporary developments in narratology, especially works that added a perspective to the inquiry into narrative which was informed by developments in cognitive science[4]. David Herman's 2002 book *Story Logic* (Herman, 2002) can be seen as the culmination of a major shift (the 'cognitive turn') in narratology (for an overview of the development, see Herman, 2013). Herman redefines narrative as a cognitive function for sense-making that is not tied to any specific form. This move has important implications for a discussion centered on the question whether video games and other forms of interactive expressions can be narratives. Yet, two years after Herman's book came out (and more than a decade after cognitive perspectives started to make inroads in narratology (e.g., Ibsch, 1990), Aarseth seems unaware of the impact of this development and claims a disconnect between a "cognitive perspective" and "proper narratologists" (Aarseth, 2004a). Furthermore, anybody who understands narrative in a wider context – Aarseth claims – has fallen prey to an "ideology of narrativism:"

> [...] the notion that everything is a story, and that storytelling is our primary, perhaps only, mode of understanding, our *cognitive perspective* on the world. [...] Ironically, most proper narratologists, who actually have to think about and define narratives in a scholarly, responsible, and accurate way, are not guilty of this overgeneralization.
>
> *Aarseth, 2004a [my emphasis]*

Why do the ludologists ignore the 'cognitive turn?' Certainly, the positioning of games versus narrative and narratology becomes even harder to defend with the advent of cognitive narratology. Ever since, narrative can no longer as easily be relegated to a Eurocentric model comprised of non-avant-garde print novels and Hollywood movies; simultaneously, it becomes even harder to portray narratology as being exclusively concerned with studying that very model. In other words, the ludology argument applies an artificially restricted and outdated representation of narratology, rather than discussing contemporary developments in narratology and their implications for the study of interactive narrative artefacts in the digital medium. What I am saying here is certainly not a new insight, since Marie-Laure Ryan already made that very point in *Avatars of Story* (Ryan, 2006), although she did not explicitly mention the cognitive perspective. Ryan describes the ludologists' argument as positioned against a 'myth' – a crude scapegoat version of the actual academic discipline of narratology. In her view, the ludologists take Prince's original (Prince, 1987) definition of narrative (which can be seen as rejecting mimetic forms) as the central tenet of narratology and ignore additional positions as well as Prince's own later modifications (e.g., in the revised edition of the Dictionary of Narratology (Prince, 2003)). Interestingly, Aarseth's later effort at 're-contextualizing' ludology (Aarseth, 2012; 2014b) includes a somewhat similar assessment:

> Tragically, in the field of game studies the term "narratology" has changed meaning and does not refer to the academic discipline of narrative theory, but to a more or less mythical position taken by an imagined group of people who are seen to believe that games are stories. It is high time, and hopefully not too late, to reinstate the original meaning and function of narratology, and ground the debate in narratological terminology and theory.
>
> *Aarseth, 2012*

Indeed. However, the question is: who actually did create this "mythical position"? The analysis of the ludologists' publications presented so far paints a pretty clear picture, which is also supported by Ryan's critique – the categorial confusion of narrative and narratology, the use of outdated positions in narratology and the ignorance of the cognitive turn certainly amount to the creation of a "mythical position." Aarseth's statement – as a main perpetrator of this 'myth' – is therefore deeply, if maybe involuntarily, ironic.

The lack of a smoking gun and the turn to 'fiction' in 'Half-Real'

For all the rhetoric against the supposedly imperialist tendencies of narrative analysis, the ludologists fail to provide convincing evidence of this alleged development. As already mentioned, Janet Murray's interpretation of Tetris as a narrative of an overwhelming onslaught of tasks in a late capitalist society (Murray, 1997) becomes one of their favorite targets despite the fact that it constituted only half a page in a book of 200 pages. Certainly, Murray's analysis of Tetris as a symbolic drama is open for criticism. However, it is a valid form of interpretation and – especially given her background in literature studies – one that is neither particularly surprising nor wrong on an absolute level. The difference between her analysis and Markku Eskelinen's (2001) is not between wrong or right – as he alleges – but rather in its level of abstraction. Eskelinen is concerned with a more concrete level and Murray operates on a more abstract one. Properly identifying this aspect would have certainly helped to put the debate on a more solid foundation.

Half-Real: entrenching the ludological position

Juul's book *Half-Real* (2005) marks the end of the 'hot phase' of the ludology vs. narratology debate. His book is sometimes even described as ending the narratology vs. ludology debate. This, however, is in conflict with the actual text, as Juul reiterates ludological positions and further reinforces the dichotomic view of games vs. narratives.

Juul repeats Aarseth's claim of imperialist "narrativism" and accuses the 'narratology' side of a totalizing claim that games would be *better* if they would be more like narratives:

> The description of games as storytelling systems often overlaps with the prescriptive idea that video games (or "interactive narratives") would be *better* if they were more like stories.
>
> *Juul, 2005 [Juul's emphasis]*

Yet, Juul offers no actual evidence for this alleged 'claim of superiority' and neither does Aarseth a year earlier (Aarseth, 2004a). What Aarseth does present is Murray's 2004 pronunciation "games are always stories" (Murray, 2004). Yet, this remark works in exactly the same way as her symbolic reading of Tetris, which becomes clear when we read the whole sentence. "Games are always stories, even abstract games such as checkers or Tetris, which are about winning and losing, casting the player as the opponent-battling or environment-battling hero." (Ibid) What Murray does here, is to interpret games as abstract hero stories. Certainly, Murray could have described her approach more clearly, especially for an audience not familiar with methods in literature studies. And of course, we can debate her particular interpretation. However, and most importantly for the present discussion, the claim of superiority – 'games are better as stories' – is not present. Juul does present an alleged piece of evidence in the form of Brenda Laurel's doctoral thesis "Toward the Design of a computer-based interactive Fantasy System" (Laurel, 1986). Laurel's work is essentially a design fiction, where she lays out a speculative architecture for a first-person interactive drama experience. While Juul alleges her vision to be about video games, he does not offer any actual quotes in support of this interpretation. In contrast, Laurel clearly positions interactive drama as an experience that shares some qualities with video games, but also possesses distinct ones:

> Such an experience would afford the user pleasures that are both similar to and distinct from those offered by viewing or writing a play or by playing a video game. *ibid*

It is for these kinds of experiences that Murray proposes the term "cyberdrama" (Murray, 2004). Instead of redefining games, her interest is therefore in novel forms of narrative and for her, this means to overcome dichotomic conceptions. "We hear, for example, that games and stories are opposed and what makes a good story makes a bad game and vice versa. But the more useful question is, how do we make a better cyberdrama?" (ibid) This perspective, she reminds us, is actually not that different from the one Aarseth developed in 1997 when he coined the term "cybertext" (Aarseth, 1997):

> Espen Aarseth (1997) uses the term "ergodic literature," which he defines as "open, dynamic texts where the reader must perform specific actions to generate a literary sequence, which may vary for every reading." Some such term is needed to mark the change we are experiencing, the invention of a new genre altogether, which is narrative in shape and that includes elements we associate with games.
>
> *Murray, 2004*

What we see here is another example of the apparent transformation in Aarseth's position from a proponent of novel narrative forms, including games, in *Cybertext*, to someone advocating a separation of the two concepts only a few years later. The issue with this 'ludological turn' in perspective is that it happened without an accompanying explanation. As long as this explanation remains elusive, it is prudent to divide Aarseth's work into a phase before ludology and one since.

Juul in *Half Real* proceeds with a dismissal of Murray's vision of the Holodeck (Murray, 1997):

Janet Murray's book *Hamlet on the Holodeck* (1997) describes the similar utopia of a holodeck – a completely immersive and transparent environment in which a user/player can engage in a well formed [sic] story. While this is in itself an overwhelming technical challenge, the logical problem is that there is no compelling argument demonstrating that a well formed [sic] "narrative" would be a more interesting *player* experience.

Juul, 2005

Again, his interpretation is not supported by any actual quotes from Murray's work and Juul instead just reiterates the assumed dichotomy. Logically, his argument against Laurel and Murray is problematic: first an assertion is made about their presumed totalizing tendencies and then exactly these presumed tendencies are criticized. Another way – supported by both authors' actual words – would be to state that while some scholars focus on rule-based game experiences, others work on interactive narrative experiences.

We are therefore faced with a perplexing situation: the ludologists aim their arguments at an imaginary opponent, who in reality could be an ally in the quest to explore and understand the expressive possibilities of the digital medium. What makes matters worse is that these arguments are often based on interpretation alone, unsupported by actual quotes and in some cases (e.g., with Laurel's positioning of interactive drama) even in direct contrast to clearly stated positions.

Reinforcing the dichotomy

By the time of the publication of *Half-Real*, the dichotomic framing of narrative and games had been well established in Games Studies. Juul himself describes the alleged dichotomy as being "[…] between the open structure of games and the closed structure of stories." (Juul, 2005) However, the understanding of story/ narrative as a "closed structure" only' applies to a subset of narrative forms and thus constitutes an instance of narrative fundamentalism. Games can be narratives provided we do not expect them to adhere to the model established by a subset of western literary and cinematic forms. In other words, Juul here does not actually compare video games and narrative, he only compares video games and a subset of narrative. This restricted variety of narrative can never be a first-class member of an interactive experience, according to Juul. At best, in the guise of "game fiction" (Juul, 2005) it might provide context along with an opportunity for identification with game characters and can become entirely superfluous once the interactor has understood well enough what they can do. This is precisely the point Juul makes in *Half-Real*:

It is a common characteristic that with sustained playing of the same game, the player may become less interested in the fictional/representational level of the game and more focused on the rules of the games

ibid

Yet, what Juul ignores here are games in which narrative is essential such as adventure games and role-playing games (RPGs). This is also the case for many games which appeared after the publication of *Half-Real*, for example, narrative-focused shooter games like *Bioshock* (2K Games, 2007), action-adventure games like *The Last of Us* (Naughty Dog, 2014) and *The Last of US 2* (Naughty Dog, 2020), action RPGs like *Mass Effect* (Electronic Arts, 2007) or *The Witcher 3* ("The Witcher 3 [Video game]," 2015), open-world experiences like *Red Dead Redemption 2* (Rockstar Studios, 2018), as well as the first-person experience narratives (FPEN) *Dear Esther* (The Chinese Room, 2008), *Gone Home* (The Fullbright Company, 2013), *Firewatch* (Campo Santo, 2016), and many others.

Interestingly, Juul inadvertently provides an argument for research on IDN as his concern with narrative seems also to be with the lack of control over a given player's fantasy. While he characterizes "game fiction" as "optional" he also sees it as an aspect beyond the control of the game designer, an "ambiguous" quality, "imagined by the player in uncontrollable and unpredictable ways." (Juul, 2005) This remark betrays an uneasy awareness of the expressive power of interactive digital narrative. It also incidentally describes the reason for research into interactive digital narratives – the need for a better understanding of the potential, challenges, and practices of IDN.

The long-term consequences of the narratology vs. ludology debate

While the debate's 'hot phase' might seem to have ended in 2005, it has never actually come to a conclusion and its longer-term consequences are still tangible today, nearly two decades later. The original ludology papers are still frequently cited and their questionable claims still influence both the academic discourse and the professional practice by way of game design education. Indeed, Matthew Kapell takes the unresolved questions the debate poses as the reason for a collection of essays in 2015 (Kapell, 2015) while Ian Bogost evokes the ludology argument again in a 2017 article in the *Atlantic*, "Video Games Are Better Without Stories" (Bogost, 2017).

Moreover, we can find the ludologists' claims uncritically repeated and treated as historical fact in more recent papers. For example, the following quote from a 2018 book chapter presents an argument by Frasca as a 'fact' ("points out" instead of 'argues' or 'claims'):

> Gonzalo Frasca (2003) points out that this means games offer distinctly different rhetorical possibilities; games offer different tools for conveying opinions and feelings than do more traditional media that depend heavily on the mechanism of narrative representation.
>
> *Neys & Jansz, 2018*

By uncritically repeating Frasca's argument, the authors connect the "mechanism of narrative representation" to "traditional media" and thus marginalize non-traditional, novel forms of narrative. This assertion is problematic and at the very least would need further discussion, which is not provided. Another set of examples are in recent journal articles that take the claimed divide between narratology and ludology and the alleged roles of Jenkins and Murray as 'narratologists' as historic fact:

> In the late 20th century, discussions regarding the ontological nature of video games were centered on the issue of whether they should be observed from the perspective of narratology (Jenkins, 2004; Murray, 1999; Ryan, 2004) or ludology (Frasca, 1999; Juul, 2001).
>
> *Vargas-Iglesias & Navarrete-Cardero, 2019*

Another example:

> Ludology considers games as nothing more than a simulation like a game of chess, with the entertainment stemming from the confrontation of set rules and challenges. Ludologists such as Gonzolo Frasca believe that researchers ought to treat video games not as narrative texts but as "rules-based systems structured around game play mechanics rather than representational narratives." However, narrativists view video games as an inherent medium to telling stories. Narrativists such as Janet Murray claimed that "games are always stories" and the ludological theory as restrictive.
>
> *P. Eapen & Eapen, 2021*

These quotes are testimony to a problematic development that clearly shows the need for continued attention to this topic. In particular, the uncritical references to earlier arguments and their presentation as historical fact are problematic.

For the present discussion, two related consequences are the most pertinent: first, research on interactive forms of narration was marginalized, creating an analytical void; and second, since the phenomenon of interactive digital narration did not just disappear, terminology and analytical approaches originating in literary studies have more recently been used to fill this void (e.g., Ensslin, 2014; Mukherjee, 2015). The problem with the latter development is that concepts originally developed to analyze (print) literary narratives are applied to IDN without proper scrutiny in regard to the validity of the respective underlying assumptions, appropriateness of categories and resulting limitations to analytical insights. This is exactly the danger Aarseth has been warning about in regard to the limitations of inherited vocabulary in detecting "empirical differences" and thus preventing necessary "theoretical innovation." (Aarseth 2012)

Similarly, Timothy J. Welsh wonders about the influence of established frameworks and asks in a review of Ensslin's book "Literary Gaming," (Ensslin, 2014) whether video game narrative has 'matured,' as Ensslin suggests, on its own terms, or rather started to produced artifacts that "sufficiently resemble already established artistic practices and critical traditions" (Welsh, 2015). This is an important concern – should we really understand (some) games as literature, as Ensslin suggests in her book, or rather be particularly careful in applying literary models? I side with

Aarseth's concern here – once we use the lens of established frameworks, our view becomes restricted and all we can see is what this particular framing allows us to see.

Unfortunately, there is an ironic twist here – by conceiving games studies as oppositional to narrative and narratology, the ludologists are at least partly responsible for the lack of theoretical development in understanding interactive forms of narration which has resulted in a theoretical void. As we can see, what has been used to fill this void are long-established narratological categories as evidenced, for example, by Ensslin's and Mukherjee's books – testimony to the very theoretical imperialism that ludology was concerned with in the first place. In the next section, I will discuss this perspective in more detail.

Theoretical imperialism

In the book *Videogames and Storytelling* (2015), Souvik Mukherjee foregrounds a specific humanities' tradition as the privileged understanding of the phenomenon at hand. Mukherjee's framework combines Roland Barthes' extension of "textuality" to cover different mediated forms beyond the printed word, Jean-Jacques Derrida's understanding of "writing" as the central concept of all mediated expression, as well Gilles Deleuze and Felix Guattari's work on the "machinic." He takes these concepts together as ground truth for analyzing mediated expressions from which all other perspectives are judged. However, no actual argument for the privileged status of these perspectives is provided. The references to Barthes, Derrida, and Deleuze/Guattari together with the supporting perspective of "remediation" (Bolter & Grusin, 2000) are taken as sufficient evidence to support the approach. To Mukherjee, the question then becomes one of making game studies compatible with existing perspectives in the humanities, "how games 'plug into' aspects of humanities studies in ways that are vital." Yet, in Mukherjee's view, the 'plugging into' can only happen in the terms set by existing frameworks in the humanities. From this perspective, Murkherjee criticizes the ludologists for their audacity to declare video games a specific object requiring specific lines of inquiry that differ from those prevalent in the humanities. Beyond that, his critique seems unaware of the inherent discrepancies of the ludological argument and thus he simply accepts the ludologists' positioning and characterization of the so-called "narratologists." Conversely, Mukherjee's project is focused on criticizing what he understands as the unwarranted separatism of games studies from the humanities. The differences in technological basis between video games and earlier forms like books and film do not warrant a difference in the analytical approach, according to him:

> Following Derrida's argument, all technology, being forms of writing, are not prostheses. Instead of being prosthetic, they also inform the (non) centres of each other; at the same time, these elements are separate objects in themselves. Poole's example of football as not being technology-specific (and therefore, perhaps, embodying 'pure' play) while video games are entirely dependent on computers, therefore, rests on a questionable notion of technicity. Just as

football can be played using 'scrunched up paper' (as well as in a FIFA video game or board-game), video games are not limited to the computer. It can be played on the various consoles, mobile phones, handheld devices or even in books which, as some examples in the later chapters will show, sometimes exhibit clear signs of being proto-video games.

p. 11

This is a curious argument, especially the one about video games not being confined to computers, since all his listed alternatives to the computer are equally technical, digital platforms and thus provide no support for an argument against the technical basis of video games as an essential distinguishing aspect. Equally, that some paper-based forms might be seen as "proto-video games" is not an argument against the specific status of actual video games. Incidentally, Murray considered the same aspect already in 1997 in *Hamlet on the Holodeck* with the opposite conclusion in a chapter on proto-works which she termed "harbingers" (Murray, 1997).

When it comes to the so-called "narratologists," Mukherjee copies the misconstruing of Murray's argument – which is as about new forms of narrative in the digital medium and not about all games – practically unmodified from the ludologists as being about video games. "The ambitiousness of Murray's *agenda for video games* emerges more clearly in the following assertion" [my emphasis]. Curiously, the author seems aware of alternative conceptions of IDN as a separate form ("some critics even see them as an entirely new phenomenon quite separate from earlier narrative and ludic media.") yet he does not concern himself further with this perspective.

By this time, Mukherjee's agenda and method are clear. He follows an argument by Derrida to negate the "prosthetic" character of technology and instead takes any kind of difference in representation as a question of different "assemblages:"

> The first thing to observe is that if video games are rapidly gaining importance then this is so because of the multiplicity of networks (socio-cultural, political or economic) to which they connect. In themselves, too, they are characterised by multiplicity: they have a multiplicity of endings and game events take place in multiple points in time. Only by studying the multiple nature of video games is it possible to gain a fuller understanding of the growing influence of video games and to envisage their role in the future. To do so, however, the methodology of analysing games in terms of opposing binaries, out of which emerges the assumption of video games as one core essence, needs to be challenged. Instead of binaries, perhaps a model that considers games as a multiplicity of assemblages would be more appropriate.

ibid

On this basis, any observable differences to traditional forms are relegated to a secondary question of different "assemblages" and "supplementarity" under the proper theory-imperialistic order of established frameworks in the humanities.

> Throughout this book, supplementarity will be used to describe Derrida's concept of originary presence and interiority, and will provide the framework for rethinking the binaries of game/ story, game/ machine and story/ machine. Revisited in terms of this framework, the debates around the storytelling capabilities of video games will be seen as being problematic and, in some respects, lacking credibility.
>
> *ibid*

Instead of considering and addressing the "debates about storytelling capabilities of games" directly, they are declared problematic and even invalid. Yet, what we should worry about is whether a given analytical framework is able to concretely detect and analyze specific aspects of the object in question. Instead of being concerned with fitting into an established academic tradition, we should focus on improving the understanding of the object of our inquiry. This means we need to strongly consider the limitation imposed by frameworks not originally intended to understand dynamic interactive artifacts. It is certainly the case that Mukherjee is aware of the need for theoretical innovation with regard to the understanding of games. However, this insight is severely undermined by a perspective that allows innovation only within established humanities frameworks.

Cybertext Poetics

In contrast to Murkherjee, Eskelinen presents an effort at a 'grand unified theory' coming from the side of ludology. In his book *Cybertext Poetics* (Eskelinen, 2012b) Eskelinen merges literary narratology (mainly Genette (Genette, 1980)) and Aarseth's earlier (pre-ludology) work on cybertexts. (Aarseth, 1997) This approach might be somewhat surprising, given Eskelinen's seemingly staunch opposition to established narratology in the heyday of the ludology vs. narratology debate. Indeed, his attempt to solve "four persistent and strategically chosen problems in four separate, yet interconnected fields: literary theory, narratology, game studies, and digital media" (Eskelinen, 2012b) is yet another testimony to the unresolved nature of the issues underlying the narratology vs. ludology debate. Interestingly, Eskelinen's problem analysis bears resemblance to my own. "The problems in the first three fields stem from the same root: hegemonic theories are based on a subset of possible media behaviors that is far too limited, and this limitation seriously undermines their explanatory and analytical power." (ibid) In principle I would like to agree here; however, it is not immediately clear how these problems can be solved by re-introducing one of the supposedly hegemonic theories (here, Genette's) ludology was initially focused on rejecting. It is also interesting to see that 'texts' (in the semiotic meaning as an assemblage of signs) are Eskelinen's overarching category, despite Aarseth's apparent rejection of the term. "Are games texts? The best reason I can think of why one would ask such a crude question is because one is a literary or semiotic theorist and wants to believe in the relevance of one's training." (Aarseth, 2004a)

Unfortunately, Eskelinen's book fails to provide convincing evidence of the usefulness of this approach. Rather, the persistent distinction between digital and non-digital forms in this volume is at odds with the stated goal to provide an all-encompassing model and points to the limitations of a perspective that, on the one hand, insists on media-agnosticism (cybertexts are not media specific) and, on the other hand, is aware of the specific characteristics of the digital medium (digital cybertexts vs. non-digital ones).

Beyond the dichotomic view

Juul's understanding of narrative in *Half-Real* (Juul, 2005) is more nuanced than his earlier rejection of video games as a narrative medium. However, he seems unable to escape the 'fixed narrative/rules-based game' dichotomy. As I have shown earlier, several of his allegations appear ideologically motivated, and even entirely in opposition to clearly stated positions (e.g., by Brenda Laurel). Another problematic argument in *Half-Real* is the claimed inability to consolidate different perspectives on the meaning of "narrative:"

> [...] the term narrative has such a wide range of contradictory meanings and associations for different people and in different theories that it is practically meaningless unless specified in great detail.
>
> *ibid*

This statement might seem innocent enough, however, it presupposes that: (a) no common ground between different theoretical positions can be found, and that (b) exclusive, detailed specifications are the only way to elucidate meaning. This perspective prevents the consideration of more inclusive definitions such as the one Barthes offers (cited earlier and repeated here for convenience).

> There are countless forms of narrative in the world. Among the vehicles of narrative are articulated language, whether oral or written, pictures still or moving, gestures, and an ordered mixture of all those substances. Narrative is present in myth, legend, fables, tales, short stories, epics, history, tragedy, *drame* [suspense drama], comedy, pantomime, paintings (in Santa Ursula by Carpaccio, for instance), stained-glass windows, movies, local news, conversations.
>
> *Barthes & Duisit, 1975*

Or the one by David Herman:

> [Narrative is a] forgiving, flexible cognitive frame for constructing, communicating, and reconstructing mentally projected worlds.
>
> *Herman 2002*

Barthes and Herman's perspectives can accommodate games as narratives. The latter's inclusive understanding of narrative – influenced by advances in cognitive science – has been the productive basis for many narratology scholars over the past two decades. In other words, more inclusive perspectives are certainly not "practically meaningless" but they do constitute a challenge for a project that insists on a dichotomy between games and narratives. And this particular dichotomy is not between equals, as Juul's understanding of the influence of the digital medium shows. In this respect, Juul points out that modern digital forms change the classic game model:

> While video games mostly conform to the classic game model, they also modify the conventions of the classic game model. Games *have* changed. So while it makes sense to see games as a fairly well defined form, this book is also about how video games modify and supplement the classic game model.
> *Juul, 2005 [Juul's emphasis]*

This remark makes Juul's narrative fundamentalism quite obvious – he perceives the changes to expressive forms affected by the digital medium, but admits the effect only in regard to games – an artificial restriction that is not supported by arguments. As a thought experiment, I would like to modify Juul's statement.

> While interactive digital narratives mostly conform to the classic narrative model, they also modify the conventions of the classic narrative model. Narratives *have* changed. So while it makes sense to see narrative as a fairly well defined form, this book is also about how interactive digital narratives modify and supplement the classic narrative model.

Or, in a more inclusive variant, that would cover both games and narratives:

> While interactive digital forms mostly conform to their respective classic non-interactive models, they also modify the conventions of the respective classic non-interactive model. Interactive digital forms *have* changed. So while it makes sense to see types of mediated expression as fairly well defined forms, this book is also about how interactive digital forms modify and supplement the respective classic non-interactive model.

This modification ends the special role claimed only for games by Juul and other ludologists. It emancipates narrative from an artificial restriction to certain traditional forms – from narrative fundamentalism. That the latter is still very much alive over a decade after Juul's book becomes obvious in Ian Bogost's 2017 article in the Atlantic. "Video games are better without stories. Film, television, and literature all tell them better." (Bogost, 2017) The underlying assumption for this claim is that narrative in video games has to conform to the model provided by the earlier forms mentioned. And surely, Bogost is right – traditional media are better in presenting the traditional forms of narrative we conventionally associate them with. Yet, this fundamentalist position ignores both established forms of narrative outside of the tight confines of the dominant canon of Eurocentric mainstream film, television, and literature as well as the possibility for novel forms of narrative. IDN is located in this larger, more inclusive space of narrative.

Future work: A Grand Unified Theory of Narrative

The developments that led to the establishment of a dominating dichotomic per-spective in games studies and manifestations of theoretical imperialism point to the need for a *Grand Unified Theory of Narrative*, and this is how we should under-stand the legacy of the narratology vs. ludology debate, by exposing foundational problems of our understanding of the phenomenon of narrative. A grand unified theory of narrative must be able to identify which aspects are media-specific and which are not. Ideally, such an effort would first identify characteristics of print narrative, cinematic narrative, oral narratives, interactive digital narrative, and so forth, and then proceed to identify commonalities across media, without put-ting printed, mostly Eurocentric literary expressions in a privileged position to start with. Unfortunately, this ideal perspective is also currently unrealistic, pre-cisely because an established print-literary understanding of narrative already exists, exerting a dominant normative influence.

Yet, similar to the way the normative influence of colonialist and patriarchal conceptions has been challenged and ultimately reduced through continuous schol-arly and practical efforts, we must continue to add to the specific understanding of different narrative forms. A crucial element in this regard is an increased awareness for media-specific aspects. Traditionally in the humanities, the medium has been ignored, as we can learn from N. Katherine Hayles, "within the humanities and especially in literary studies, there has traditionally been a sharp line between representation and the technologies producing them." (Hayles, 2002) What Hayles talks about here, is equivalent to the 'Cartesian split' between body and mind, an influential perspective that postulated the independence of the mind from the body. Developments in neurosciences, the study of experience and consciousness (phenomenology) and a general acknowledgment of the importance of embodied perspectives have increasingly challenged the dogma of a separation between body and mind. Yet, when it comes to the study of narrative, the dogma of 'media agnos-ticism' – the study of narrative expressions as independent from their medium is very much alive and thus Hayle's assessment is still valid today. The best chance we have to overcome this "media blindness" (Hausken, 2004) is by acknowledging media specificity and in focusing on understanding media-specific forms better. The question of media-specificity should not be reduced to one of granularity in our analytical tools and to categories that are assumed to be transmedial, two of the strategies used in Jan-Noel Thon's "Transmedial Narratology" (2016). While Thon's effort is certainly impressive, our knowledge of many aspects specific to IDN is still limited. This is why, at this point in time, I advocate to concentrate on adding to the specific understanding of interactive digital narrative, an effort that amounts to the creation of a specific IDN theory. Once our knowledge of interactive digital narratives has grown significantly, we can engage in another attempt at a unified, cross-medial theory of narrative.

Narrative indifference

Before closing this part, I want to draw attention to what we can understand as narrative fundamentalism's 'evil twin,' – *narrative indifference*. While the former restricts narrative to a small subset of the actual space, the latter fails to provide any definition or model. Concretely, this means the use of terms like 'story,' 'narrative,' 'fiction,' or 'storytelling' without any direct explanation or definition of what these terms mean. In such situations, an inaccessible implicit definition is being used, which relegates the concrete meaning to the field of speculation. This issue here is not only a question of academic rigor, but one that also has severe consequences in the practice, for example, in interdisciplinary projects when contributors from different fields collaborate. Without a clear definition of terms in the word field around narrative, much energy and time can be wasted, as a game designer might have a very different idea of what, for example, the term 'story' entails in comparison to someone with a background in film or theater. Crucially, the success of interactive narrative projects depends on a shared understanding of key terms. Indeed, a former member of my research lab, who has successfully managed award-winning transmedia projects, spends considerable time and energy to alleviate the problem and enable a productive collaboration between diverse contributors. However, even within teams from the same discipline, a shared understanding of what 'story' and related terms mean is not guaranteed and therefore it is a best practice to work with explicit definitions.

From a scholarly perspective, inaccessible definitions constitute an impediment to evaluation and further development. How can we situate a new analysis or technical solution vs. earlier ones when we do not know what definition of key terminology is being used? Consequently, a paper on any aspect of IDN without such a definition is problematic and its contribution to the field is limited.

This tendency is at its worst when the implicit definition changes even within a single contribution. An instance in this regard is a paper from McCoy et al. on *Prom Week* (McCoy, Treanor, Samuel, Reed, & Mateas, 2013). Here, the authors variously refer to the term 'story' as a "personally meaningful" game experience ('story' is the experience), as a "campaign," (now 'story' is the progression) as "gameplay," (and now 'story' is the activity), as a "collection of levels [...] where the player can take social actions" ('story' here is more restricted to mean social actions). In addition, they write about "player agency at the story level" (this means 'story' is only one layer affected by player agency within the game) and the "player's path through the story" (now 'story' seems to mean 'story world'). In each of these instances, 'story' refers to different concepts without any clear indication of the underlying definition.

This example is particularly unfortunate since *Prom Week* is an important work in the field of IDN. However, by leaving the meaning of key terminology to individual interpretation, it is near impossible to assess this contribution in relation to earlier work and to use it as a basis for future research. Instead of clearly situating the contribution in the scholarly and professional discourse around IDN, this paper only offers an isolated description. As a result, the impact of the research and development on *Prom Week* has unfortunately been less than what this important work deserves.

Summary

For the understanding of interactive digital narrative, we are faced with a dual challenge of *narrative fundamentalism* and *narrative indifference*. The former is an ideological and normative perspective that artificially restricts the phenomenon of narrative to certain traditionalistic Eurocentric forms (the novel and the Hollywood-style movie) and thus precludes a recognition of IDN as a novel expression requiring the development of specific theoretical concepts and design approaches. *Narrative fundamentalism* is particularly prominent in pronouncements of universality of narrative structures (e.g., story arc, monomyth) in design practice, but also as an important factor in the ludology vs. narratology debate, where it is used to proclaim an essential opposition between narrative and games with long-term consequences for the conception of narrative in games.

Narrative indifference describes the tendency of failing to provide any definition of narrative and related terminology which precludes the proper assessment and positioning of a given contribution. For the further development of IDN, it is crucial to overcome both of these issues. To do so, I will develop a specific model and framework for the analysis of interactive digital narrative in part three.

Notes

1 I considered the following translations: A Scholtz, 2008; I Bywater, 1920; S H Butcher, 1902.
2 Witkowski, W. (2021): Videogames are a bigger industry than movies and North American sports combined, thanks to the pandemic, www.marketwatch.com/story/videogames-are-a-bigger-industry-than-sports-and-movies-combined-thanks-to-the-pandemic-1160 8654990
3 Review aggregator GameRankings.com reports a score of 82.7% based on seven reviews, Macworld magazine declared *Myst* "Game of the Year" and several articles in mainstream media outlets (New York Times, Wired, Entertainment Weekly, San Francisco Chronicle) lauded the game as an artistic achievement.
4 Another influential development in narratology, the question of "natural" narratives following Monika Fludernik's 1996 groundbreaking book (Fludernik, 1996) is equally missing from the debate.

References

2K Games. (2007). BioShock. Novato, California, U.S.: 2K Games.
Aarseth, E. J. (1997). *Cybertext*. JHU Press.
Aarseth, E. J. (2001). Computer Game Studies, Year One. *Game Studies*, 1(1).

Aarseth, E. J. (2004a). Genre Trouble. In N. Wardrip-Fruin & P. Harrigan (Eds.), *First Person: New Media as Story, Performance, and Game*. Cambridge, MA: MIT Press. Retrieved from www.electronicbookreview.com/thread/firstperson/vigilant

Aarseth, E. J. (2004b, January 5). Espen Aarseth responds. Retrieved November 26, 2017, from http://electronicbookreview.com/thread/firstperson/cornucopia

Aarseth, E. J. (2012). A Narrative Theory of Games (pp. 1–5). Presented at the Foundations of Digital Games 2015. http://doi.org/978-1-4503-1333-9/12/05

Aarseth, E. J. (2014a). Ludology. In M. J. P. Wolf & B. Perron (Eds.), *The Routledge Companion to Video Game Studies*. Routledge. http://doi.org/10.4324/9780203114261.ch23

Aarseth, E. J. (2014b). Ludology. In *The Routledge Companion to Video Game Studies*. Routledge.

Apperly, T. (2019, March 26). On the Persistence of Game Studies Dull Binary. Retrieved August 17, 2022, from https://critical-distance.com/amber/cache/e14dfa4228cef783d 0f2c901ac08fcd5/

Aristotle Transl S H Butcher. (1902). Poetics. (S. H. Butcher, Trans.) (pp. 1–33). Retrieved from http://classics.mit.edu//Aristotle/poetics.html

Barthes, R., & Duisit, L. (1975). An Introduction to the Structural Analysis of Narrative. *New Literary History*, 6(2), 237. http://doi.org/10.2307/468419

Bogost, I. (2017, April 24). Video Games Are Better Without Stories. Retrieved April 24, 2017, from www.theatlantic.com/technology/archive/2017/04/video-games-stories/ 524148/?utm_source=atlfb

Bolter, J. D., & Grusin, R. (2000). *Remediation: Understanding New Media*. Cambridge, MA: MIT Press.

Butler, J. (1999). *Gender Trouble*. London, New York: Routledge.

Calleja, G. (2013). Narrative Involvement in Digital Games. Presented at the Foundations of Digital Games.

Calleja, G. (2015). Game Narrative: An Alternate Genealogy. In Digital Interfaces in Situation of Mobility. Digital Interfaces in Situation of Mobility.

Campagna, F. (2018). Games | Game Design | Game Studies: An Introduction. *Design Issues*, 34(2), 83–84.

Campbell, J. (1949). *The Hero with a Thousand Faces*. New York, NY: Harper & Row.

Campo Santo. (2016). Firewatch. Portland, OR: Panic.

CD Project RED. (2015). The Witcher 3. Warsaw: CD Project.

Chatman, S. B. (1980). *Story and Discourse: Narrative Structure in Fiction and Film*. Ithaca and London: Cornell University Press.

Crenshaw, K. W. (2017). *On Intersectionality: Essential Writings*. The New Press. NYC

Cyan. (1993). Myst. Eugene, Oregon: Broderbund.

de Beauvoir, S. (2014). *The Second Sex*. Random House.

Delgado, R., & Stefancic, J. (2017). *Critical Race Theory*. New York University Press.

Dontnod Entertainment. (2015). Life is Strange. Dontnod Entertainment.

Dundes, A. (1984). *Sacred Narrative*. Univ of California Press.

Dundes, A. (2005). Folkloristics in the Twenty-First Century. *The Journal of American Folklore*, 118, 385–408.

Electronic Arts. (2007). Mass Effect [Video game]. Edmonton: Electronic Arts.

Ensslin, A. (2014). *Literary Gaming*. Cambridge, MA: MIT Press.

Eskelinen, M. (2001). The Gaming Situation. *Game Studies*, 1(1). Retrieved from www.game studies.org/0101/eskelinen/

Eskelinen, M. (2004, September 1). Markku Eskelinen's response. Retrieved November 26, 2017, from www.electronicbookreview.com/thread/firstperson/astragalian

Eskelinen, M. (2012a). *Cybertext Poetics*. London, New York: Bloomsbury Publishing USA.

Eskelinen, M. (2012b). *Cybertext Poetics*. New York, NY: Bloomsbury Publishing USA.

Field, S. (1979). *Screenplay: The Basics of Film Writing*. New York: Random House Publishing Group.

Finnegan, R. (2012). *Oral Literature in Africa*. Open Book Publishers.

Fludernik, M. (1996). *Towards a "Natural" Narratology*. Routledge.

Frasca, G. (1999). Ludology Meets Narratology: Similitude and Differences between (Video) Games and Narrative. Retrieved December 3, 2017, from www.ludology.org/articles/ludology.htm

Frasca, G. (2003). Ludologists Love Stories, Too: Notes from a Debate that Never Took Place. DIGRA Conf.

Freebird Games. (2011). To the Moon. Freebird Games.

Freytag, G. (1863). Die Technik des Dramas.

Fullerton, T., Swain, C., & Hoffman, S. S. (2008). *Game Design Workshop (2nd ed.)*. Burlington, MA: Morgan Kaufmann.

Genette, G. (1980). *Narrative Discourse, an Essay in Method*. Ithaca: NY: Cornell UP.

Green, R., & Larson, J. (2014). That Dragon, Cancer. Retrieved March 29, 2015, from http://thatdragoncancer.com/

Hausken, L. (2004). Coda. In *Narrative Across Media* (pp. 391–403). University of Nebraska Press.

Hayles, N. K. (2002). *Writing Machines*. Cambridge, MA: MIT Press.

Herman, D. (2002). *Story Logic*. Lincoln, NE: University of Nebraska Press.

Herman, D. (2013). Cognitive Narratology. In P. Hühn, J. C. Meister, J. Pier, & W. Schmid (Eds.), *The Living Handbook of Narratology*. Hamburg: Hamburg University. Retrieved from www.lhn.uni-hamburg.de/article/cognitive-narratology-revised-version-uploaded-22-september-2013

Hudson, K. (2013). The Novelist. Orthogonal Games.

Ibsch, E. (1990). The Cognitive Turn in Narratology. *Poetics Today*, 11 (2), 411–418.

Ion Storm. (2000). Deus Ex. London, UK: Eidos Interactive.

Jenkins, H. (2004). Game Design as Narrative Architecture. In N. Wardrip-Fruin & P. Harrigan (Eds.), *First Person: New Media as Story, Performance, and Game*. Cambridge, MA: MIT Press. Retrieved from www.electronicbookreview.com/thread/firstperson/lazzi-fair

Jennings, P. (1996). Narrative Structures for New Media. *Leonardo*, 29(5), 345–350.

Juul, J. (1999a). *A Clash between Game and Narrative*. Danish Literature.

Juul, J. (1999b). *A clash between game and narrative: A thesis on computer games and interactive fiction*. University of Copenhagen.

Juul, J. (2001). Games Telling Stories. *Game Studies*, 1(1).

Juul, J. (2005). *Half-Real*. Cambridge, MA: MIT Press.

Kapell, M. W. (2015). *The Play Versus Story Divide in Game Studies*. McFarland.

Kopp, R. (2013, January 21). Overcome Kishotenketsu to Improve Your Communication with Americans. Retrieved June 2, 2018, from www.japanintercultural.com/en/news/default.aspx?newsid=240

Laurel, B. (1986). *Toward the Design of a Computer-Based Interactive Fantasy System*. Ohio State University.

Laurel, B. (1991). *Computers As Theatre*. Boston, MA: Addison-Wesley.

LeRay, L. (2017, January 3). Developing A Cat's Manor in Saudi Arabia for a Western Audience. Retrieved November 21, 2017, from www.gamasutra.com/view/news/285904/Developing_A_Cats_Manor_in_Saudi_Arabia_for_a_Western_Audience.php

Lunenfeld, P. (2010). Story Arc. In *Routledge Encyclopedia of Narrative Theory*. New York: Routledge.

Mäyrä, F. (2020). Game Culture Studies and the Politics of Scholarship. *G|a|M|E Games as Art, Media, Entertainment*, (9), 11–31.

McCoy, J., Treanor, M., Samuel, B., Reed, A. A., & Mateas, M. (2013). Prom Week: Designing Past the Game/Story Dilemma. Foundations of Digital Games 2015.

Mukherjee, S. (2015). *Video Games and Storytelling*. Springer. http://doi.org/10.1007/978-1-137-52505-5

Murdock, M. (1990). *The Heroine's Journey*. Shambhala Publications.

Murray, J. H. (1997). *Hamlet on the Holodeck: the Future of Narrative in Cyberspace*. New York: Free Press.

Murray, J. H. (2004). From Game-Story to Cyberdrama. In N. Wardrip-Fruin & P. Harrigan (Eds.), *First Person: New Media as Story, Performance, and Game*. Cambridge, MA: MIT Press.

Murray, J. H. (2005). The Last Word on Ludology vs Narratology in Game Studies. Retrieved July 2, 2015, from https://inventingthemedium.com/2013/06/28/the-last-word-on-ludology-v-narratology-2005/

Murray, J. H. (2011). *Inventing the Medium: Principles of Interaction Design as a Cultural Practice*. Cambridge, MA: MIT Press.

Naughty Dog. (2014). The Last of Us [Video game]. Tokyo: Sony Computer Entertainment.

Naughty Dog. (2020). The Last of Us 2. Tokyo: Sony Entertainment.

Neys, J., & Jansz, J. (2018). Engagement in Play, Engagement in Politics: Playing Political Video Games. *In The Playful Citizen* (pp. 1–21). Games and Play. http://doi.org/10.5117/9789462984523/ch02

Núñez-Pacheco, R., & Phillip, P.-T. (2021). Divergent Theoretical Trajectories in Game Studies: a Bibliographical Review. *Artnodes*, (28). https://doi.org/10.7238/artnodes.v0i28.380176.

OED Online. (n.d.). arc, n. Retrieved June 11, 2016, from www.oed.com.othmerlib.chemheritage.org/view/Entry/10245?rskey=gMstLd&result=1

Phillips, A. (2020). Negg(at)ing the Game Studies Subject: An Affective History of the Field. *Feminist Media Histories*, *6*(1), 12–36.

Pope, L. (2013). Papers, Please. 3909 LLC.

Prince, G. (1987). *A Dictionary of Narratology*. Lincoln, NE: University of Nebraska Press.

Prince, G. (2003). *A Dictionary of Narratology*. Lincoln, NE: University of Nebraska Press.

Quantic Dream. (2018). *Detroit: Become Human*. San Mateo, CA: Sony Interactive Entertainment.

Quinn, Z., & Lindsey, P. (2013). Depression Quest. The Quinnspiracy.

Rockstar Studios. (2018). Red Dead Redemption 2. Rockstar Games.

Rothstein, E. (1994, December 4). *A New Art Form May Arise From the "Myst."* New York Times. New York, NY.

Ruiz, S. (2006). Darfur is Dying. interFUEL. Retrieved from www.gamesforchange.org/game/darfur-is-dying/

Ryan, M. L. (2001). Beyond Myth and Metaphor: The Case of Narrative in Digital Media. Retrieved November 30, 2017, from www.gamestudies.org/0101/ryan/

Ryan, M. L. (2006). *Avatars Of Story*. Minneapolis: University Of Minnesota Press.

Ryan, M. L. (2009). From Narrative Games to Playable Stories: Toward a Poetics of Interactive Narrative. Storyworlds: *A Journal of Narrative Studies*, *1*(1), 43–59. http://doi.org/10.1353/stw.0.0003

Schell, J. (2008). *The Art of Game Design: a Book of Lenses*. Amsterdam; Boston: Elsevier/Morgan Kaufmann.

Scheub, H. (1985). A Review of African Oral Traditions and Literature. *African Studies Review*, *28*(2/3), 1–72. http://doi.org/10.2307/524603

Simons, J. (2007). Narrative, Games, and Theory. *Games Studies*, *7*(1). Retrieved from http://gamestudies.org/0701/articles/simons

Starbreeze Studios. (2013). Brothers: A Tale of Two Sons. 505 Game.

Tale of Tales. (2008). The Graveyard. Ghent: Tale of Tales.

Tale of Tales. (2009). The Path. Ghent: Tale of Tales.

Tale of Tales. (2015). Sunset. Ghent: Tale of Tales.

The Chinese Room (2008). Dear Esther. Portsmouth, UK: The Chinese Room.

The Fullbright Company. (2013). Gone Home. Portland, OR: The Fullbright Company.

Thon, J. N. (2016). *Transmedial Narratology and Contemporary Media Culture*. Nebraska.

Valve. (1998). Half-Life. Oakhurst, CA: Sierra Studios.

Vargas-Iglesias, J. J., & Navarrete-Cardero, L. (2019). Beyond Rules and Mechanics: A Different Approach for Ludology. *Games and Culture*, 13, 155541201882293. http://doi.org/10.1177/1555412018822937

Vogler, C. (2007). *The Writer's Journey*. Studio City, CA: Michael Wiese.

Voorhees, G. (2019). Genre Troubles in Game Studies: Ludology, Agonism, and Social Action. *Kinephanos*, (May 2019). Retrieved from www.kinephanos.ca/2019/genre-troubles-in-game-studies-ludology-agonism-and-social-action/

Walk, W. (2018, May 14). The Myth of the Monomyth. Retrieved May 31, 2018, from www.gamasutra.com/blogs/WolfgangWalk/20180514/318014/The_Myth_of_the_Monomyth.php

Wardrip-Fruin, N., & Harrigan, P. (2004). *First Person-New Media as Story, Performance, and Game*. Cambridge, MA: MIT Press.

Watson, K. (2005). Queer Theory. *Group Analysis*, *38*(1), 67–81.

Watts, N. (2010). *Write a Novel and Get It Published: A Teach Yourself Guide*. McGraw-Hill.

Welsh, T. J. (2015). Literary Gaming [Book Review]. *American Journal of Play*, (Spring), 396–398.

Wright, W. (2000). The Sims [Video game]. Redwood City, CA: Electronic Arts.

Yorke, J. (2014). *Into the Woods: A Five-Act Journey Into Story*. The Overlook Press.

Part 3

SPP

A model and analytical framework for IDN

The move to IDN theory

In the previous part, I have shown that narrative fundamentalism – restricting narrative to a limited number of manifestations – is a major factor in discussions about interactive digital narrative (IDN). On that basis, problematic and misleading arguments have been made about IDN which result in misconceptions. For instance, when it comes to games, the concern for interactive narratives is neither a movement to take over the discipline of game studies nor a means to reform games. Inclusive conceptions of narrative – such as the ones by Roland Barthes and Lionel Duisit (Barthes & Duisit, 1975) or by David Herman (Herman, 2002) (see previous part) – provide a foundation for a formal model of interactive digital narrative forms. Unfortunately, they also do not deliver much more than that, as these perspectives have been developed and applied in the context of understanding static artefacts – print literature and movies – and the resulting analyses are limited in their capacity to understand novel dynamic forms of narrative expression. The cause of these limitations lies in several fundamental issues which arise from the application of narratology for IDN analysis. These issues stem from a conceptual basis of media-independence with consequences for the ability to detect and analyze novel phenomena.

Media-independence is a fundamental issue in narratology – conceptually, this academic discipline has long understood its object of analysis as independent of the medium, yet the discipline's insights are overwhelmingly based on the analysis of printed literary texts and then are often universally applied, regardless of the medium. This situation has been criticized as a case of ignorance toward the importance of the respective medium by N. Kathrine Hayles (2002) and as outright "media blindness" by Liv Hausken (2004), as discussed in the previous part of this volume. This means that applying a framework intended to understand print

DOI: 10.4324/9781003106425-3

literature to IDN will analyze these interactive works as if they were a form of print literature and thus restrict our understanding of the specific aspects of the novel phenomenon. A typical outcome of such an approach is the fallacy of collapsing the interactivity inherent in all forms of narrative consumption – interpretation and speculation – with the kind of interactivity afforded by the digital medium, the ability to plan an action and engender actual changes to the artifact and its virtual word. I have described this aspect as the difference between *interactivity 1* (interpretation and speculation) and *interactivity 2* (planning and execution) in the introduction. Certainly, both types of interactivity exist, yet in order to fully understand IDN, we need to be able to analyze the specific characteristics of *interactivity 2*.

Concrete testimony to the limitations of a project focused on adapting literary narratology to understand IDN is Marie-Laure Ryan's struggle with recognizing interactivity as an integrated aspect. Her strategy is to position interactivity outside the realm of narrative, as a technical aspect and a problem of design only. She claims that "interactivity is not a feature that facilitates the construction of narrative meaning" – a sentence so central to Ryan that she repeats it verbatim in two publications (Ryan, 2002; 2006).[1] Ryan here conceives of narrative meaning-making in the manner afforded by traditional, non-interactive forms and therefore takes the presence of cinematic 'cut scenes' as evidence for her claim. Yet, cut scenes might equally be taken as evidence for narrative fundamentalism – for the inability to use the potential of interactivity for meaning-making. What we see here is an example of the analytical limitations arising from the application of legacy frameworks designed originally for print literature and thus we should not expect them to detect the importance of interactivity and other specific qualities of IDN.

More recent efforts to address the issue of media-independence have resulted in a "media-conscious narratology" (Ryan & Thon, 2014), or "transmedial narratology" (Herman, 2004; Thon, 2016). However, the focus here is still on preserving as much of the established instruments of print narratology as possible, creating an imbalance between supposedly "transmedial" categories and media-specific ones. Concretely, transmedial narratology distinguishes between "medium-free" concepts, those that are "transmedially valid yet not medium-free" and "medium- specific" ones. In the "medium-free" category, there are "character, events, setting, time, space, and causality" (Ryan & Thon, 2014). Yet, this categorization only makes sense if the concepts are taken as highly abstract with limited application for concrete analysis. We need to ask whether a character we can only view or read about is really the same ontological and epistemological entity as a character we have control over. While the role of the interactor varies between different forms of IDN, their status toward the main character is often closer to that of an actor than that of a protagonist perceived by a viewer or reader. Furthermore, a reactive non-player character (NPC) is not the same entity as a minor character encountered in a print literary narrative. If we want to understand what character means in IDN, media-specificity is key and the same condition applies for the other supposedly "medium-free" categories. For example, a 3D space an interactor can explore is a very different category from space which is described or shown in print literature and film.

In addition, transmedial narratology features a combinatorial perspective in which variants of IDN, such as narrative video games, are described as only the sum of its parts, for example in the following definition offered by Jan-Noel Thon for video game narrative in his book *Transmedial Narratology and Contemporary Media Culture*:

> [Video game narrative is a] combination of interactive simulation, scripted events, and cutscenes (the latter of which in particular can, of course, integrate multimodal configurations from many other representational media), which are sometimes arranged in a nonlinear narrative structure that may result in a number of very different narrative representations, depending on player performance, player decisions, and similar parameters.
>
> *Thon, 2016*

While this approach improves earlier narratological positions, it is still rooted in them. Thon's description here might be classified as an observation from the outside and is correct as such, but with a limited understanding of the inner workings of IDN due to analytical categories never intended to describe dynamic phenomena. IDN are a coherent dynamic representation in their own right, a multi-variant and multilinear expression certainly influenced by and built on earlier "representational media," but predicated on interactivity and the shift to dynamic systems. The material basis of IDN differs considerably from that of the print medium or film and is instead routed in computation. Under these conditions, the elements are connected in a cybernetic feedback loop and might change dynamically independently (e.g., a character in an role-playing game (RPG) or the structure in a procedural narrative system) but also together (e.g., character development can have an impact on the progression and outcome). In that sense, IDN systems are larger than the sum of their parts and expose the limitations of mechanical thinking (cf. Koenitz & Eladhari 2021, also see Bellini 2022).

Trying to understand IDN by applying the perspective of the novel, movie, and play, or a combination of earlier forms, means to frame IDN as a variant of these traditional forms, effectively looking at oranges and describing them as variants of apples. And as long as we keep doing that, we should not be surprised to find oranges deficient in their role as apples. Unfortunately, that is what has happened to IDN for a long time – this novel expression was described using the framing of different phenomena. And exactly that is the problem. IDN are neither deficient video games nor are they enhanced movies or literary works. They are a specific expression and need their own conceptual framework to understand them. Applying the analytical framework of literary-based narratology to IDN, even in its postclassical and 'transmedial' versions, carries too great a danger of failing to detect or misunderstand the specific aspects and qualities of the novel phenomenon. What is needed instead is a 'material turn' of IDN theory that makes provision for the specific qualities of IDN.

The emphasis on difference does not mean to deny that lines of continuation to earlier forms of narrative expression exist – they certainly do – but that it makes sense to concentrate on specific aspects for the present discussion on what separates IDN from earlier forms. Once we have built up this knowledge, we are in a better position to compare IDN and traditional forms at some point in the future. Indeed, similar reasons have led to specific film theory and film studies as a discipline distinct from literary studies. The difference between dynamic and fixed representations is at least as significant as the one between textual representations and moving images. For these reasons, especially the difference in material basis and the limitations of adapted analytical frameworks, there is a need for IDN theory as a conceptual basis for the analysis and creation of IDN artifacts. How we conceptualize IDN is not only a concern for scholars – it equally affects the practice. For example, if we subscribe to a belief in the universal existence and applicability of the hero's journey, our designs and finished works will be limited by that structural concept.

The vocabulary question

There are also pragmatic reasons for the move to IDN theory and vocabulary. Much confusion around the topic of narrative is due to its relationship with an abundance of diverse traditions and associated vocabulary that lacks precision. In the general discourse so far, we cannot be sure what is actually meant when someone uses words like "storytelling," "story," or "narrative" – are these words interchangeable? In everyday usage, we might feel so, but for scholars and professionals, these words have acquired specific meanings, accessible only to the specialized group to which they belong. The newspaper journalist's written story is neither the one that the film director creates with the means of cinematic storytelling nor the one that the theater director produces with a stage production, and neither is it the one an author of a novel writes. All these narrative forms have specific conventions, genres, structures, and means of distribution. They might share a topic or narrative material like characters or setting, and they even might be intended to serve the same purpose, but their production methods and resulting material artifacts are quite different. In addition, all of these forms engage their audiences in specific ways. And yet, this specialization has not resulted in a more granular, precise vocabulary when it comes to the word field around narrative. A newspaper journalist, film director, stage director and novelist might all use terms like "storytelling," "story," and "narrative" but mean quite different things. This issue becomes most obvious in transmedial projects, where often considerable effort is spent on defining a shared lingo – essentially an agreed meaning for vocabulary within a particular project – that is crucial to facilitate productive collaboration.

In addition, the specific characteristics of IDN – for example, procedural generation – make new vocabulary necessary in the professional context as celebrated narrative designer Emily Short points out, as quoted in an article in *The Verge*. "Without words to describe [procedural storytelling], it's very hard to discuss." (Gordon, 2021)

The educational challenge

Unfortunately, a limited understanding of narrative and the use of the same impre-cise vocabulary also permeates our education systems. In many countries, the cur-riculum on narrative is almost exclusively based on teaching Eurocentric, traditional literary forms and the texts of stage plays. Other forms, for example oral storytelling traditions, avant-garde forms like surrealist and postmodern novels, comics, the per-formative aspect of stage plays, and even movies are often ignored. This state of affairs has consequences we need to be aware of when approaching the subject of IDN. It basically means that while many people have some foundational understanding of literary narratives, this 'standard knowledge' is severely limited when it comes to the diversity of narrative forms and structures. Whenever they encounter a novel form of narrative such as IDN, many people will therefore fall back on frameworks of references for understanding literary narratives they have encountered at school. Consequently, most conversations about IDN require a considerable amount of explanation to address misconceptions and explain specific characteristics. While outside the scope of this volume, there is a need to develop new school curricula to teach a more inclusive and expansive understanding of narrative.

Foundations of IDN theory

The question of what interactive digital narrative is, and what it is not, marks the beginning of IDN theory. This demarcation is necessary given the challenges described earlier – of narrative fundamentalism, narrative indifference, and impre-cise vocabulary. I will now extend the initial considerations from the introduction and discuss them in more detail. I have described IDN to mean all kinds of works that apply computation to enable audiences as interactors to influence a narrative in a non-trivial way and have offered the following definition:

> Interactive digital narrative is a narrative expression in various forms, implemented as a multimodal computational system with optional analog elements and experienced through a participatory process in which interactors have a non-trivial influence on progress, perspective, content, and/or outcome.

In addition, it is important to distinguish and emancipate IDN from other forms of narration.

> IDN is *not* the simple addition of computational interaction to traditional forms of narrative.

Interactivity is not an 'add-on feature' to legacy narrative forms; instead, the move to interactivity requires a re-thinking of narrative strategies and analysis.

> IDN is *not* the future of the novel or the movie, and its purpose is *not* to replace earlier forms.

Neither the novel, movie, or stage play have been waiting to be "interactivized" – they are fine the way they are and we can be certain that further developments of these forms will happen. Instead, the point of IDN is to enable the expression of the human condition in novel and hitherto impossible ways.

The specificity of IDN: understanding the difference to traditional narrative

The next question is how IDN differs from traditional static forms of narrative, for example, print literature and film. IDN takes interaction as a central aspect and thus is concerned also with a process in which a participant engages with the computer program to produce the output. The following illustration shows a key difference between fixed narrative forms in traditional media and interactive digital narrative (Figure 3.1). In this high-level view, the dark shaded areas represent aspects not fully covered by existing narratological frameworks – the digital computer system (software and hardware) and the participatory interactive process that are necessary to produce an output.

On the side of more traditional narrative forms – for example literature – only the output in the form of a book is available for analysis. A comparative view of film would introduce three additional steps below the initial output (the filmscript) – production, editing/post-production, and the final output as a movie. However, these additions do not change the fact that the object for analysis is fixed.

On the side of IDN, we can record the output – for example, by means of screen recording or with a video camera. This kind of product of an IDN work – a recording of a single 'playthrough' – is fixed and might be understood as a narrative in a more traditional sense and analyzed with existing narratological tools and methods. However, such an analysis would ignore the essential aspect of IDN, the two additional elements: the nature of the artifact as dynamic system employing a software/hardware combination and the participatory process of interaction.

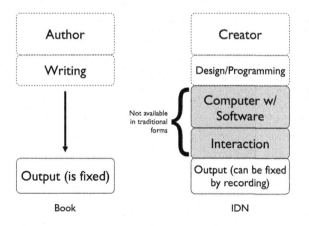

FIGURE 3.1 Comparison of literary narrative in traditional media (left) and IDN (right)

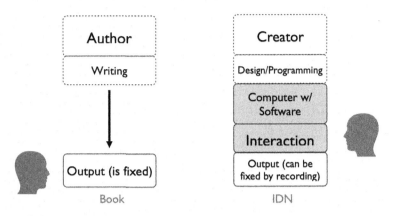

FIGURE 3.2 Difference in audience position between literary narrative in traditional media (left) and IDN (right)

The latter aspect leads to another important difference to traditional forms – the position and function of the audience in respect to the work. The reader/viewer encounters a fixed, static output, whereas the audience of an IDN work is involved in a participatory process to produce the output (Figure 3.2).

Montfort: the distinction of the IDN artifact and the missing connection

A key issue with the existing understanding of IDN and the need for IDN theory becomes apparent in the work of Nick Montfort, especially his research on interactive fiction (IF) works such as *Zork* (Lebling, 1980) or *Planetfall* (Blank, 1983).

Montfort explicitly points out the lack of an appropriate theory for IDN in the form of IF in that "[…] there is no theory to help us understand works in the interactive fiction form directly" (Montfort, 2003b, p. 23) and, consequently, proceeds to outline such a theory. Montfort starts by emphasizing the differences to "narrative," here understood as a function of legacy media artefacts. "A work of IF is not itself a narrative, it is an interactive computer program." (Montfort, 2005, p. 25) Therefore, Montfort explains, key narratological concepts are not applicable – for instance *story* (in contrast to discourse) as defined by Gerald Prince (Prince, 1987):

> […] interactive fiction is not a story in the sense of the things that happen in a narrative, […] "the content plane of narrative as opposed to its expression or discourse; the 'what' of a narrative as opposed to its 'how'" (Prince, 1987).
> *[Montfort's quote] Montfort, 2003a*

While Montfort clearly acknowledges the differences between IF and traditional notions of narrative, he still considers narratology a useful framework for the analysis of IF works:

An IF work is always related to story and narrative, since these terms are used together in narratology, even if a particular work does not have a 'story' in this ordinary sense.

Montfort, 2003b, p. 25

This statement is surprising, given his earlier remark that emphasizes the lack of an appropriate theory. Montfort attempts to solve this conflict by positioning IF works as "potential literature," a term Montfort borrows from the French Oulipo group and their experiments with literature based on mathematical formulas.

Interactive fiction has the potential to produce narratives, usually as a result of the interactor typing things to effect action in the IF world.

Montfort, 2003a

In this way, Montfort establishes a distinction between the IF artifact as a computer program and narrative as the output. The two categories are no longer mapped onto each other but are subject to a complex relationship. This is a key insight, equally valid for other forms of IDN, and one that provides a productive direction for the development of IDN theory. What is still missing, however, is a formal description of this relationship and a narrative perspective on both the artifact/computer program and the interactive process that leads to narrative output. It is the purpose of IDN theory to describe these elements (artefact, interactive process, output) and their relationships. Later in this part, I will introduce a framework for this purpose. Before doing so, I would like to acknowledge earlier developments in understanding the potential and qualities of the digital medium that provide grounding for my framework. Then, I will describe *instantiation* as a crucial aspect of IDN that helps to understand the specificity of the digital medium.

The digital medium and its affordances

Brenda Laurel in her seminal works on interactive drama (Laurel, 1986) and human-computer interaction (Laurel, 1991) first recognized the expressive potential of digital computers as a distinct "interactive, representational medium." This perspective puts the computational medium on equal footing with electronic media and print, overcoming notions of a 'multimedia platform' merely emulating earlier media forms.

The next important step is provided by Janet Murray in *Hamlet on the Holodeck* (Murray, 1997) with the introduction of a descriptive and analytical framework consisting of affordances (essential characteristics) and aesthetic qualities (the kind of experiences designers aim at creating). Murray describes four affordances – *procedural, participatory, spatial,* and *encyclopedic* – and three aesthetic qualities – *immersion, agency,* and *transformation* – to which she later adds the meta-quality of the *kaleidoscopic* (Murray 2011, 2016, 2018). She takes the computer's ability to "execute a set of rules" (1997, p. 71) – to be an engine that runs instructions – as the *procedural* affordance.

The *participatory* affordance captures the computer's ability to react to user input and respond in a predictable manner. The procedural and participatory affordances together create the phenomenon of interactivity (in the sense of what I previously described as *interactivity 2*) and are thus the defining categories of the digital medium from which all other aspects originate. In the strictest sense, what Murray describes here is *digital* interactivity, in contrast to a broader understanding of the term that would describe for example a conversation between two people as interactive.

The *spatial* affordance describes the ability of the digital medium to represent space and how digital artifacts are experienced as the traversal of a space. The *encyclopedic* affordance is Murray's term for the computer's ability to handle and represent huge amounts of data. Murray emphasizes this quality in the light of the digital medium's potential to incorporate lengthy plots and a multitude of different perspectives.

Next, Murray focuses on the user experience by defining the aesthetic qualities of *immersion, agency,* and *transformation. Immersion* describes the ability of a digital artifact to hold our interest and minimize distraction by offering an experience that feels "expansive, detailed, and complete." (Murray, 2011) She sees *agency* as the experience of "making something happen in a dynamically responsive world" that results in a coherent reaction by way of "clear and immediate feedback on the result of [interactors'] actions." (Murray, 2011) Agency is thus the experience of affecting meaningful and intelligible changes in the digital artifact. Murray observes that the resulting experience is a transformation in a dual sense – by changing the virtual artefact and as an experience of change for the interactor. This transform-ation can be enhanced by replay, but even a single playthrough is transformative, Murray explains, as the interactor becomes aware of choices not made and paths not taken. Finally, Murray uses the term "kaleidoscopic" (Murray 2011, 2016, 2018) to describe the ability of the digital artefact to enable and allow for changing arrangements as well as different perspectives reminiscent of the way a kaleido-scope offers a novel arrangement of its set of elements with every turn. The "kal-eidoscopic" affords novel perspectives and new insights and can be understood as a meta-level of the previous three qualities. In part four, I will return to this topic with a discussion of the relationship between these aesthetic qualities.

Laurel's recognition of computers as a digital medium together with Murray's definition of affordances and aesthetic qualities provide a basis for IDN theory. In the next section I will describe instantiation as an additional factor distinguishing IDN from traditional narrative forms.

Instantiation: an essential aspect of the digital medium

I will now examine an essential aspect of the digital medium – instantiation – more closely. Before I can do so, I want to acknowledge other applications of the term. In computer science, instantiation describes the concrete realization of re-usable collections of code during run-time in object-oriented programming. More con-cretely, *instances* (realized copies) are understood to be objects that are derived from

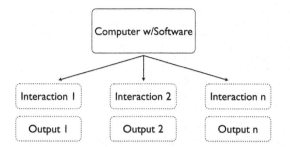

FIGURE 3.3 Instantiation in the interactive digital medium

classes, which are, in turn, blueprint definitions consisting of properties (or variables) and behaviors (or methods). An instance is thus an object created when the software is being processed on a computer (is running) that inherits the methods defined in the blueprint that has the variables filled with concrete values. *Classes* thus never manifest by themselves at runtime, but only by means of their derived *instances.*

Conversely, in linguistics, instantiation is brought up by Michael Halliday (systemic functional linguistics), who is concerned with establishing a connection between particular utterances and language in general, overcoming Ferdinand de Saussure's distinction between *parole* and *langue* (Halliday, 1985; 2006).

What both concepts share is the idea of a mechanism by which concrete occurrences originate from a more abstract structure. This general description also applies for IDN, as every concrete output originates from a digital artefact, which, in turn, incorporates the elements and schemes to engender different outputs. With regard to IDN, the term *instantiation* describes the relationship between the artefact (computer/software system) and the output (Figure 3.3). By means of interaction, output is generated from the artefact (computer with software).

Any particular output is a specific instantiation of the computer/software system, which means that the same system can potentially generate a wide variety of different outputs, an aspect already described by Lev Manovich. "A new media object [...] can exist in different, potentially infinite versions. [It] typically gives rise to many different versions." (Manovich, 2001)

For example, in the case of *Gone Home,* an interactor can choose from several alternate routes through the virtual building, pick up other objects and get stuck solving puzzles at different times, yielding divergent outputs. While in many cases, the number of possible outputs will be relatively small, with the advent of procedurally generated content – for example, trillions of planets in the video game *No Man's Sky* (Hello Games, 2016) – and procedural narrative[2] being deployed in more recent video games such as *Hades* (Kasavin, 2020), or *Wildermyth* (Worldwalker Games, 2021), the number of outputs can become very large.

Instantiation is an important aspect of the digital medium and one that differentiates it from legacy media. In particular, instantiation exposes the differences regarding the status of the artefact and the role of the recipient-turned-participant.

Instantiation and aura

I will now consider the notion of instantiation in relation to earlier theoretical perspectives. Walter Benjamin's analysis of the impact of technologies of reproduction on works of art and their aura provides a foundation for this discussion. Of particular interest here is his treatment of the relationship between original and copy. A comparison to the digital medium will show how this relationship has changed and what role instantiation plays.

A key concept in Benjamin's understanding of media is *aura,* yet his description of aura varies over time, which leaves the term open to interpretation. In his famous 1936 essay *Das Kunstwerk im Zeitalter seiner technischen Reproduzierbarkeit,* (The Work of Art in the Age of Mechanical Reproduction) Benjamin offers a description of aura as a unique experience of nature, of being situated in space and time in combination with the awareness of a "distance, however close." (Benjamin, 1963)

> Ein sonderbares Gespinst von Raum und Zeit: Eine einmalige Erscheinung einer Ferne, so nah sie sein mag. An einem Sommernachmittag ruhend einem Gebirgszug am Horizont oder einem Zweig folgend, der seinen Schatten auf den Betrachter wirft, bis der Augenblick oder die Stunde Teil an ihrer Erscheinung hat – das heißt die Aura dieser Berge, dieses Zweiges atmen.
>
> *Benjamin, 1963, p. 57*

> A peculiar amalgam of space and time: a unique appearance of a distance, however close it may be. On a summer afternoon resting, following a mountain range in the distance or a branch, that is casting its shadow on the observer, until the moment or the hour becomes a part of its appearance – this means to breathe the aura of these mountains, of this branch.
>
> *author's translation[3]*

Benjamin describes *aura* also as a quality related to the authority of an original work, which is present for example when standing in front of the actual *Mona Lisa* painting in the Louvre in Paris. However, according to Benjamin, the advent of mass production endangers this particular quality by making art works available in the form of mass-produced copies (i.e., Mona Lisa postcards or posters), bereft of any aura. Additionally, mass-distributed technical "intermediaries" such as film reduce aura, in comparison to the live performance of the stage play. Therefore, Benjamin's concern with aura is tightly coupled with the question of the original artwork or performance and its relation to mass-produced and distributed copies.

Ever since, scholars and artists have come to a more nuanced understanding of aura as a quality that can also be associated with the technologies of reproduction itself. For example in 2003, Hans Ulrich Gumbrecht and Michael Marrinan conclude that the opposite to Benjamin's prediction has happened. "Aura has definitely not disappeared as Benjamin anticipated, rather it has conquered the field of art's technical reproduction." (Gumbrecht & Marrinan, 2003) A further complication in this regard is the advent of the digital medium that challenges the original/copy distinction with its ability to create and distribute indistinguishable copies. Commenting on this development, Douglas Davis proclaims in 1995. "There is no longer a clear conceptual distinction between original and reproduction in virtually any medium." (Davis, 1995)

For the present discussion, I will extend the argument of Jay Bolter (Bolter et al., 2006) who concluded that digital artifacts have aura, provided they make the audience appreciate the distance to nature or art, effectively creating a "distance, however close." According to Bolter, digitally mediated experiences in physical environments create aura by introducing a "sense of distance-through-proximity" building on the "presence of the authentic." (ibid)

Going back to the concern with original and copy, this means that it is the digital copy that has now acquired the quality of aura. This statement might seem surprising at first, but it will become clearer with the help of George Legrady, another scholar and artist. Two salient steps in Legrady's analysis identify what has changed in the digital medium. First, he observes that the digital artwork by itself has "none of the physical properties normally associated with commodity objects" and thus has the quality of "immateriality" (Legrady, 2019). What Legrady means by immaterial is that code and assets only exist as bits on a digital storage medium (cloud or local storage), which by itself only materializes as a form of transport and not as the digital work itself. This indicates that there is no original in the digital medium— at least not in the sense of the term as applied by Benjamin for earlier mediated forms. The next step in understanding is Legrady's observation that digital art only attains physical manifestations when the software/hardware combination is placed in physical space and the work is being processed there (the computer program is running). Legrady – similarly to Bolter – locates aura at the interplay between interactive digital art and the associations evoked by the real spaces in which they are presented. Digital aura would therefore be most apparent in digital interactive installation pieces and augmented reality (AR) projects, yet it would also exist in any digital work that manifests in a physical location on a physical device.

However, neither of these two authors explicitly points out the crucial aspect of instantiation. Yet, without interaction, without the participation of the audience, without instantiation, there is only a work sitting idly in a physical location and no unique experience comes into existence. Digital aura is the production of a unique experience in a physical location *through an act of instantiation*. Since the digital 'original' is immaterial and has no aura, it is the realized, *instantiated* 'copy' that attains aura. When it comes to aura, the relationship between copy and original is thus the reverse of what Benjamin described for non-digital art. The concept of instantiation is a specific quality of the digital medium that needs to be reflected in a theory of IDN. The next step in the development of IDN theory is the question of an appropriate definition of narrative.

A definition of narrative for IDN

During the 20th century, scholars have characterized narrative in a variety of ways. In the context of IDN, a suitable definition of narrative must accommodate the specific qualities of the digital medium. Established definitions need to be scrutinized in this light with a special focus on Murray's affordances and phenomenological qualities, as well as the process of instantiation.

Prince defines narrative as involving the representation of at least two events, connected in a temporal sequence: "the representation of at least two real or fictive events in a time sequence, neither of which presupposes or entails the other." (Prince, 1982, p. 4) He later augments this definition to allow single events and includes both the functions of narrator and audience, which might not be explicitly assigned in every narrative:

> the recounting [...] of one or more real or fictitious events communicated by one, two or several (more or less overt) narrators to one, two or several (more or less overt) narratees.
>
> *Prince, 2003, p. 58*

Prince's definition leaves room for the procedural quality in the process of recounting but does not cover the participatory element in the digital medium. Narrative for Prince is a directed communication from narrator(s) to the audience as recipients. This stance is not compatible with Murray's participatory affordance and the concept of agency, because one cannot have agency in the role of a reader or a spectator.

This does not mean that reading a novel or viewing a movie are inherently passive – indeed these are highly active mental activities. However, these mental activities do not fulfill the requirement for agency as they cannot be turned into executable plans that result in meaningful changes to the narrative artefact (cf. the discussion of *interactivity 1* and *interactivity 2* in the introduction).

Similar to Prince, Jeremy Hawthorn's definition of narrative theory as "concerned only with the issue of how the events which make up this particular story are narrated" (Hawthorn, 1992, p. 130) implies a narrator ("are narrated") and is consequently problematic for participation and agency.

Gérard Genette's basic definition of narrative emphasizes a change of state:

> [...] an action or an event, even a single one [...] because there is a transformation, a transition from an earlier to a later and resultant state."
>
> *Genette, 1983, p. 18*

While this initial definition could work for IDN, Genette also emphasizes the act of narration and the temporal location of narrative in the form of a story:

> I can very well tell a story without specifying the place where it happens [...] nevertheless, it is almost impossible for me not to locate the story in time

with respect to my narrating act, since I must necessarily tell the story in a present, past, or future sense.

p. 215

This assumption is challenged in IDN, since the "narrating act" is transformed into an act of creating and designing a dynamic narrative artefact (we could call that the "designing act") that lets the user experience a narrative by participating in it (the "participating act"). Furthermore, the procedural quality of the digital medium complicates the temporal relationship Genette refers to – it is conceivable that in a highly procedural narrative, the location in time would not be set a priori, and would change during the course of the experience. For example, a specific situation could be experienced either in the present or as a flashback, depending on the participant's choices.

Moving beyond these earlier perspectives, David Herman (Herman, 2000; 2002) and other narratology scholars (e.g., Ibsch, 1990; Ryan, 2006) augmented narrative theory with aspects drawn from cognitive science to create what is now understood as the "cognitive turn" in narratology. In particular, Herman is concerned with "story logic," which he considers to be a basic cognitive function in contrast to mathematical logic. For him, "storyworlds" designate the cognitive structure used to comprehend narratives, the narrative macro-design in contrast to the narrative micro-design (for example the role of verb semantics). Herman describes narrative as a cognitive structure that can be evoked by different coding strategies and media forms. In this vein, Herman defines narrative as a "forgiving, flexible cognitive frame for constructing, communicating, and reconstructing mentally projected worlds." (Herman, 2002, p. 49) This definition decouples narrative from specific forms of media and therefore opens up the space for experiments and alternative forms. Herman's perspective also removes the requirement for specific roles of narrator and narratee and is therefore compatible with both Murray's framework of affordances and phenomenological qualities. And since his definition does not require a specific fixed artifact, it is also compatible with instantiation and therefore it is suitable also as definition of narrative for IDN.

Thus, IDN can now be characterized more precisely as:

> Interactive digital narrative is a narrative expression in various forms, implemented as a multimodal computational system with optional analog elements and experienced through a participatory process in which interactors have a non-trivial influence on progress, perspective, content, and/or outcome where narrative is understood as *a flexible cognitive frame for mentally projected worlds*.

Story and discourse in IDN

Before introducing my model of IDN, I like to reflect on a basic tenet of 20th century structuralist narrative theory – the distinction between fabula/story/

histoire (or the "what" of a narrative) and syuzhet/discourse/plot[4] (or the "how" of a narrative). First introduced by Russian formalist Viktor Shklovsky (2017, org. 1917), the separation of *content* (story) and its internal temporal-spatial order from its *presentation* (discourse) has been fruitful for analyzing narrative in legacy media. For instance, a discontinuous discourse could then be understood to present a continuous story. While this dichotomy still plays a role in contemporary narratology, it has also been the subject of criticism, for example with regards to the hierarchical relationship between the two terms by poststructuralists (see Culler, 1981).[5] In addition, the concrete meaning of the terms is open to interpretation and fluctuates in different academic perspectives, as Nitsche (2008) points out, which can lead misunderstandings.

> [Some scholars] interpret fabula as plot rather than story (Bruner 1990, 43); or read sjuzet as story and fabula as events (Brooks referring to Ricoeur in Brooks 1984, 14), which means that the range of interpretations of the original terms has become so great as to be potentially confusing [...].
>
> *Nitsche, 2008, p. 48*

For IDN, Nick Montfort has already problematized the direct application of the distinction, as mentioned earlier in this part (*reproduced* here again for convenience):

> [...] interactive fiction is not a story in the sense of the things that happen in a narrative, [...] "the content plane of narrative as opposed to its expression or discourse; the 'what' of a narrative as opposed to its 'how'" (Prince, 1987).
>
> *[Montfort's quote] Montfort, 2005*

Montfort has good reason to reject the category of *story*, as the "what" in IDN is not static and immutable as in literature or cinematic forms, but instead dynamically constructed.

In post-classical narratology, there have been some further developments of the story/discourse concept. For instance, Ryan understands narrative as comprised of story as the "cognitive representation" and narrative discourse as the "representation encoded in material signs." (Ryan, 2006, p. 7) From her perspective, the two categories cannot be understood as separate. Instead, she effectively collapses them by equating narrative with story while proposing to understand "narrativity (or 'storiness')" as a "scalar property." (ibid) Ryan's understanding of story and discourse as interdependent aspects avoid many of the problems that would otherwise appear in relation to IDN. In a procedural environment that requires a participatory process, both story and discourse are subject to change. However, this is also where the compatibility ends, as Ryan's perspective does not account for a multitude of different instantiations originating from the same dynamic artefact.

For instance, in Mateas & Stern's *Façade* (Mateas & Stern, 2005a; 2005b), the interaction directly affects the discourse (as the presentation encoded in material signs) as the graphics and sound/voice on the computer screen constantly react and adjust. In addition, the content of each instantiation is determined by the inter-play between the interactor's actions (textual input, movements, interactions with objects), the drama manager AI – which selects the next narrative element ("beat") by considering an internal plan of narrative progression – and the pre- and post-conditions of the available narrative elements. When an interactor types a question directed at one of the two virtual characters, text (the question the interactor has written) appears on the screen, followed by a reaction from the characters. Both action and reaction are connected in a feedback loop (input/output) and both are visible in the presentation, but also affect the narrative content and carry it further.

This dynamic relationship between malleable content and malleable presentation applies in general to IDN and not only to the case of *Façade*, since an interactor's contribution to the experience in principle affects both presentation/discourse and content/story (often simultaneously). Consequently, the binary distinction between the two fixed categories of story and discourse no longer applies and is therefore not appropriate to describe IDN works.

The cybernetic perspective: toward system art

Given the limitation of literary-based models, it is prudent to consider perspectives that describe phenomena similar to IDN. Roy Ascott's theory of cybernetic art (Ascott, 1964; 1968) is particularly relevant in this regard. Ascott urges artists to look at the scientific discipline of cybernetics, the study of "control and communication in animal and machine" (Wiener, 1948), and to create art inspired by cybernetics' concern with the behavior and regulation of environments, as well as organiza-tional, systemic structures.

As mentioned in the introduction, the connection between cybernetics and inter-active narrative was first made by Aarseth (1997). He derives his term cybertext expli-citly from cybernetics and describes a "cybertextual process" (Aarseth, 1997, p. 1). In his effort to create a media-agnostic framework, Aarseth classifies even paper-based works as "cybertextual machines." This is a problematic extension of the term, as cybernetics is commonly concerned with phenomena that are complex and dynamic and where a feedback loop exists between the phenomena and the interactors. Cybernetics' original topic was the question how to hit fast-moving targets – the planes and submarines of WW2 – a problem, which could not be solved with the fixed artillery tables in use at the time. Wiener's essential insight was that a complex relationship existed in which parameters, such as the plane's speed, heading, velocity of the projectile, and reaction time of the gunner, are connected in a feedback loop. A paper-based artifact by itself does not exhibit this kind of complex behavior. With the introduction of a human actor and their creativity, it might be possible to simulate something resembling a cybernetic system with a paper-based artifact in our mind, but we need to be aware of the categorial difference between actual cybernetic phe-nomena and a simulated one. The framework I will develop describes works in the digital medium for which feedback loops as a result of procedurality (the ability to execute a set of commands and react to input) are a foundational characteristic.

Ascott's perspective further develops Wiener's more technical concept by merging it with artistic sensibility, and thus provides additional insights for a theory of IDN. The combination of art and cybernetics, Ascott argues, will have a profound impact on art practice and audiences' experience. His concept of a "cybernetic art matrix" (Ascot 1966) proposes a tight integration between art and computation and foreshadows the importance of interaction for the digital medium. In addition, Ascott offers a high-level perspective on the discrete elements involved and the differences in contrast to traditional art forms. In particular, Ascott observes a change in the artistic focus from product to process, from structure to systems and thereby turning the "observer" into a "participant." (Wheeler and Zureck, quoted in Ascott, 1990) Ascott describes the shift as follows, essentially foreshadowing the procedural and participatory nature of the digital medium as "behavior."

> When art is a form of behaviour, software predominates over hardware in the creative sphere. Process replaces product in importance, just as system supersedes structure.
>
> *Ascott & Shanken, 2003, p. 157*

This perspective overlaps with Murray's affordances of the digital medium, especially the *procedural* and *participatory* categories. Thus, Ascott's definition of cybernetic art and IDN are closely aligned in the focus on process, the importance of interaction, and the concept of the audience as participant. Ascott's vocabulary and conceptual perspective therefore provides another stepping stone for IDN theory.

The SPP model

I will now introduce the SPP (system, process, product) model (Figure 3.4) as a core element of IDN theory. This model takes into account the procedural nature of IDN and the reactive and generative aspect of the computational *system*. It also describes the participatory *process* and identifies the output as an instantiated *product*. These categories are informed by a material view, oriented on cybernetics and computation. In addition, I take the perspective of creators into account and consider which categorial divisions would be operational for them. In that sense, the

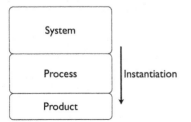

FIGURE 3.4 High-level view of IDN

SPP model represents a 'material turn,' which is also a contribution to reduce the division between theory and practice.

In the SPP model, *system* describes the digital artifact, the combination of software with the hardware on which the software is executed. This includes the executable programming code and assets – digital representations of pictures, movie clips, sounds, and text, as well as links to more resources on a local network or the internet. Additionally, system refers to the hardware – keyboards, mice, displays, and other hardware (e.g., sensors) used in a realized IDN. The sum of what the IDN system contains are 'potential narratives,' following Montfort's (Montfort, 2005) use of "potential literature."

Once a user starts to engage with the system, a *process* is created. The actions of the user as interactor, and the opportunities provided by the system, define and shape the process. The resulting *product* of interactive digital narrative – a single "playthrough" session – represents an instantiated narrative.[6] Given the participatory process, instantiation and the procedural nature of IDN, many different narrative products can originate from the same source (the system). Each instantiated playthrough can be recorded and this product may be analyzed in terms of traditional narratology, as a static narrative. While product is a necessary category for a model of interactive digital narrative, it is crucial to realize that any concrete product represents only one particular instantiation. Product alone is therefore severely limited as a representation of an IDN work. A full analysis of any interactive digital narrative necessarily includes an examination of process and system.

Overall, the SPP model takes IDN as a narrative expression in various forms, implemented as a computational *system* (with optional analog elements) containing potential narratives, which is experienced through a participatory *process* that results in *products* representing instantiated narratives.

Retellings: second-order narratives

So far, the SPP model does not cover an additional narrative category related to IDN – the narratives produced by interactors retelling their experience. Any kind of oral, written or visual retellings of the experience fall in this category. For example, players of *The Sims* have created retellings of their experiences and put them online. This aspect has been most thoroughly described by Eladhari as "re-tellings" (Eladhari, 2018), who also emphasizes the potential of retellings as a source for IDN criticism. To accommodate this important category, the SPP model is extended to recognize *retelling* as an additional product, derived from process (interactors retelling their experiences). The different products can thus be distinguished as *recording* (objective product) and *retelling* (subjective product) (Figure 3.5). The retelling is an interactor's recollection of the experience, that can cover multiple playthroughs and might include contextual information. In contrast, the recording is a direct record of a single experience.

The additional category of *retelling* is instrumental in understanding narrative aspects of IDNs that are similar to *The Sims* (Wright, 2000). In this game series

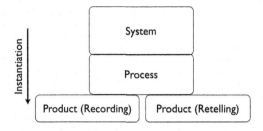

FIGURE 3.5 High-level view of IDN with retellings category

(first version in 2000, currently version four since 2014), the interactor controls the lives of a range of artificial characters that exist in a virtual society broadly similar to the contemporary US, including social aspects like dating, child raising, and economic pressures to earn money, but also opportunities for self-expression through architecture and community building. Will Wright, *The Sims'* creator, has called the game a "dollhouse for adults" (Baker, 2012), while Murray described it as a "novel-generating system." (Murray, 2004) *The Sims* can be understood as a successful IDN, yet its *process* is light in direct narrative experiences – instead, the game offers dramatic situations in line with its overall topic of human existence in relation to western-style economic and societal success. Consequently, *The Sims* excels in generating *retellings.* We might thus classify *The Sims* as an 'authoring-tool IDN' for interactors.

The addition of the category of *retelling* is a good opportunity to take stock and have another look at IDN elements and consider them as different narrative entities.

System – the protostory defining *potential narratives*

Process – the *narrative experience* as a function of progress, evaluation, planning and execution

Product (recording) – the fixed *instantiated narrative* of a single experience

Product (retelling) – A *retold narrative* about the experience by an interactor

Protostory and its elements

With a general model in place, it is now time to focus on the contents of the IDN system. For that purpose, I introduce the concept of *protostory* along with elements contained in it – *procedural components, assets, UI, narrative design*, and *narrative vectors*.

Protostory describes the concrete content, internal structure, and outward appearance of an IDN system as a space of potential narratives that is connected to any instantiated narrative through a participatory process. The dynamic and flexible relationship between an IDN system's protostory and a particular realized narrative marks the difference from a purely mechanical way of reproduction that produces the same copy every time. Conceptually, protostory is a prototype – a procedural blueprint, that defines the space of potential narrative experiences contained in one IDN system. As an analytical category, protostory describes the IDN artifact as containing discrete but interconnected parts and a particular organization – the *narrative design*.

As I have discussed earlier (in the section on *Story and Discourse in IDN*, p. 117), given the dynamic quality of IDN afforded by procedurality and participation, presentation layer and content cannot be clearly separated in an IDN system since an action by an interactor can affect both the content and its presentation. In other words, the static content and presentation of legacy media give way to a space providing the malleable material for potential narratives instantiated through a participatory process. For this reason, in the SPP model, protostory has no protodiscourse equivalency *as two separate entities*.[7] To be clear – there are certainly aspects with a discursive (presentation) function in IDN, yet these exist within the protostory. It is the understanding of a fixed relationship between two separate entities, which is not adequate for IDN analysis.

Procedural components, assets, user interface, narrative design and narrative vectors

I will now describe the elements of the protostory – *procedural components, user interface* (UI), and *assets* provide material used in the *narrative design*. (Figure 3.6)

Procedural components require computational processing to enable the IDN experience. For example, a 3D environment by itself is only a static *asset* and in order to be used as an element in an IDN work, several procedural components need to be added. The basic requirements are a physics system defining where the floor is and how movement works, but also a collision-detection system to prevent the interactor from going through walls.

If there are obstacles placed within a 3D or 2D environment (e.g., a door that can be opened with a key), procedural rules need to be defined which check whether certain conditions have been fulfilled (e.g., if a key is present and, if found, will allow passage). In turn, this means that a key object exists somewhere and that the interactor needs to be able to execute an action (e.g., a mouse click on the key) to retrieve it, requiring additional rules and conditions to be defined. More advanced *procedural components* enable the creation of new items or structures by

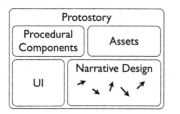

FIGURE 3.6 Protostory and narrative design

interactors, control character traits, and allow an interactor to rise in social status and abilities by means of achievements. They can also embody societal rules (e.g., to assure that the interactor is treated according to a certain rank) or define rules of engagement within a multi-player experience. Concrete examples of such *procedural components* exist in role-playing games like *The Elder Scrolls V: Skyrim* (Bethesda Game Studios, 2011), *World of Warcraft* (Blizzard Entertainment, 2004), *Mass Effect* (Electronic Arts, 2007), *The Witcher 3: Wild Hunt* (CD Project RED, 2015), and *Genshin Impact* (Mihoyo, 2020). Time functions are yet another example of *procedural components* (e.g., a simulated day which progresses during the experience, or to create time pressure for the interactor in specific situations). Artificial intelligence (AI) functions which process natural language input, generate environments or objects (text, audio, visuals) on-the-fly, or decide on the sequencing of elements (planner systems) are on an even more advanced level from a computational perspective.

The *UI* (user interface) describes aspects interactors are directly concerned with. This includes the perspective – whether it is first person or third person – and also the available modes of interaction: screen-based point-and-click, movement in 3D space according to the rules set in the *procedural components*, text input with keyboard, VR controllers, custom controllers, and so forth. The *UI* often appears to be transparent and is recognized as a separate element mostly when an interactor accesses the title's settings. However, in some works, for example in role-playing games or the discussion forum mode of *Fort McMoney* (Dufresne, 2013), the *UI* becomes more obvious as an integral part of the experience. Other examples of prominent *UI* aspects are in-experience camera functions and diaries.

Assets are all the static elements being used in an IDN work and include 2D images, 3D models of characters, landscapes and buildings, text, video, sounds, music, and recorded speech.

Narrative design is the arrangement of the material provided by the other elements, the procedural logic applied in an IDN, and how the elements are exposed through a *UI* to enable a participatory process. The sequencing of narrative material, the overall structure, and the definition of possibilities for interaction are part of the *narrative design*.

Narrative vectors describe sub-structures within a narrative design, which serve several important functions in lieu of conventional narrative structures. *Narrative vectors* provide motivation to the interactor, help to retain a level of authorial control, and move the narrative forward. The closest equivalent in legacy media is *plot points* (e.g., Field, 1979), a term used to describe "milestones" within a story, yet narrative vectors provide additional functions. For instance, they convey important information to the interactor, set boundaries to prevent an interactor from getting lost, and facilitate particular dramatic events, turns, and endings.

Narrative vectors do not work as isolated structures, but rather in connection with the preceding and following parts of the narrative. For example, in a IDN murder mystery, a narrative vector could be the occurrence of a murder or the disappearance of an important witness, but also the breakdown of the interactor's car as a means to prevent them from leaving the crime scene before all clues are gathered. Whether a specific vector appears in a particular instantiated experience depends on the interactor's choices and the overall interactive narrative design. For instance, a 'new murder event' vector only appears as long as the interactor (as detective) has not caught the perpetrator; the 'witness disappears' vector only appears if the interactor waits too long with the interview; and the 'car breakdown' vector is only needed when the interactor actually overlooks important clues. Outside of these situations, the interactor as detective might have all the freedom possible to conduct the investigation and thus narrative vectors might be best understood as loosely connected in terms of structure.

Together, the elements of the protostory describe the dynamic system of an IDN work. For example, the *narrative design* of the video games *Dear Esther* (The Chinese Room, 2008), *Oxenfree* (Night School Studio, 2016), and *Mutazione* (Die Gute Fabrik, 2019) combines their respective *assets* of an island landscape and the *procedural components* of the physics system/movement rules of the game engine used. Further aspects of these three titles are distinct, as *Dear Esther* presents a first-person *UI* to a 3D world, while *Oxenfree* and *Mutazione* use a third-person 2.5 D (2D with depth information) view. Further differences are in the sequencing as part of the *narrative design*. In *Dear Esther* and *Mutazione*, the narrative develops chronologically, while in *Oxenfree* the interactor moves forward and backward in time, and the time jumps represent *narrative vectors*. In *Dear Esther*, *narrative vectors* exist, for example, when attempting to go into the sea or by entering a tunnel to the next chapter while in *Mutazione*, conversations with other characters take the function of narrative vectors.

Finally, the opportunities for interaction vary considerably between these IDN works. *Dear Esther* is about exploring the island and in doing so, visiting voice-over fragments that piece together the past and current condition of the interactor. *Oxenfree* allows the interactor to explore the island, to converse with other characters by means of dialogue options, and also to jump in time and location using a radio and forcing the interactor to re-orient themselves. *Mutazione* provides a rhythm of days during which the interactor can explore the island and engage in conversations and activities with the inhabitants. A focus of activity is on creating and tending to gardens in several locations.

Narrative experience: the triple hermeneutics of IDN

The interactor engages with the system in the interactive process, instantiating products. How can we understand this narrative experience in more detail? Murray's aesthetic categories of immersion, agency, and transformation are useful to understand different aspects of the experience of IDN. Yet, this perspective is not sufficient to fully understand the experience of IDN because Murray's categories exist on a higher level of abstraction. It is equally important to understand the fundamental interpretive mechanics of IDN experiences, which exist on a lower level. The work by Veli-Matti Karhulahti who applied Giddens' concept

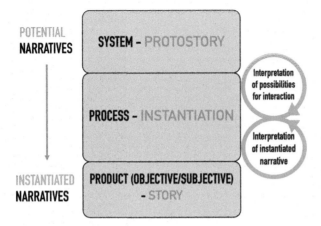

FIGURE 3.7 The double hermeneutic of the IDN experience

of *Double Hermeneutics* (Giddens, 1987) to the understanding of video games (Karhulahti, 2012) is instrumental in this regard. Karhulahti's fundamental insight is that the interactive nature of the experience engenders two interpretive activities that occur simultaneously, which we can understand as two combined hermeneutic circles – one concerned with interpreting the narrative trace instantiated up until the current point and the other evaluating the current opportunities for interaction. Previously, together with Tom van Nuenen and Christian Roth, we have applied this perspective to the SPP model as a hermeneutic strip (Roth, van Nuenen, & Koenitz, 2018) (Figure 3.7).

I am now extending this perspective in order to accommodate the effect of replay. Repeat experiences, as we can, for example, learn from Alex Mitchell (Mitchell & McGee, 2012), are an essential aspect and pleasure of IDN. Interactors can explore the possibility space again to revisit earlier decisions, change perspectives, or visit different locations. In this way, interactors produce memories of traversals that affect future engagements with the work (see Figure 3.8). This means that starting from the second engagement, a third hermeneutic circle is added to the experience – the reflection of earlier traversals. In the framework of the SPP model, this aspect is represented as a triple hermeneutic (Figure 3.9). The three circles of interpretation ask – What has happened so far and how could it continue? What can I do right now? What did I do the last time(s)?

Using the SPP framework for analysis

In this section, I will demonstrate the use of the SPP framework for the analysis of IDN works, highlighting some advantages of this approach. For this purpose, I will use *Unpacking* (Witch Beam, 2021), *Afternoon, A Story* (Joyce, 1987), *Façade* (Mateas & Stern, 2005b), and *Save the Date* (Cornell, 2013). These works represent different forms of IDN, ranging from hypertext fiction to interactive drama to video game.

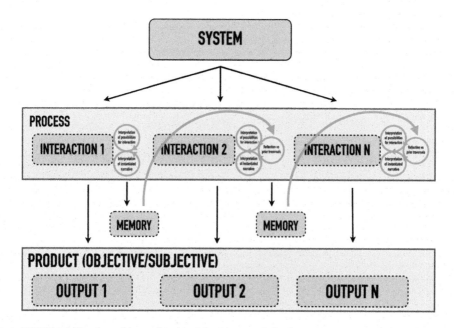

FIGURE 3.8 Replay adds a reflection of prior traversals via memory

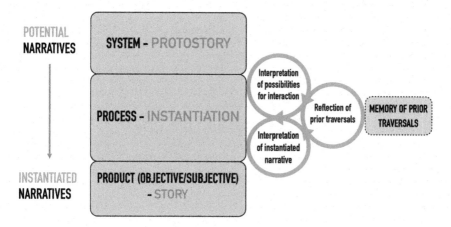

FIGURE 3.9 The triple hermeneutic of the IDN experience

A first benefit of the SPP framework is the ability to analyze diverse works through a common lens.

Protostory and the elements contained in it, together with the triad of system, process, and product, provide the basic categories for analysis. At the same time, the framework is designed to be flexible in order to cover a range of different forms and implementations. A given work might use few procedural elements, for example, some hypertext fictions or some interactive documentaries, while others might have few static assets and apply procedural generation techniques. Similarly, some IDN manifestations will be focused on screen-based text, while others will be multimodal and/or location-based.

Example analysis 1: Unpacking

Taking *Unpacking* as an example, I will now go through the analysis step-by-step. *Unpacking* conveys the narrative of a child growing up into adulthood by unpacking items from moving boxes at various stages – starting as small child and ending with an apartment meant for 'settling down.' The experience depicts growing up through different room styles appropriate for different ages, but also by means of changing items and significant evocative objects that are kept for sentimental reasons. The experience works mostly without text and there are no direct explanations in regard to the meaning of a specific apartment or age. Yet, it succeeds in conveying the experience of a girl growing into a young woman with particular interests, who first moves in with a boyfriend, moves out, and then settles in with a girlfriend.

Step 1: identify material

The dynamic nature of IDN means that a static snapshot is not sufficient in principle, as UI modalities and content can change during the course of the experience. Therefore, assuming an 'analyst-as-interactor' position, the analysis begins with a first playthrough of the IDN work, taking stock of the material encountered (Figure 3.10). The following list of questions is a starting point for this task and more questions should be added if needed.

- Is there screen-based text with hyperlinks?
- Are there dialogue trees?
- Does the experience take place within a 3D environment?
- Can the interactor move around freely?
- What is the UI perspective – first person or third person?
- What UI modes exist – screen-based point and click, text input with keyboard, VR controllers, custom controllers?
- What rule systems exist?
- Is there a physics system used in a 3D environment?
- Are there societal rules?
- Are there changeable character traits?
- Is there an inventory system?
- Can objects be combined to produce different objects?
- Is there time pressure?
- Are there elements which are procedurally generated?
- What, if anything, can the interactor generate – text on screen, building of structures?
- Is there a system for note or picture taking?

FIGURE 3.10 Assets and UI in an episode of *Unpacking*. Image courtesy of Which Beam

Step 2: categorize material

The next step is to categorize the identified material into *assets, UI*, and *procedural components*. For *Unpacking*, this step will produce the following list:

Assets: 2.5D depictions of various rooms, moving boxes, household and personal items, background sound, click sounds, 2D assets for *UI* (camera interface, menu, sticker book, picture book)

UI: first-person view, menu with basic functions, point and click on objects to place them and to change rooms, arrows to navigate between rooms, zoom in/out, camera function for picture taking, end of episode indicator, fast playback option at the end of episodes to show where the objects have been placed, stickers for special placement (i.e., electrical device in sink), a book of 'stickers' to collect them.

Procedural components: rule system for general placement of unpacked items, particularly significant items have special placement rules, movement rules in and between rooms.

Step 3: identify narrative design

The next step is to consider the *narrative design*. This is where the elements identified in the previous step are arranged to create the experience. Narrative design is the structure which connects and sequences the elements to provide opportunities for interaction. A description of the *narrative design* includes a visualization of the structure. For *Unpacking*, there is a clearly identifiable structure, as there are eight episodes, spanning 21 years, representing eight different apartments in which the protagonist grows up from being a child to becoming a young adult. The episodes are arranged chronologically, which is represented in the numbered sequence in Figure 3.11.

Within each episode, the interactor can unpack at their own speed, there is no time pressure. Each episode uses the material supplied by *assets, UI*, and *procedural components*. Between the episodes is a 2D intermission, informing the interactor of their accomplishment of completing the previous episode and enabling the continuation of the experience. A visual representation of *Unpacking's* full protostory is shown in Figure 3.12. Out of space constraints, not all aspects of the elements

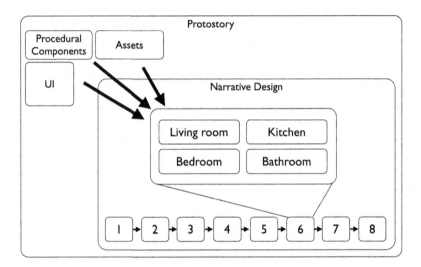

FIGURE 3.11 Narrative design of *Unpacking*

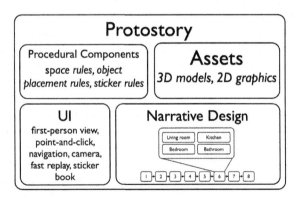

FIGURE 3.12 *Unpacking* protostory

can be listed in this depiction and therefore it needs to be combined with a list as shown under step 2.

Step 4: add developer information

Not all elements can be identified in steps 1 and 2 as they might be opaque to the analysist as interactor, especially when procedural components are being used. A case in point is *Façade* (see example analysis 3), where the drama manager function and the atomic narrative units of beats cannot be identified without information from the developer. For *Façade,* this type of information is available through published academic papers (Mateas & Stern, 2005a; 2005b); in other cases, it can come from developer interviews, or presentations at conferences such as the Game Developer Conference (GDC). If found, this information should be used to update the list of categorized material and the narrative design. This step is optional and is not necessary in the case of *Unpacking,* where material and structure can be clearly identified.

Step 5: apply system, process, and product progression

Next, by applying the differentiation between *system, process,* and *product,* we now see that any instantiated narrative product is derived from the elements contained in the protostory by means of a participatory process (Figure 3.13). The different elements of the protostory are interconnected and depend on each other. What an interactor experiences in an IDN work is a dynamic composition of these elements, structured for interaction by the user interface (UI). The result is an instantiated narrative product, which is a subset of the space of potential narratives described by the protostory. In the case of *Unpacking,* the overall sequence does not change; however, there is considerable variety within each episode as the interactor can place many objects wherever they want.

The result of this analysis is an understanding of *Unpacking* as an IDN work – a dynamic construct, distinct from earlier mediated expressions – which conveys a narrative mostly through sequencing and interaction with evocative objects and spaces. Using this perspective, it is now possible to analyze and compare

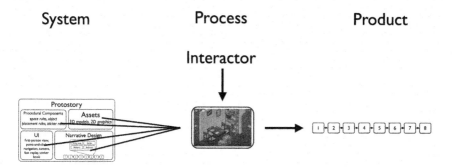

FIGURE 3.13 Functional relations in *Unpacking*

particular instantiated narratives (*products*) in the form of *recordings* or *retellings*. Equally, the process can be further examined, bringing in the perspective of triple hermeneutics.

Example analysis 2: Afternoon, A Story

Michael Joyce's hypertext fiction narrative *Afternoon, A Story* (Joyce, 1987), conveys fragmented narrative of a psychotic state. To achieve the desired effect, his *narrative design* consists of an extensive web of textual *assets* (lexias – short pieces of text that do not exceed a single screen) containing seemingly disjointed texts, yet connected by hyperlinks. The mechanics of hyperlinks afforded by the authoring environment storyscape constitute the *procedural components*. Finally, the *UI* category contains the user interface of clickable words in the text, together with additional navigational options in the form of a row of buttons.

All possible paths an interactor can take are defined in the *narrative design* through the sequencing of lexias connected by hyperlinks and the procedural element of guard fields that enable conditional links. This means some links will only appear when specific other lexias have been visited before. The concrete structure is an intricate web with more than 800 nodes containing lexias and an even larger number of connecting links. *Narrative vectors* in *Afternoon* manifest as combinations of lexias and links that are designed to create specific experiences, for example, the re-visiting of a particular passage after the interactor has gathered additional knowledge (Figure 3.14). This means that in a concrete experience, the interactor could be returned to a description of a car accident after they learned that the protagonist suspects his son to be involved in it.

Using the differentiation between *system*, *process*, and *product* (Figure 3.15), we see how the organization of the narrative design facilitates the dynamic assembly of protostory elements (assets, UI, procedural components) in the process. The result is an instantiated narrative product, which is a subset of space of potential narratives described by the protostory.

The elements *procedural components*, *assets*, *UI*, *narrative design*, and *narrative vectors* provide categories for a fine-grained analysis of the content and structure of an

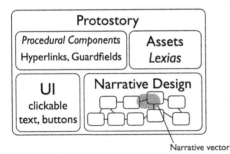
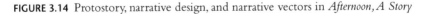

FIGURE 3.14 Protostory, narrative design, and narrative vectors in *Afternoon, A Story*

System   Process   Product

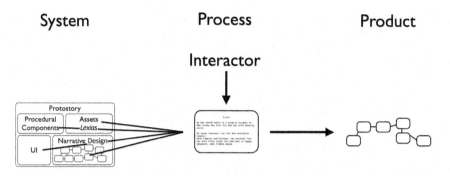

FIGURE 3.15 Functional relations in *Afternoon, A Story*

TABLE 3.1 Protostory elements in *Afternoon, A Story*

Element	Function	Afternoon, A Story
Procedural components	Provide rules like physics systems, societal rules, spatial configurations, interaction processing, and also generative components	Hyperlinks, guardfields
Assets	Provide static material for narrative design	Texts for the lexias (ca. 800)
UI	Enable agency through interaction	Words clickable by an input device, additional buttons for navigation and display of available links
Narrative Design	Arrangement of content, mechanics of the relationship between elements	The connected web of lexias through hyperlinks, also the mechanics of conditional "guardfields"
Narrative Vectors	Parts of the narrative design to guide the user and create specific effects	An example for a narrative vector is a structure to revisit a lexia with additional information

IDN (Table 3.1). Furthermore, this framework describes the functional relations between the elements that enable the presentation of a portion of the work to the user, provide agency, and record the resulting narrative path. Further analysis is possible by investigating the process as well as the objective and subjective products.

Example analysis 3: Façade

Michael Mateas and Andrew Stern apply sophisticated artificial intelligence (AI) algorithms in their seminal work *Façade* (see Mateas & Stern, 2005a; 2005b) to create a large range of narrative possibilities. In this interactive one-act drama,

FIGURE 3.16 The interactor communicates with Grace and Trip by typing text. Image courtesy of Michael Mateas

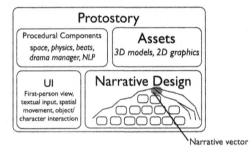

FIGURE 3.17 Protostory elements in *Façade*

the interactor encounters married couple Grace and Trip, whose relationship has soured to the point where every utterance and action can trigger bad memories and unravel subdued aggression. The challenge is to save Grace and Trip's marriage by persuading them to see a therapist. The interactor communicates with the virtual characters by typing natural language phrases (Figure 3.16). Moving within the space of a virtual apartment, approaching the characters, and picking up objects are additional modes of interaction.

The protostory in *Façade* (Figure 3.17) contains the elements of the IDN system, including 2D and 3D assets, AI procedural components and the narrative design. In experiencing *Façade*, the interactor instantiates a particular narrative product by communicating with Grace and Trip, by moving within the space of their apartment, and by using the available props. Unlike the meandering structure of *Afternoon*, *Façade* can end rather abruptly – for example, when the interactor is thrown out for trying to kiss Grace or Trip. Therefore, a given instantiated narrative could be short, with an abrupt ending and underdeveloped characters (Figure 3.18), or a longer one, in which either of the characters appears more developed and sympathetic.

System   Process   Product

Interactor

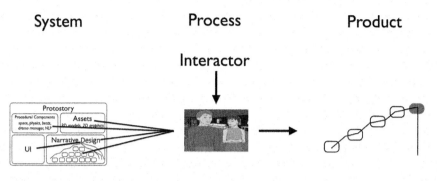

FIGURE 3.18 Functional relations in *Façade*

TABLE 3.2 Protostory Elements in *Façade*

Element	Function	Façade
Procedural components	Provide rules like physics systems, societal rules, spatial configurations, interaction processing, and also generative components	Three-dimensional space of apartment, physics system, narrative unit "beats," AI functions to understand natural language input,
Assets	Provide static material for narrative design	Character and object graphics, 3D model of apartment, pre-recorded audio replies from characters
UI	Enable agency through interaction	First-person view, textual input, spatial movement, object/ character interaction
Narrative Design	Arrangement of content, mechanics of the relationship between elements	Drama manager component implementing story arc, pre- and post-conditions of beats
Narrative Vectors	Parts of the narrative design to guide the user and create specific effects	Failure (getting thrown out) and significant progress

Table 3.2 provides an overview of protostory elements. *Procedural components* include a 3D space of the apartment (in the sense of the rules which define what movements are possible, not the 3D model, which is an asset) with a physics system. The AI responsible for recognizing textual input (described as natural language processing (NLP) in Figure 3.17) is also a procedural component as are the algorithmic narrative units called "beats" and the drama manager managing their sequencing (Mateas & Stern, 2005b). *Assets* are the 3D model of the apartment, as well as the graphics for props and the characters of Grace and Trip. Pre-recorded utterances by the characters provide additional material. The *user interface* affords movement in

space as well as interactions with objects and characters through gestures like kissing or hugging. Finally, textual input enables the communication with the characters and the AI system behind it.

The narrative design in *Façade* combines a story arc implemented using the procedural component of a drama manager as well as the pre- and post-conditions of the different beats. Narrative vectors are formed by the drama manager component as a response to the interactor's input and by consulting the conditions of the current beat and phase in the narrative. A narrative vector is active, for example, when an interactor is kicked out or when Trip and Grace reach the therapy part of the experience and are able to rescue their marriage.

Example analysis 4: Save the Date

Save the Date (Cornell, 2013) is a computer game in which the interactor has to save his dinner date from dying. The interactor's task is to make choices that prevent an encounter with death (Figure 3.19) – a difficult task since the grim reaper constantly appears in the form of freak accidents and random violence. However, the system helps the player in their undertaking by means of cross-session memory – for example, the player will find an additional choice to avoid a dish with peanuts after the date has died form an allergic reaction in a previous session. At a later stage, the work also breaks the fourth wall and enters in a meta-narrative discussion with the "date" that alerts her of her status as a character in a video game.

The *protostory* (Figure 3.20) contains the necessary elements to experience this narrative. In *Save the Date,* the interactor instantiates a particular narrative product

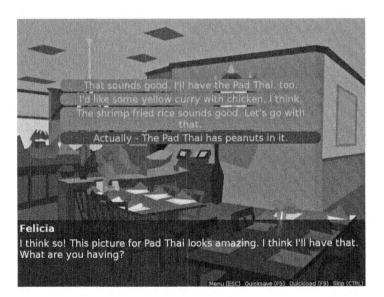

FIGURE 3.19 Conversational choices in *Save the Date*

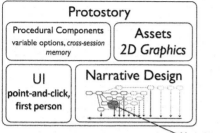

FIGURE 3.20 Protostory, narrative design, and narrative vectors in *Save the Date*

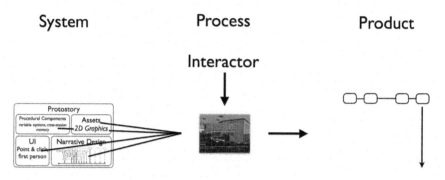

FIGURE 3.21 System, process, product in *Save the Date*

by making conversational choices in terms of location, food items, and overall communication with the date (Figure 3.21). Initially, the traversals will be short, abruptly ending with the date's death (Figure 3.21), but with additional knowledge and options gained through replay, subsequent experiences will become longer.

Table 3.3 shows the elements of the protostory in *Save the Date*. The *procedural components* are the variable options available to the interactor and the cross-session memory; the *assets* are 2D location backdrops together with textual descriptions. The user interface consists of clickable hotspots, for example, on conversation choices. Finally, the narrative design reflects cross-session memory by a range of alternate paths and provides the change to a meta-narrative dialogue.

SPP: focus on specificity

With the SPP framework, an analysis can focus on describing IDN-specific aspects and narrative strategies. The example analyses show these advantages. In the case of *Unpacking,* the analysis describes how a narrative design can combine a fixed episodic structure with the freedom of placing objects within the virtual spaces to create many opportunities for interaction. It also shows how a narrative can be conveyed with little text, mostly by sequencing, as well as evocative spaces and

TABLE 3.3 Protostory elements in *Save the Date*

Element	Function	*Save the Date*
Procedural components	Provide rules like physics systems, societal rules, spatial configurations, interaction processing, and also generative components	Variable choices available to the interactor, cross-session memory
Assets	Provide static material for narrative design	2D backdrop graphics, text used in the game, sounds
UI	Enable agency through interaction	First-person, point-and-click, interface to load/save current state and reset cross-session memory
Narrative Design	Arrangement of content, mechanics of the relationship between elements	Structure with many alternative paths to accommodate cross-session memory (additional options in next session), change to meta-narrative dialogue in later stages
Narrative Vectors	Parts of the narrative design to guide the user and create specific effects	Failure to save the date by picking a dish that causes death by allergic shock, for example

objects, leaving room for the interactor to fill in the narrative gaps. For *Afternoon, A Story*, the aesthetics and participatory possibilities provided by the *Storyspace* authoring system and its playback engine can now be analyzed as part of the protostory in the form of procedural components, assets, and UI. In the case of *Façade*, there is no longer a need to describe the overall structure in terms of legacy perspectives ("Aristotelian tension arc") – instead the focus can be on the design of a possibility space containing potential story paths, which takes every concrete instantiated path as the result of the interaction between its narrative design and the interactor's decisions. Conversely, the virtual space of the couple's apartment and the possibilities afforded by the physics engine become an integral part of the examination of the protostory and allow a more complete understanding of the work. For *Save the Date*, the mechanics of cross-session memory and its realization in the form of an iterative narrative structure become the focus for the analysis of the narrative design, while the ability to reset session memory through the UI can be described as an integral narrative function.

System narratives

I will end this part by considering the specific qualities of IDN as systemic representations in comparison to more traditional forms, and how the SPP model and its associated vocabulary capture the difference. I have previously drawn on

Ascott's cybernetic art theory and it is now time to expand on this topic, especially his interest in depicting and exposing dynamic systems and processes instead of static objects (Ascott, 1964). Ascott sees the advent of computational processes as both an opportunity for artists and a challenge to existing art practices. In his view "cybernetic" processes influence a constantly growing sphere in our life and therefore should become a target for artistic reflection. However, Ascott deems established ways of artistic expression in the form of static artifacts insufficient to represent dynamic systems. He therefore calls on artists to learn about cybernetic systems and then to apply these lessons and use the underlying technology to create art works. Today Ascott's call is as valid as it was in the 1960s, especially in the light of the complexity of many contemporary issues.

Certainly, traditional narratives are also concerned with dynamic processes – the development of a storyline, or the mutations displayed by a character during the course of a narrative – however, these processes are fixed descriptions, "products" in Ascott's terms, that cannot be changed. Ascott instead envisions dynamic artworks as reactive systems modifiable by participants. Many installation pieces fall in this category, but also kinetic art works and software art. Works in this particular manner are not made to depict the characteristics of a static object, but instead expose the workings of a complex system.

Similarly, IDN offers the means to depict highly complex contemporary issues as dynamic systems – and these representations we can understand as *system narratives*. For instance, IDN has the potential to represent a central concept of chaos theory, the ripple effect, which describes how tiny effects and decisions can lead to large-scale phenomena – most famously illustrated with the image of the wing flap of a butterfly starting a chain of effects that lead to a hurricane (Lorenz, 1963). The experience of the consequences of decisions interactors have made themselves in the process of engaging with a protostory is a powerful artistic strategy in IDN works. It is intensified further when the user is aware of many different possible choices and alternate paths, a "transformation through variety." (Murray, 1997)

By combining agency with the awareness of different consequences, IDN can offer compelling experiences not available in static media narratives. This radical change can be expressed by associating traditional narratives and IDN with answers to different questions. While traditional narratives address questions like – "How did this happen?" "How will this character develop?" "Will the protagonist succeed in this challenge?" IDN is concerned with consequences of actions and associated questions. "What will happen next if I make this decision?" "How will the overall outcome change if I go this route?" "What can I do here?" "What are the rules of this particular experience/situation?"

E.M. Forster understands the essential quality of any kind of narrative to be the desire of wanting to know what will happen next, a wish driven by a deeply engrained "primeval curiosity" (Forster, 1927). IDN can take this desire to the next level by adding agency over "what happens next." The promise of IDN is to combine the desire of "finding out" with the pleasure of agency. By exploring

TABLE 3.4 Comparison of Legacy Narrative and IDN

Category	Legacy narrative	Interactive digital narrative
Narrative object	Story	Protostory
Narrative presentation	Plot	Narrative design/narrative vectors
Composition	Fixed	Dynamic and procedural
Participation	In the reception	Participatory process to instantiate potential narratives
Engagement	Speculation, interpretation	Speculation, interpretation, planning, execution
Size	Limited by practical factors (e.g., page count)	Encyclopedic (no practical limit)
Manifestation	Linear	Spatial, and multi-linear
Object	Plot/character	Plot/character/system

and testing the limits of a given protostory and discovering the narrative vectors embedded in its narrative design, an interactor experiences this pleasure.

With the addition of system narratives, the theoretical framework for IDN can now be compared to legacy narrative terminology (Table 3.4).

Summary: SPP model and system narratives

The SPP model described in this part addresses the conceptual and analytical gap between the IDN artifact as a computer program and the instantiated output as a narrative that became first evident in the work of Montfort (2005). In the SPP model, the artifact is described as a dynamic *system* which facilitates an interactive *process* involving the audience as interactors resulting in objective (recorded) and subjective *products* (retellings). In addition, *double* and *triple hermeneutics* describe the experience of interactors in the first and subsequent playthroughs of an IDN work. This framework facilitates the examination of aspects outside of the focus of traditional narrative studies and thus overcomes limitations inherent in attempts to adapt legacy theoretical positions. Several example analyses are provided to show the application of the framework. Furthermore, understanding IDN works as *system narratives* distinguishes this expression from fixed representations and helps to identify their creative opportunities, in particular for the representation of complex topics.

Notes

1 A later formulation does not fundamentally change this aspect. "While narrativity is a type of meaning, interactivity, when put in the service of entertainment, is a type of play" (Ryan, 2009) and a more recent perspective still relegates interactivity to the technical aspect of mediality, outside a semiotic or cultural dimension (Ryan, 2014).

2 For a technical description of such a system see for example (Mason, Stagg, & Wardrip-Fruin, 2019).

3 I offer a new translation in order to put more emphasis on the temporal aspect ("until the moment or the hour becomes a part of its appearance"), which is missing for example in Michael W. Jennings' translation:

"A strange issue of space and time: the unique appearance of a distance, however near it may be. To follow with the eye while resting on a summer afternoon a mountain range on the horizon or a branch that casts its shadow on the beholder is to breathe the aura of those mountains, of that branch."

Benjamin, W., & Jennings, M. W. (2010). The Work of Art in the Age of Its Technological Reproducibility [First Version]. Grey Room, (39), 11–38.

4 I am aware that plot can also be described as an element of discourse. I am following here the usage of Nitsche (see next page).

5 Consequently Richard Walsh (2001) reverses the positions by taking syuzhet as the main category from which fabula is understood.

6 Noah Wardrip-Fruin (2009) shares the concern for process, which he distinguishes from "output." However, his focus is in describing the aesthetics of "expressive processes" and in foregrounding the evaluation of a work based on these aesthetics.

7 I am clarifying here my position (also in line with my earlier publications e.g. (Koenitz 2015)) to avoid potential misunderstandings caused by the mentioning of "protoprocess" in Koenitz et al. (2016).

References

Aarseth, E. J. (1997). *Cybertext*. JHU Press.

Ascott, R. (1964). The Construction of Change. *Cambridge Opinion*.

Ascott, R. (1968). The Cybernetic Stance: My Process and Purpose. *Leonardo*, 1(2), 105. http://doi.org/10.2307/1571947

Ascott, R., & Shanken, E. A. (2003). *Telematic Embrace*. Univ of California Press.

Baker, C. (2012). Will Wright Wants to Make a Game Out of Life Itself. Retrieved June 20, 2022, from https://web.archive.org/web/20141229200435/ www.wired.com/2012/07/mf_iconswright/all

Barthes, R., & Duisit, L. (1975). An Introduction to the Structural Analysis of Narrative. *New Literary History*, 6(2), 237. http://doi.org/10.2307/468419

Bellini, M. (2022). Interactive Digital Narratives as Complex Expressive Means. *Frontiers in Virtual Reality*, 3. https://doi.org/10.3389/frvir.2022.854960

Benjamin, W. (1963). *Das Kunstwerk im Zeitalter im Zeitalter seiner technischen Reproduzierbarkeit*. Frankfurt/Main: Surhkamp.

Bethesda Game Studios. (2011). The Elder's Scrolls V: Skyrim. Bethesda, Maryland: Bethesda Softworks.

Blank, M. (1983). Planetfall [Video game]. Cambridge, MA: Infocom.

Blizzard Entertainment. (2004). World of Warcraft. [Virtual Game World].

Bolter, J. D., MacIntyre, B., Gandy, M., & Schweitzer, P. (2006). New Media and the Permanent Crisis of Aura. *Convergence: the International Journal of Research Into New Media Technologies*, 12(1), 21–39. http://doi.org/10.1177/1354856506061550

CD Project RED. (2015). The Witcher 3. CD Project.

Cornell, C. (2013). Save the Date. Paper Dino Software.

Davis, D. (1995). The Work of Art in the Age of Digital Reproduction. *Leonardo*, 28(5), 381–386. Retrieved from http://links.jstor.org/sici?sici=0024-094X%281995%2928%3A5%3C381%3ATWOAIT%3E2.0.CO%3B2-M

Die Gute Fabrik. (2019). Mutazione. Steam.

Dufresne, D. (2013). Fort McMoney. National Filmboard of Canada & Arte. Retrieved from www.fortmcmoney.com

Eladhari, M. P. (2018). Re-Tellings: The Fourth Layer of Narrative as an Instrument for Critique. In R. Rouse, H. Koenitz, & M. Haahr (Eds.), *Interactive Storytelling: 11th International Conference for Interactive Digital Storytelling, ICIDS 2018* (Vol. 11318, pp. 65–78). Cham: Springer Berlin Heidelberg. http://doi.org/10.1007/978-3-030-04028-4_5

Electronic Arts. (2007). Mass Effect [Video game]. Edmonton: Electronic Arts.

Field, S. (1979). *Screenplay: The Basics of Film Writing*. New York: Random House Publishing Group.

Forster, E. M. (1927). *Aspects of the Novel*. Arnold.

Genette, G. (1983). *Narrative Discourse*. Cornell University Press.

Giddens, A. (1987). *Social Theory and Modern Sociology*. Stanford University Press.

Gumbrecht, H. U., & Marrinan, M. (2003). *Mapping Benjamin: the Work of Art in the Digital Age. Writing Science* (Orig. printing, pp. XVI–349 S.). Stanford, CA: Stanford University Press.

Halliday, M. (1985). Systemic Background. In *Systemic Perspectives on Discourse: Selected Theoretical Papers from the 9th International Systemic Workshop*. Ablex Publishing Corporation.

Halliday, M. A. K. (2006). *On Language and Linguistics*. A&C Black.

Hausken, L. (2004). Coda. In *Narrative Across Media* (pp. 391–403). University of Nebraska Press.

Hayles, N. K. (2002). *Writing Machines*. Cambridge, MA: MIT Press.

Hello Games. (2016). No Man's Sky [Video game]. Guildford, UK: Hello Games.

Herman, D. (2000). Narratology as a Cognitive Science. *Image and Narrative*.

Herman, D. (2002). *Story Logic*. Lincoln, NE: University of Nebraska Press.

Herman, D. (2004). Toward a Transmedial Narratology. In M. L. Ryan, J. Ruppert, & J. W. Bernet (Eds.), *Narrative Across Media: The Languages of Storytelling* (pp. 47–75). Lincoln, NE: University of Nebraska Press.

Ibsch, E. (1990). The Cognitive Turn in Narratology. *Poetics Today*, 11 (2), 411–418.

Joyce, M. (1987). Afternoon, A Story. Eastgate.

Karhulahti, V.-M. (2012). Double Fine Adventure and the Double Hermeneutic Videogame (pp. 19–26). Presented at the Proceedings of the 4th International Conference on Fun and Games.

Kasavin, G. (2020). Hades. San Francisco: Supergiant Games.

Koenitz, H. (2015). Towards a Specific Theory of Interactive Digital Narrative. In H. Koenitz, G. Ferri, M. Haahr, & T. I. Sezen (Eds.), *Interactive Digital Narrative* (pp. 91–105). New York: Routledge.

Koenitz, H., Dubbelman, T., Knoller, N., & Roth, C. (2016). An Integrated and Iterative Research Direction for Interactive Digital Narrative. In F. Nack & A. S. Gordon (Eds.), *Interactive Storytelling 9th International Conference on Interactive Digital Storytelling, ICIDS 2016* (Vol. 10045, pp. 51–60). Cham: Springer International Publishing. http://doi.org/10.1007/978-3-319-48279-8_5

Koenitz, H., & Eladhari, M. P. (2021). The Paradigm of Game System Building. *Transactions of the Digital Games Research Association*, 5(3). https://doi.org/10.26503/todigra.v5i3.123

Laurel, B. (1986). *Toward the Design of a Computer-Based Interactive Fantasy System*. Ohio State University.

Laurel, B. (1991). *Computers As Theatre*. Boston, MA: Addison-Wesley.

Lebling. (1980). Zork [Video game]. Cambridge, MA: Infocom.

Legrady, G. (2019). Intersecting the Virtual and the Real: Space in Interactive Media Installations. In M. Rieser & A. Zapp (Eds.), *New Screen Media: Cinema/Art/Narrative*. Bloomsbury Publishing.

Lorenz, E. N. (1963). Deterministic Nonperiodic Flow. *Journal of Atmospheric Sciences, 20*(2), 130–141.

Manovich, L. (2001). *The Language of New Media.* Cambridge, MA: MIT Press.

Mateas, M., & Stern, A. (2005a). Procedural Authorship: a Case-Study of the Interactive Drama Façade. Presented at the Digital Arts and Culture 2007.

Mateas, M., & Stern, A. (2005b). Structuring Content in the Façade Interactive Drama Architecture (pp. 93–98). Presented at the Proceedings of the First AAAI Conference on Artificial Intelligence and Interactive Digital Entertainment, Marina del Rey, California: AAAI Press.

Mitchell, A., & McGee, K. (2012). Reading Again for the First Time: A Model of Rereading in Interactive Stories. In D. Oyarzun, F. Peinado, R. M. Young, A. Elizalde, & G. Méndez (Eds.), *Interactive Storytelling: 5th International Conference, ICIDS 2012,* San Sebastián, Spain, November 12–15, 2012. Proceedings. Berlin, Heidelberg: Springer Berlin Heidelberg. http://doi.org/10.1007/978-3-642-34851-8.pdf

Montfort, N. (2003a). Toward a Theory of Interactive Fiction. Retrieved February 11, 2016, from http://nickm.com/if/toward.html

Montfort, N. (2003b). *Twisty Little Passages: An Approach to Interactive Fiction.* Cambridge, MA: MIT Press.

Montfort, N. (2005). *Twisty Little Passages.* Cambridge, MA: MIT Press.

Mason, S., Stagg, C., & Wardrip-Fruin, N. (2019). Lume (pp. 1–9). Presented at Foundations of Digital Games (FDG), 14th International Conference, New York, New York, USA: ACM Press. http://doi.org/10.1145/3337722.3337759

Murray, J. H. (1997). *Hamlet on the Holodeck: the Future of Narrative in Cyberspace.* New York: Free Press.

Murray, J. H. (2004). From Game-Story to Cyberdrama. In N. Wardrip-Fruin & P. Harrigan (Eds.), *First Person: New Media as Story, Performance, and Game.* Cambridge, MA: MIT Press.

Murray, J. H. (2011). *Inventing the Medium: Principles of Interaction Design as a Cultural Practice.* Cambridge, MA: MIT Press.

Murray, J. H. (2016). (2nd edition). *Hamlet on the Holodeck.* New York: The Free Press.

Murray, J. H. (2018). Research into Interactive Digital Narrative: A Kaleidoscopic View. In R. Rouse, H. Koenitz, & M. Haahr (Eds.), *Interactive Storytelling: 11th International Conference for Interactive Digital Storytelling, ICIDS 2018* (Vol. 11318, pp. 3–17). Cham: Springer Berlin Heidelberg. http://doi.org/10.1007/978-3-030-04028-4_1

Night School Studio. (2016). Oxenfree. Glendale, CA: Night School Studio.

Nitsche, M. (2008). *Video Game Spaces.* Cambridge, MA: MIT Press.

Prince, G. (1982). Narrative Analysis and Narratology. *New Literary History, 13*(2), 179–188. http://doi.org/10.2307/468908

Prince, G. (1987). *A Dictionary of Narratology.* Lincoln, NE: University of Nebraska Press.

Prince, G. (2003). *A Dictionary of Narratology.* Lincoln, NE: University of Nebraska Press.

Roth, C., van Nuenen, T., & Koenitz, H. (2018). Ludonarrative Hermeneutics: A Way Out and the Narrative Paradox. In R. Rouse, H. Koenitz, & M. Haahr (Eds.), *Interactive Storytelling: 11th International Conference for Interactive Digital Storytelling, ICIDS 2018* (pp. 93–106). Cham: The 3rd International Conference for Interactive Digital Storytelling. Retrieved from https://doi.org/10.1007/978-3-030-04028-4_7

Ryan, M. L. (2002). Beyond Myth and Metaphor: Narrative in Digital Media. *Poetics Today, 23*(4), 581–609. http://doi.org/10.1215/03335372-23-4-581

Ryan, M. L. (2006). *Avatars Of Story.* Minneapolis: University of Minnesota Press.

Ryan, M. L. (2009). From Narrative Games to Playable Stories: Toward a Poetics of Interactive Narrative. *Storyworlds: a Journal of Narrative Studies*, 1(1), 43–59. http://doi.org/10.1353/stw.0.0003

Ryan, M. L., & Thon, J. N. (Eds.). (2014). *Storyworlds Across Media: Toward a Media-Conscious Narratology*. Lincoln, NE: University of Nebraska Press.

Ryan, M. L., & Thon, J. N. (2014). Storyworlds across Media: Introduction. In M.-L. Ryan & J. N. Thon (Eds.), *Storyworlds across Media*. Lincoln, NE: University of Nebraska Press.

Shklovsky, V. (2017). Art as Technique. In J. Rivkin & M. Ryan (Eds.), *Literary Theory: An Anthology* (Vol. 3). Wiley.

The Chinese Room. (2008). Dear Esther. Portsmouth, UK: The Chinese Room.

Thon, J. N. (2016). *Transmedial Narratology and Contemporary Media Culture*. Nebraska.

Wardrip-Fruin, N. (2009). *Expressive Processing: Digital Fictions, Computer Games, and Software Studies*. Cambridge, MA: MIT Press.

Wiener, N. (1948). *Cybernetics Or Control and Communication in the Animal and the Machine*. Cambridge, MA: MIT Press.

Witch Beam. (2021). Unpacking. Humble Games.

Wright, W. (2000). The Sims [Video game]. Redwood City, CA: Electronic Arts.

Worldwalker Games. (2021). Wildermyth. Austin, TX: Worldwalker Games.

Part 4

IDN DESIGN

In this part, the focus is on the practice of creating IDN, on interactive narrative design. I will start with a high-level overview and identify overarching topics. Then I will address frequent misunderstandings and, finally, provide foundational elements toward a specific practice in the form of design principles, sanity checks, and a concrete process for creating IDN works.

IDN design can be traced back to experiments in computer science in the 1960s (Ryan, 2017; Weizenbaum, 1966), and yet, more than half a century later, it is still emerging as a fully recognized design discipline. There are several reasons for this state of affairs. First, the significance of IDN design is often downplayed and instead portrayed as a mere extension of long-established practices, especially of screenwriting. In this view, IDN works are essentially interactive versions of non-interactive narratives, much in the same way as cinematic adaptations are versions of literary originals. This view is problematic as it ignores the considerable changes and resulting creative opportunities afforded by the digital medium. When it comes to IDN design, practices for adaptation established in non-interactive media are inadequate – what is needed instead is a reconsideration of narrative under interactive conditions. Most importantly, on the conceptual level, IDN works represent a shift away from singular 'one-to-one' mappings and an embrace of multiplicity – of 'one-to-many' mappings. Instead of having one authoritative, pre-authored narrative, there are now multiple narratives, shaped in part by an audience-turned-participant.

As such, IDN design means to embrace complexity, and question as well as subvert simplistic mono-authorial perspectives. This paradigm shift has considerable implications for designers. It also marks IDN design as part of a wider effort of sense-making in a complex, postmodern reality, related to critical, reflective, and participatory design practices (S. Bardzell, Bardzell, Forlizzi, Zimmerman, & Antanitis, 2012; Björgvinsson, Ehn, & Hillgren, 2010; Sengers, Boehner, David, &

DOI: 10.4324/9781003106425-4

Kaye, 2005), but also feminist perspectives such as "Troubling Design" (Søndergaard, 2020). To emphasize the difference to non-interactive practices in this volume, I use the term 'IDN design' instead of 'narrative design.' Readers are welcome to substitute "narrative design" or "interactive narrative design" whenever they encounter this term. The benefits from the emphasis on the specificity and novelty of the task at hand is visible in the related field of game design, where effort and attention to the topic has spurred the continuous development of the professional practice, established game design as a subject in higher education, and led to a considerable number of textbooks and academic publications.

A second reason for the delay in recognition for the field of IDN design is the lack of a shared knowledge about IDN design elements. In contrast, creators of traditional forms of narrative can rely on a rich body of established design conventions for structuring and presenting narrative material – from the Aristotelian concept of unity of time and place to the rules of the Commedia dell'Arte, classical French theater, and the pacing and stock characters of the 20th century detective novel. Even the comparatively young narrative medium of film has established many helpful conventions, including continuity editing and rules for framing particular shots. In the evolving field of interactive digital narrative, few design conventions exist, and the ones that do are often shared with other digital manifestations and not directly focused on narrative – for example, a highlighted word in on-screen text will be conventionally understood as a clickable hyperlink or that an inventory function exists to hold items. Indeed, Janet Murray has described the search for design building blocks as one of the central challenges for designers of interactive works (Murray, 2011) and even a decade later, this concern is still at the forefront of IDN design practice and research. The scarcity of generalized design principles and the absence of a body of shared design knowledge also increases the lure of available non-interactive design conventions. This creates a vicious circle – the lack of available IDN design building blocks lead to an increased application of non-interactive design conventions, which, in turn, become normalized and decrease the interest in specific IDN design building blocks. This condition affects not only practicing IDN designers, but also creates a considerable obstacle for creatives from other narrative disciplines interested in the expressive potential of interactivity, as the specific advantages of IDN can appear to be minimal when only adaptive strategies are used. Additionally, education in IDN design is impacted by this situation and for the same reason might be tempted to fall back on adaptation strategies and present IDN design as a variant of screenwriting, instead of as a specific discipline.

A third reason is the scarcity of formal training in IDN design. Professionals in this area carry different titles, from "narrative designer" to "game writer" to "interactive director," and are mostly self-trained, because specialized training is still the exception rather than the rule. Most university-level game design programs feature only a single course on narrative design, which cannot do more than provide an introduction to the topic and is insufficient as a preparation for a career as IDN designer[1]. At the time of writing, no full degree program exists that covers the different manifestations of interactive digital narratives – from video games to interactive documentaries.[2] As I mentioned in the introduction, there are only a small number of bachelor's programs covering particular areas of the overall IDN design space, such as video game narrative or interactive documentaries, and a single master's program at the University of Westminster focusing on non-fiction content. As a consequence of this situation, in the games industry, several game studios and production companies have resorted to in-house training in order to fill the need for interactive narrative designers. Unfortunately, such uncoordinated and idiosyncratic efforts engender the creation of silos in the form of company-specific design approaches and vocabulary which is often inaccessible from the outside (either because this knowledge is treated as trade secret and/or because of the lack of documentation), not easily transferable, and requires re-learning when switching positions between companies. This problematic situation will not change before full degree programs in interactive narrative design and study are established – the biggest step forward this field of design can, and should, take. To realize this goal, it is crucial to increase research efforts in IDN design and contribute to a body of design knowledge that will form the basis of future educational programs. I will do so in this part by considering the specificity of IDN design, discussing common fallacies, and identifying successful design principles as well as best practices. I will conclude the part with a set of concrete steps for IDN prototyping.

IDN design is specific

Fundamentally, IDN is a specific human expression enabled by the affordances of the digital medium and not simply a merger of traditional narrative forms like the novel or movie with interactivity. A successful IDN creator is not simply someone who combines the talents of a film scriptwriter/novel author and that of an interaction designer – a notion we might understand as the 'additive perspective.' Rather, "cyberbards" (Murray, 1997) succeed in creating narrative experiences by means of the active involvement of their audiences. This is a fundamental aspect of IDN design – the realization that the audience has an active role, no longer as readers or viewers, but as "interactors" (ibid). The designer of an IDN work no longer produces a finished object in the sense of a printed book or the theatrical release of a movie. Instead, they create artifacts that can be considered *purposefully incomplete*, as they require the active engagement by an audience to be fully realized. Roy Ascott already described this aspect for cybernetic art in 1964. "I make structures in which the relationships of parts are not fixed and may be changed by the intervention of a spectator. [...] To project my ideas, I set limits within which he [sic] may behave." (Ascott, 1964 p.37) This is exactly what the SPP model (described in the previous part) shows – the digital *system* affords a participatory *process* which results in *products* as output. The IDN designer creates the dynamic *system* – the protostory – that enables and shapes the participatory *process* in order to facilitate narrative experiences which are realized by the audience as interactors. What happens in the IDN *process* is a shared responsibility connecting the IDN designer and their audience. This is why Murray reminds us that IDN audiences *actively create belief* (Murray, 1997), in contrast to Coleridge's understanding of the *suspension of disbelief* (Coleridge, 1894) for non-interactive media. Overall, we might understand IDN design as the art of creating 'participatory narrative systems.' The artifacts resulting from such a practice will be different from traditional narrative forms as Henry Jenkins reminds us, using the case of narrative-focused games as an example. "If some games tell stories, they are unlikely to tell them in the same ways that other media tell stories. Stories are not empty content that can be ported from one media pipeline to another." (Jenkins, 2004) Therefore, it is not the aim of IDN design to create the same experience that non-interactive narrative forms offer. From this perspective, the question of the "narrative paradox" (Aylett, 1999) – described as the problem of balancing authored narrative coherence and interaction opportunities for the audience – is problematic in itself, as it can be seen as asking for an impossible hybrid that connects the coherence of static narrative forms with the dynamic of IDN. The trap to avoid here for IDN design is to project expectations from non-interactive forms onto IDN. To be clear, IDN design should certainly strive for narrative coherence, but what we understand as coherence in IDN will be different from the same notion in earlier forms of narrative because IDN designers create dynamic artifacts where the responsibility for the coherence of the narrative experience is shared between creator and audience.

In terms of concrete design strategies, this means that the IDN designer cannot rely on established practices. What works for fixed, static expressions like a film or novel does not automatically apply to the dynamic and participatory systems the IDN designer creates. The designers of *Tale of Tales,* Auriea Harvey and Michael Samyn, describe this change:

> We are not story-tellers in the traditional sense of the word. In the sense that we know a story and we want to share it with you. Our work is more about exploring the narrative potential of a situation. We create only the situation. And the actual story emerges from playing, partially in the game, partially in the player's mind.
>
> *Newheiser, 2009*

The differences in affordances, potential for interaction, and status of the audience need to be taken into account. Much energy can be wasted in an ultimately futile effort to adapt non-interactive practices for interactive conditions. Simple adaptations often fail in this regard, effectively turning the respective works into unconvincing and deficient variants of non-interactive narrative. In such cases, interactivity appears as an afterthought and audiences might have been better served with the initial forms of a book or film. Consequently, Janet Murray warns us about "unproductive attempts to apply legacy [design] conventions to new digital frameworks." (Murray, 2011) In IDN design – as Murray points out – invention is a necessity, as there are often no applicable prior examples.

We might wonder how this perspective can still be correct after more than half a century of IDN design practice and a decade after Murray wrote the above words. Certainly, a considerable number of excellent practitioners exist who have invented and perfected many effective building blocks for IDN design. However, in the absence of a recognized design discipline and academic field, and a shared vocabulary, there is still little in terms of an established and shared body of IDN design knowledge. Consequently, embracing the specificity of IDN means to accept a considerable intellectual and artistic challenge, which at times might seem intimidating and even frustrating. Novel design principles are as much the fruit of intuition as they are the result of trial and (often repeated) error. Yet, it is also incredibly exciting to work on a creative frontier and help charter a novel territory of human expression.

In the professional sphere, venturing into the unknown also means to take on considerable economic risks. The challenge for a new form of expression is also an economic one. Investors and managers are much more easily convinced of the 'tried and tested' ways of design principles inherited from traditional non-interactive forms of narrative (cf. Wolfgang Walk's description of the economic risks of foregoing the "hero's journey" in communication with clients (Walk, 2018)). It is therefore not surprising that specific approaches to IDN design can often be found in productions by small, independent companies or solo producers. Examples in this vein include *Dear Esther* (The Chinese Room, 2008), *The Path* (Tale of Tales, 2009), *Gone Home* (The Fullbright Company, 2013), *Kentucky Route Zero* (Cardboard Computer, 2013–2020)[3], *Sunset* (Tale of Tales, 2015), *Firewatch* (Campo Santo, 2016), *Oxenfree* (Night School Studio, 2016), *Florence* (Mountains, 2018), *Mutazione* (Die Gute Fabrik, 2019), and *Disco Elysium* (ZA/UM, 2019). In contrast, big-budget productions such as *The Last of Us* (Naughty Dog, 2014), *The Last of Us 2* (Naughty Dog, 2020), or *Unchartered 4 – A Thief's End* (Naughty Dog, 2016) often rely heavily on 'cinematics' – digital movies that are interjected at intervals into the gameplay for narrative development. As a case in point, the protagonist's relationship to his romantic partner is shown in *Unchartered 4* in non-interactive 'cut scenes' (running into several minutes) and experienced in an interactive fashion in *Florence*[4] where, for example, the interactor has to make space in a cupboard in order for the partner to move in (Figure 4.1).

IDN creators are system designers

It is important to fully consider what it means to be a designer of an interactive system, and not a novel author or scriptwriter. This shift is as crucial as it is difficult, since it means to give up a considerable amount of artistic control and release it into the hands of an active audience of interactors. In this regard, it is helpful to embrace a notion of 'sit back and watch with amazement' what interactors will do with an IDN work. There is a different kind of joy and reward from seeing interactors' performances and participatory co-creation happening. Conversely, agency can also be a problematic as interactors might use their capabilities in ways not intended by the creator. A case in point is *The Sims* (Wright, 2000) – as already described before – a simulation where interactors manage the lives of in-game characters

FIGURE 4.1 Interactive experience of a relationship in Florence: making space for the partner to move in – objects on the shelf need to be taken away and put in the storage box so that the partner's objects can be placed there. Image courtesy of Mountains studio

in a society determined by economic pressure and the pursuit of goods to build and decorate elaborate houses, which also includes relationships and children. Will Wright intended this hugely successful simulation game as a "dollhouse for adults" (Baker, 2012) and certainly never envisioned that some interactors would figure out ways to trap and torture the in-game characters in cellars they created for this purpose. This anecdote is a warning about the potential negative aspects of highly dynamic systems. Another example is the failure of Microsoft's infamous AI chatbot "Tay," which was taught racist remarks and perspectives by some audience members and had to be taken down for spreading racism within 16 hours of the original launch. There is a specific ethical responsibility that comes with the ability to bestow the power of agency and co-creation on the audience. The IDN creator as system designer needs to take this aspect into consideration – that interactors' agency impacts the creator's intention, but also has an effect on interactors' own experience and on others in multiplayer settings. Agency should certainly not mean the power to hurt others or enable oppressive behavior. Yet, there is no easy solution that enables only desirable behaviors and prevents undesirable ones when a dynamic system reaches the level of possible combinatorics displayed by *The Sims*. The functions that enable ethically problematic actions can be the same ones that also enable prosocial behavior.

A first step in addressing problematic actions by interactors might be in scripting the audience – in the sense of Murray's "scripting the interactor" (Murray, 1997) – for ethical behavior in the first place. In the longer run, what is needed are behavior rules that function in a dynamic context. The best analogy we might have in this regard are the rule systems of democratic societies that aim to guarantee freedoms while simultaneously preventing harm to its members. This analogy is productive in showing us that there is no single correct approach, just as there are many different ways to organize a democracy. For example, the US presidential system differs in important ways from that in France, while Germany's federal system of governance is distinct from the one in Australia. Additionally, countries' laws are not static and are adjusted to address changing conditions – for example, global warming or demographic changes within a society. Similarly, dynamic IDN systems and the kind of interactions they enable might change over time – for example, because of technological advances or when the interactor population reaches particular levels in a multiplayer experience.

The ethical dimension of IDN design is of particular importance if we use IDN to educate and inform. What is our intention? What sources and databases are we using? How are we representing differing opinions? What are we (potentially) excluding due to our own biases or the biases of the algorithms we use? Are we excluding certain parts of the audience? While an in-depth discussion about ethical aspects in IDN creation is outside the scope of this volume, these questions need to be addressed in future work. As a starting point, I have developed an initial ethics framework for IDN design together with Agnes Bakk and Jonathan Barbara. The 12 rules from that framework are reproduced in the next part of this volume.

Frequent misunderstandings in IDN design

IDN design is an emergent field that is still in the process of emancipating itself from more established practices in creating print literature, film, and stage drama. The result of this situation is a considerable number of misunderstandings. In the following section, I will address particularly important cases. Recognizing the specificity of IDN design and the changed role of the creator as system designer are crucial first steps in overcoming these issues.

General issues

Design is not the finished meal or mistaking descriptions for prescriptions

In a previous part, I categorized game designer Jesse Schell's comments on IDN (Schell, 2008) as narrative fundamentalism. From a design perspective, these remarks about supposedly universal rules governing narrative warrant further discussion. We need to consider the analytical foundation of such rules carefully before we apply them. A crucial question in this regard is whether the rules are *descriptive* or *prescriptive/generative*. The issue here is the fallacy of misconstruing the question of IDN design as a question of narrative analysis. Existing theoretical frameworks are for the most part meant to analyze narrative artifacts ex-post and therefore do not tell us how to create them. Consequently, the issue with concepts like Campbell's *hero's journey* is not only in their inherent narrative fundamentalism, but also in that they analyze the finished product and not the design process. This difference is not unique to IDN design and also exists for non-interactive narrative design; but is particularly important when the result of the designer's activity is a system, a dynamic IDN artifact with multiple perspectives, paths, and/or endings, and not a fixed product.

The contrast becomes clearer when we compare IDN design to cooking: descriptive models like the hero's journey *describe* how the finished meal manifests to the audience. Yet, what we need to understand is that IDN design is the equivalent of a recipe, a *prescription* of how the elements are put together. The way an IDN artifact was actually designed can only be partially inferred from the finished work, irrespective of how well the analysis has been done. At best, it might be possible to identify all the ingredients. Yet, in order to understand how to cook a risotto, bake a cheesecake or understand the intricate process to make ramen broth, we need an ingredient list *and* instructions.

In addition, we need to be aware that every analysis and description of a finished artifact is an interpretation. What is the designer's understanding of the structure of the Netflix IDN production *Bandersnatch* (2019)? Unless the original design documentation is released, we cannot be sure and therefore different interpretations of the underlying structure exist (Figure 4.2, Figure 4.3, Figure 4.4). For example, the mappings in Figure 4.3 and Figure 4.4 show a further influence of the first dead end (accepting to work at the company), while the first mapping (Figure 4.2) does not. Equally, all three mappings depict the password entry and consequences slightly differently. This does not mean that any of these representations are *wrong* in absolute terms, but rather that we need to be aware of their epistemological status as post-factum interpretations. They should therefore not be seen as representing 'the structure of *Bandersnatch*' but instead as 'an interpretation of the structure of *Bandersnatch*.'

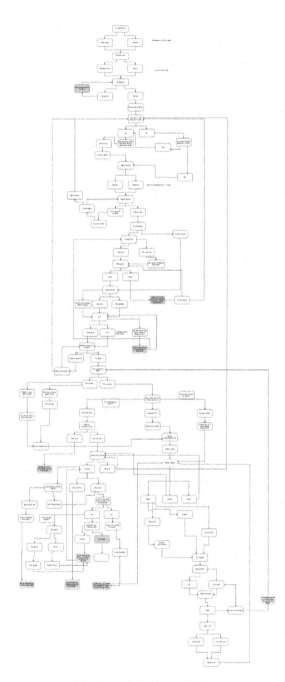

FIGURE 4.2 Mapping of *Bandersnatch*. Image courtesy of Leon Hurley. https://twitter.
com/LeonHurley/status/1078796394247393281/photo/1

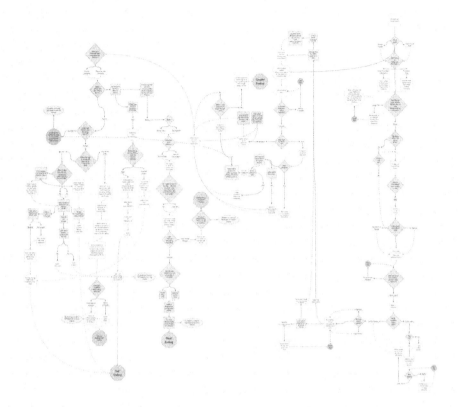

FIGURE 4.3 Alternative mapping of *Bandersnatch*. Image courtesy of IGN. www.ign. com/wikis/black-mirror/Bandersnatch_Map_-_All_Choices_and_Outcomes

Far too long have we tried to learn how to cook from descriptions of finished meals. This does not mean that descriptions are useless for designers – they are necessary to understand the results of a design process. Yet, as IDN designers we need to be aware that what we are working on is the process of putting together ingredients and creating structures, while descriptions of the result come last.

Interaction always exists with narrative, the difference to IDN is only a matter of degree

I have already discussed this issue in a previous part as the difference between *inter-action 1* (speculation) and *interaction 2* (planning and execution) but it bears repeating in the context of design. Schell is again testimony to this misunderstanding:

> When one is engaged in any kind of storyline, interactive or not, one is con-tinually making decisions: "What will happen next?" "What should the hero do?" "Where did that rabbit go?" "Don't open that door!" The difference only comes in the participant's ability to *take* action.
>
> *Schell, 2008 [Schell's emphasis]*

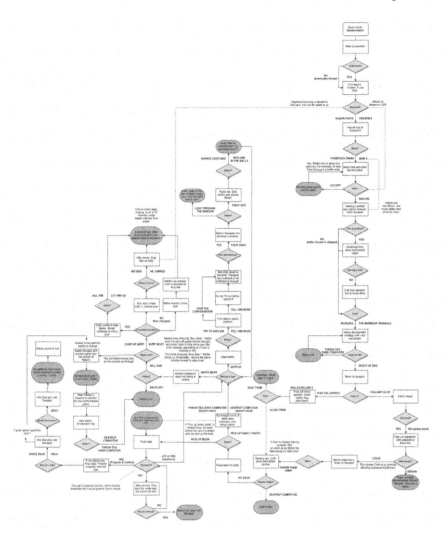

FIGURE 4.4 Another alternative mapping of *Bandersnatch* by Reddit user alpine.
Available at https://i.imgur.com/6liEhYk.png

What Schell describes here is *interactivity 1* (speculation) – the answers to the questions he presents in his text do not have any influence on the artifact. This is why the "ability to take action" is much more than a matter of degree. The difference between speculation and the ability to formulate actual plans and execute them is considerable. When we read *Lord of the Rings*, we might imagine what the Shire looks like or wonder whether Frodo will succeed in delivering the ring to Mordor, but we will not change the course of a marriage as in *Façade* (Mateas & Stern, 2005), develop the careers and private lives of characters as in *The Sims* (Wright, 2000), or act under the pressure of a totalitarian regime as in *Papers, Please* (Pope, 2013). The difference between *interactivity 1* of interpretation and speculation and *interactivity 2* of planning and execution[5] is the reason why IDN design is necessary. If we downplay this difference, we rob ourselves of much of the expressive possibilities of IDN. Consequently, Schell's proposed solution to narrative design in video games is insufficient with its emphasis on "indirect control, using subtle means to covertly limit the choices that a participant is likely to make." (Fullerton et al., 2008) Certainly, this approach has a place in the IDN designer's toolbox, but it represents only one possible means among many, and it is inadequate when we consider emergent narratives as the result of co-creation, multiplayer interaction, or procedural generation.

The universal rules of storytelling also apply to IDN

This point can be dismissed by pointing out that most so-called 'universal rules' of narrative turn out to be Eurocentric and ignorant of a plethora of non-western forms of narration (see part two of this volume). Yet, even if we sidestep the problematic claim of universality for a moment, we need to understand what this perspective means in actual design practice. The environment for the designer changes dramatically in the move from print literature and film to the procedural and participatory digital medium. Therefore, we need to carefully consider which rules are actually still usable in the new design context. Do the same rules apply when we depict character development in a movie in contrast to giving interactors the ability to develop a character? Can temporal sequencing be the same when we can no longer be sure how long the audience as participants will take in reaching a certain point in the narrative, because they might follow unexpected detours or take much longer to complete a prior task? At the very least, traditional rules will need considerable adaptation in order to be useful for IDN design and some simply do not apply in the interactive context – especially the ones predicated on full authorial control.

Unfortunately, these aspects might not seem so clear in every case. Nothing prevents a designer from applying traditional storytelling formulas in interactive situations – for example, when long cinematic 'cut scenes' are used to convey narrative progression in video games. Yet, such practices are attempts to find convenient shortcuts to sidestep the challenge of IDN design and do not constitute evidence for the existence of universal rules. At best, such practices can be understood as an early evolutionary step, as harbingers of a more fully developed form. In addition, there are productions which recreate traditional forms of narration within an interactive setting, but such works are not examples of IDN design. The digital medium can simulate earlier forms and therefore it is entirely possible to create works that fully adhere to the design conventions of earlier media such as print literature and film. These productions are digitized versions of earlier forms of narrative artifacts (e.g., ebooks) and only make use of the specific affordances of the digital medium in very limited and non-expressive capacities (e.g., search functions in ebooks).

IDN is narrative + interactivity

It might not be immediately clear in what way this phrase is a fallacy. However, there is a danger in misunderstanding interactivity in IDN as an 'add-on' to traditional forms of narrative. IDN is not a variety of an earlier form, similar to the way that film is not simply stage play + film technology, but instead a specific form which applies film technology for narrative expression. In other words, when we understand that film is not just enhanced theater, we also see that IDN is neither simply enhanced literature nor enhanced cinema.

This is a variation of the issue described above in its attempt to minimize the need for specific conceptions by re-using established design conventions and production workflows. Works embodying this perspective do not make use of the affordances of the digital medium and often feel underdeveloped and derivative. Transmedial projects that also have outputs in non-interactive forms (e.g., as a movie) are particularly susceptible to this fallacy when they try to re-purpose existing material for the interactive context. Mirka Duijn's Emmy-award winning interactive documentary *Last Hijack Interactive* (Duijn, Wolting, & Pallotta, 2014) is one of the few successful examples of repurposing material, but a key to this title's success was the creation of additional content to facilitate opportunities for interaction in the form of perspective changes.

Specific issues

In addition to the more general misunderstandings connected to the design of IDN, there are a number of concrete issues which also affect critics and audiences. Overcoming these issues is therefore also an educational effort. For example, too many audience members and critics are still focused on global agency as the only measure for a satisfying experience. Improving IDN literacy is key in order to change expectations and create appreciation for good IDN design, for the rich experience that can be offered, for example, by local agency or by acting within restraints.

Multiple endings are the only way to implement global agency

An often-discussed aspect of IDN design is the difference between local and global agency (cf. Roth & Vermeulen, 2012), with the latter taken as the more important of the two in terms of perceived impact. IDN works offering opportunities for interaction which result in a perceptible change provide *local agency*. If the interactor's actions also have a global effect during the experience and/or impact on the ending, then the artifact also offers *global agency*. Interactors might perceive works with only local agency as not giving them real impact – 'whatever I did had no impact on the outcome.' Yet, this perspective is too simplistic because different paths can be (and should be) as interesting as different endings. In this regard, I remind my students that human life can be (and often is) very interesting even though the end is invariable. An IDN offering varied paths that all lead to the same ending can be as interesting as one which has several different endings. Global agency is not only about different endings, but also about what can be changed on the way. For example, global agency exists if an interactor can choose freely how their character will get from a starting point in London to Sydney.

Narrative sequencing needs to be affected in order to have agency

This is a variant of the previous point. However, even within a fixed sequence of events, choices that affect character development and perspective can create meaningful and varied interactive experiences. The interactor character might always be born as a princess, will grow up to be a mighty empress, and die on the same day – but the interactor's perspective on the same events might be entirely different depending on choices that will add to character's benevolence or malice. Emily Short's *Blood and Laurels* is an example of this kind of IDN design as is the relationship narrative *Florence* (Mountains, 2018).

Fully developed IDN means total freedom for the interactor

This is a fundamental misunderstanding of IDN design. Total freedom does not create an interesting experience. If we have total freedom, there is no purpose, no goal, no challenge and, most likely, we will become bored. Agency – which Murray has described as the ability to make meaningful decisions and see their effects (Murray, 1997) – is not the same as being able to act in any way imaginable. Decisions become meaningful if there is a purpose – if we have a goal we want to reach and if we see the impact of our decisions – and if there is also an impact on the narrative in a perceptible way, we can talk about "dramatic agency" (Murray, 2005). It is by challenges, obstacles, and authored dramatic events that we create interest by limiting an interactor's freedom. We are used to restrictions in real life (e.g., we do not cross the road at an arbitrary moment, but instead watch out for cars, as we do not want to die). Conversely, we are prepared to accept restriction in IDN, as long as they make sense to us. In this regard Murray's concept of "scripting the interactor" (Murray, 1997) is a relevant design principle with the aim to orient the interactor, make them aware of boundaries, and help them to act in accordance with their role. Therefore, the design space for IDN is not 'anything the interactor might do,' but 'everything that makes sense for the interactor to do in the current context'. The context in this regard includes all rules and boundaries of an IDN system.

A concrete example of this understanding of meaningful agency through limitations is in the design of the critically acclaimed narrative game *Disco Elysium* (ZA/UM, 2019), as reported by lead narrative designer Justin Keenan:

> We're very clear about what the bounds of your agency represent. And for us that's because we take the politics of our games very seriously, and this is a point about agency in the real world – that at any given point you can only have so much agency over the material circumstance of the world you live in. But what you do have very profound control over is what that world represents to you.
>
> *GDC Podcast Ep. 25, 2021*

The rules and boundaries of an IDN are only designed by the creator

It is important to realize that all interactors bring real-world knowledge and prior experiences with IDN and other digital manifestations to the experience which complement the specific rules designed for a particular artifact. If an IDN artifact represents real-life space, a rule system, characters, or situations, interactors expect that their existing knowledge applies. In terms of design, this is both an opportunity and a challenge. The reason Weizenbaum's *Eliza* (Weizenbaum, 1966) experiment can appear to sustain a conversation is that it applies real-world knowledge about how the conversation in a therapy session is structured and scripts the interactor into the role of a therapy patient. Unless explicitly instructed otherwise, interactors will assume that the rules of nature apply (e.g., gravity). Equally, interactors will take rules of the society surrounding them as the default (e.g., the specific flavor of democracy they live in), as well as their cultural context as a given, unless specifically instructed otherwise.

Virtual characters in an IDN need to be realistic

This aspect of IDN design has been addressed convincingly already in the 1990s by Joseph Bates and the OZ group at Carnegie Mellon University. Bates' fundamental insight was that virtual characters powered by artificial intelligence need to be believable, not realistic (Bates, 1992). The point is not to model a complete representation of real life, but a convincing likeness or coherent situation. Characters can have any shape or form, they might have magical powers, be able to fly or jump around in time, they might not have bodies or look like a tin can, but they need to be put in a context in which their existence makes sense and is comprehensible to the interactor. Simultaneously, the interactions an audience has with virtual characters need to be convincing in the given context and whether they are realistic – for example as in *Lifeline* to talk to an astronaut on a far-away planet – does not matter in this regard.

Highly advanced artificial intelligence (AI) is a requirement for a fully developed form of IDN

There are plenty examples of engaging and enjoyable IDN works that do not apply AI methods. From this perspective, Andrew Stern's 2008 argument for AI as a fundamental requirement for any kind of larger IDN project was overstated (Stern, 2008). Without AI, we do not automatically fall into the "non-linearity hell" of an unmanageable space of combinatorics. Even at the time, content management systems (CMS) running the websites of newspapers like the New York Times, showed how large amounts of content can be handled without AI functions. In Stern's work *Façade* (Mateas & Stern, 2005), AI functions are complemented by pre-authored content in the form of narrative units (including pre-recorded voice acting), overall story structure, and graphical assets. It might be best to understand AI as one tool – albeit very powerful and useful – among several others in the toolbox of the IDN designer. AI has undoubtedly great expressive potential and advanced functions – particularly in procedural narrative generation – will be an important element of many future IDN works.

There should be no gaps in the narrative of an IDN

The holy grail of IDN design is sometimes understood as a system that can provide a seamless narrative experience, no matter what the interactor does. Setting aside the question whether such as system is technically feasible, this perspective ignores the importance of providing space for the interactor's fantasy, for their capability to fill in small gaps and thus make an experience even more 'their own.' Certainly, large jumps in the narrative progression and breaks in the causal chain should be avoided, but smaller gaps are an important means for how IDN design can provide opportunities for personalization and co-creation. For example, a first-person perspective allows interactors to create a personal image of the protagonist's appearance.

Narrative is external to gameplay

In video game design, narrative aspects are sometimes described as separate from the actual gameplay, serving in various supporting roles. One example for this dichotomic approach is Bateman's edited collection (Bateman, 2007), which is focused on fitting narrative within the boundaries of established game design workflows. The emphasis on 'narrative as a support function' is clearly articulated:

> [...] narrative strings together the events of the game, providing a framework and what can alternately be called a justification, a reason, or an excuse for the gameplay encounters.
>
> *Bateman, 2007*

Similarly, Juul (Juul, 2005) describes narrative as mostly ornamental, as an initial backdrop that becomes dispensable once a player has been drawn into the game. These perspectives are problematic in their fundamentalist conception of narrative as non-interactive and separate from the players' active experiences. Once we acknowledge the cognitive turn in narratology (see previous part), and with it the experience of gameplay as narrative (Calleja, 2013; Pearce, 2004), the clear separation of gameplay and narrative is no longer possible. On this basis, Teun Dubbelman considers "narrative game mechanics" as the means to "support the construction of engaging stories and fictional worlds." (Dubbelman, 2016) Consequently, the problem described by the term "ludo-narrative dissonance" (Hocking, 2007) might be better described as a dissonance between a narrative frame and the concrete narrative experiences of the player.

(Video game) Mechanics are the message

Mechanics alone are not the message in the way Brenda Romero (formerly Brathwaite) has framed this aspect (Brathwaite, 2009). Instead, narrative is a necessary component to provide contextual and ethical orientation. and shape the audience's understanding. Romero's work *Train* (Brathwaite, 2009) exemplifies this problem. *Train* is intended to give rise to reflections on the Holocaust through the mechanics of train transport. *Train* is a board game that instructs interactors to transport yellow play figurines in cattle train cars. Unbeknown to the interactors, they are placed in the role of railroad dispatchers transporting Jews to concentration camps and thus being complicit in their mass murder. The intended effect of *Train* is that the interactors realize what role they are enacting, resist to continue in this role, and learn a valuable lesson about being complicit. We might understand the overarching design principle of *Train* as the reverse of Murray's "scripting the interactor" (Murray, 1997) – the interactor's slow realization of what role they are enacting. Yet, in contrast to Romero's claim, the piece does not rely on its mechanics as the message but on an externalized historical narrative context of the holocaust, and specifically of the victims transported to death camps by train. The mechanics of train logistics, or NPCs in train cars, have no moral implications by themselves. The crucial moral dimension of the Holocaust is not conveyed by the mechanics. It is the historical narrative of the Shoah that does that, and *Train* relies entirely on traces planted to lead to the discovery of this narrative. This is the reason why the piece is shown in a setting that includes a broken window and typewriter with an SS character. The intended effect is thus not in the experience of the mechanics, but in the interactor's realization of what historical narrative they are re-enacting. The danger with this approach is that the interactor's knowledge of this implied narrative cannot be guaranteed, and the piece might entirely fail to convey its intended message about complacency in mass murder in a cultural setting where little knowledge of the Holocaust – or even just of the train transport aspect of the genocide – exists. However, even if the interactors come to understand what role they are in, the educational take-away – beyond the pure shock-value of realizing that they acted as part of the mechanics of mass murder – are severely limited since their role remains underspecified and lacks context.[6] What is missing in *Train* is a contextual frame of indoctrination and fear in a totalitarian system as well as the pressure of a professional situation in which train logistics are a central element of an ongoing world war. *Train* externalizes the contextual historical narratives and thus misses the opportunity to facilitate important lessons about the historical situation.

This contextual frame is exactly where *Papers, Please* (Pope, 2013) excels – a work which I already mentioned. Set in an imaginary Eastern European totalitarian state, the interactor is conscripted into the role of a customs officer and has a family to support through their earnings. The work provides a rich contextual narrative framework including a high-pressure professional situation in which the interactor is tasked with enforcing the ever-changing rules of entry to their home country. The interactor might choose to subvert the official rules of their government but suffer the consequences for themselves and their families. This crucial aspect, the potential cost of resistance in a totalitarian situation, is missing from *Train* with its focus on shock value. Sophisticated interactive narrative design that includes mechanical aspects can convey this crucial contextual information, as demonstrated by *Papers, Please*.

IDN design: creating participatory narrative systems

So far, I have considered the specificity of IDN design and described fallacies and common misunderstandings connected to the topic. It is now time to consider foundations of IDN design – elements, best practices, and prototyping methods.

IDN design elements: aesthetic qualities, principles, building blocks, and conventions

Design can be understood at different levels of abstraction, and it is important to consider where a given design element is located and how it relates to others. Distinguishing abstraction levels improves communication and provides increased granularity when describing IDN design. In the remainder of this part, I will use the following categories when describing elements of IDN:

> Aesthetic Qualities
> Design Principles
> Building Blocks/Conventions

Aesthetic qualities represent the most abstract level of design elements. Murray (Murray, 1997) has defined the aesthetic qualities of immersion, agency, and transformation as essential for successful digital interactive works. These qualities manifest in the process as the result of the interplay between the conscious decisions by the designer and the ones taken by the interactor. Building blocks are the most concrete design elements. In between aesthetic qualities and building blocks are design principles – an organizing category which is shared among several different building blocks. Applying this framework, the *principle* of "scripting the interactor" belongs to the overarching *aesthetic quality* of immersion and can be realized through a variety of different concrete *building blocks*, such as an introductory training session or explanatory text at the beginning of the experience. In this conception, the lower levels can serve several higher-level purposes, meaning that some building blocks might serve several design principles that, in turn, will contribute to several aesthetic qualities.

Aesthetic qualities

Immersion

Immersion is the ability of a work to draw us in and hold our interest (Murray, 1997). This quality is the basis for everything else and without immersion, an IDN cannot function. Conversely, we need to be aware that in a time where multitasking has long become the norm for many people in their daily lives, immersion is no longer an absolute. In a multitasking world, immersion can be interrupted and come in segments without being broken. Testimony to this changed sense of immersion are works like the *Lifeline* (a conversation with an astronaut on a far-away planet) and *Karen* (Blast Theory, 2014) (a life-coach experience), both of which purposefully interrupt the experience for long breaks. These breaks are diegetic, they are part of the experience and explained as such – the astronaut will call again when he has reached the destination of a long hike; the life coach will call the next day once she has formulated a strategy for the customer. Another example for an expanded sense of immersion is the map showing interactors which paths they have taken and which ones they missed in *Detroit: Become Human* (Quantic Dream, 2018) (Figure 4.5). Traditionally, the maps would be understood as non-diegetic – as an element effectively breaking immersion. Yet, in *Detroit: Become Human*, the maps are an essential part of the experience and thus can been seen as a means to increase immersion. Finally, I want to be clear that 'immersion' – as used here – is a result of design and not a property in contrast to the meaning in recent popular terms such as "immersive technology" or "immersive media."

Agency

Murray has defined *agency* as the ability to take meaningful decisions (Murray, 1997). Agency means more than the ability to act in an interactive environment, it includes feedback which makes the action and its effect comprehensible and consequently meaningful. This does not mean that the effects of an action need to be explained in full at all times – delayed consequences are an effective design principle – but the interactor needs to be given some feedback as acknowledgment of their action. This can be mundane – for example, attempting to open a door should result in an immediate reaction (door handle animation, a small sound, a notification) even if the door cannot be opened at the time. It can also show a more profound impact – for example, when a decision will result in a change in the character's look or role, or a permanent change in the environment.

Agency should not be misunderstood as the freedom of the interactor to do anything they want. Indeed, Fox Harrell and Jichen Zhu have convincingly argued to understand agency as knowledge "of how to perform manipulations in a particular conceptual system" (Harrell & Zhu, 2009) and remind us that agency in IDN is the result of the structure provided by the artifact in combination with the interactor's interpretation, which is "socially situated" (ibid). This is the reason why the SPP model includes the triple hermeneutic of interpretation and why I stressed earlier in this part the fact that not all rules and boundaries of an IDN are created by the designer. It is crucial for IDN design to understand the factor of situated interpretation by the interactor. For example, an IDN engaging the topic of colonialization will most likely be interpreted differently by descendants of colonized versus colonizers. Similarly, the same IDN might be perceived very

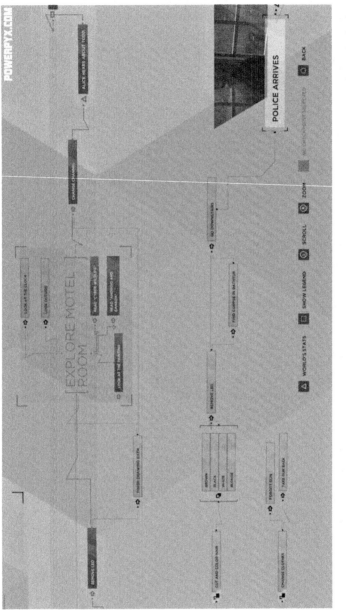

FIGURE 4.5 The progression map in *Detroit: Become Human* shows which paths the interactor has taken (dark) and which ones are still unexplored (grey)

differently depending on the location where it is experienced – for example, in an exhibition setting versus at home.

Harrell and Zhu also remind us that agency does not have to be static and can be used as a dynamic quality for expressive goals. For example, we might want to temporarily restrict agency to express that there is no choice in a certain situation or because the interactor character is trapped or arrested. The temporal removal of agency creates an increased awareness and appreciation of the quality by interactors when it is available.

Transformation

Transformation is one of the most interesting, but also challenging, aspects of IDN design. It can be seen as an extension of agency, as the longer-term effect of agency. Transformation happens on several levels, in the form of changes in the virtual world of an IDN (e.g., the development of a character, impact on the rule system, the addition of user-generated content), but also in the interactor's understanding. We can therefore describe transformation as a dual quality – of the IDN itself and transformation of the interactor's understanding through the experience of the IDN. The challenge with the former aspect in terms of design is in assuring that any changes are believable in the context of the respective narrative. Transformation of the interactor's understanding is increased through replay, as more aspects and perspectives become available when more potential narratives are realized. However, meaningful replay requires careful planning and ample material. Importantly, as Murray observes (1997), transformation through IDN already happens with a single playthrough, by means of the awareness that alternative paths exist that have not been explored. Indeed, there might be a transformational paradox – the more expansive the options for an interactor appear, the less likely replay becomes. The expansive narratives of some video games – for example, the *Mass Effect* series (Electronic Arts, 2007), *Red Dead Redemption 2* (Rockstar Studios, 2018), or *Dragon Age: Origins* (Bioware, 2009) are rarely ever replayed, yet the many available choices and consequences still resonate with interactors in a transformative way.

Kaleidoscopic

In *Inventing the Medium* (2011), Murray adds *kaleidoscopic* as an additional meta-quality that represents the variability of configuration and the complexity of the representation (Murray, 2018). This last experiential quality is an effect of skillful design that embodies a combination of the first three. We experience the kaleido-scopic when we gain an understanding and an appreciation of the variability and underlying complexity a designer wants to convey with a particular work, when immersion, agency, and transformation build on each other in a way that enables us to see interconnectedness, experience combinatorics, and explore multiple paths – to reflect on complex issues, and gain insights we might not have gained otherwise. At this point, IDN design becomes kaleidoscopic design, in Murray's words:

> Kaleidoscopic design would allow us to see how small elements combine into a larger system, to explore the possibilities of variations in components and in the rules of assembly. It would help us to better capture the complexity of systems that are currently beyond our grasp [...].
>
> *Murray, 2016*

In other words, the experience of the kaleidoscopic can be described as the joy of exploring a realm that hitherto seemed opaque and incomprehensible.

The relationship between aesthetic qualities

Aesthetic qualities do not exist in isolation and their relationship is one of dependency and reinforcement. Agency requires immersion, transformation needs agency; and the kaleidoscopic needs all three of them. Conversely, the higher-level qualities also reinforce those on the lower levels – for example, immersion is enhanced through the experience of agency, transformation, and the kaleidoscopic, while agency is deepened through transformation and the kaleidoscopic (Figure 4.6).

From a design perspective, this means that all qualities need attention – even if we might for example want to focus on agency in a given work, immersion, and transformation are still factors for design. Indeed, a designer ignores an aesthetic quality at their own peril – the result would be an imbalanced work that will most likely not provide a compelling experience. For example, in order to make an interactor aware of their agency, perceptible transformation is necessary, otherwise an interaction will feel inconsequential. At the same time, a given design aspect can serve several different qualities. For example, a 3D environment in which the interactors can move around freely will provide immersion, but also helps create the

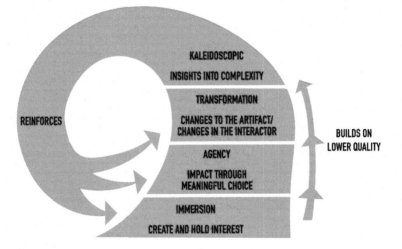

FIGURE 4.6 Relationship among aesthetic qualities

experience of agency through the ability to choose different directions. If the 3D environment can be changed, for example, when the interactor can build a house, agency is increased further, but also transformation, as the environment itself is transformed. Another example is the progression map (Figure 4.5) in *Detroit: Become Human* (Quantic Dream, 2018), which I have mentioned under immersion before, it also affects the experience of agency (by showing that decisions are meaningful and have consequences) and transformation (by showing only the paths taken), The progression maps can even be described as kaleidoscopic as they provide a view of how different decisions have led to a particular path, and how the overall system fits together.

There are no established units of measurement for aesthetic qualities and in order to establish them, more work in brain activity scanning and mapping is needed. However, we can make a relative mapping, based on established user research methods (cf. Koenitz, Roth, Knoller, & Dubbelman, 2018c; Roth, 2016; Roth & Koenitz, 2016), where the interactor's experience is evaluated through methods such as self-observation, third-party observation, interruption, think-aloud protocols, and post-factum questionnaires. The IDN design triad (Figure 4.7) is a graphical representation of such a mapping intended to help designers identify issues with the overall design of a given work. Each side of the triangle depicts the intensity of the aesthetic qualities in three bands (perceptible, well-developed, kaleidoscopic) plotted over time combined into a single structure (see Figure 4.8). Each side is turned around so that intensity is increasing outward.

The arrows extending from the center depict an increase in the respective aesthetic quality, while the arrows along the perimeter show the direction of the

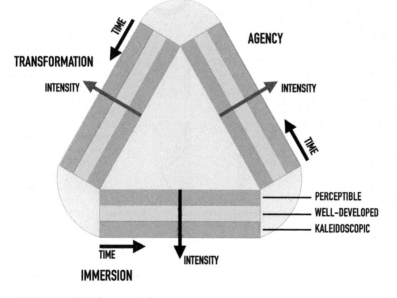

FIGURE 4.7 IDN design triad

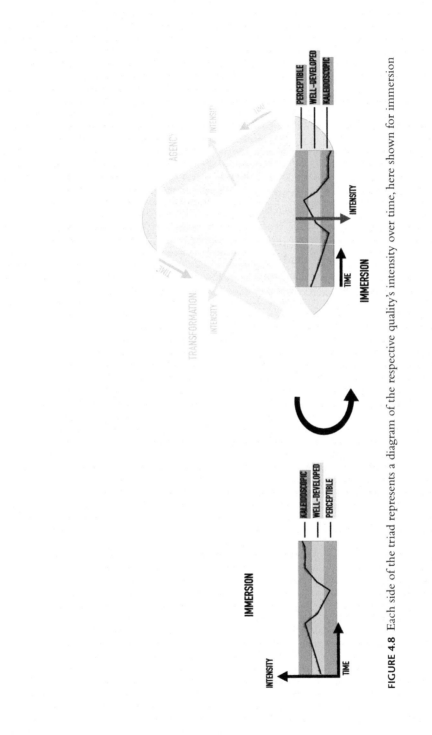

FIGURE 4.8 Each side of the triad represents a diagram of the respective quality's intensity over time, here shown for immersion

development of a quality over time. Within the triad, the aesthetic qualities in an IDN can be plotted over time, advancing in a synchronized way on all three sides. For example, a given work might start with good immersion, little agency, and very little transformation since the latter qualities need some time to develop (Figure 4.9). For a compelling experience, the aesthetic qualities of a given work need to reach the outer two bands over time. If they are mostly located within the outermost band, then the work also qualifies as kaleidoscopic. If some of the qualities are located within the inner band, then they are underdeveloped. In that regard, the border between the inner and the middle band represents the minimum threshold that the three qualities need to pass in order to be compelling. For example (Figure 4.9), an IDN work will start with strong immersion, while both agency and transformation will increase one after the other. The triad is particularly useful to identify problematic aspects in the design (e.g., the moment plotted on the right in Figure 4.9, which shows low immersion, agency and transformation and therefore needs attention, unless this is the desired experience at that moment in time).

The triad also provides a useful metaphor for the experience of the audience, in particular the simultaneity of aesthetic experiences. We can be immersed, feel agency, and experience transformation – all the same time – and this aspect becomes visible by mapping the experience of an IDN work within the space of the triad.

Aesthetic qualities as a goal of IDN design

The aesthetic qualities – immersion, agency, transformation, and the meta-quality of the kaleidoscopic – are the experiences that IDN design is aiming for. The interactor should be immersed, they should feel agency, experience a transformation of the virtual world, and of themselves and ideally also gain insights to hitherto opaque aspects or issues and experience the kaleidoscopic. These qualities first need to be understood in terms of their hierarchy and dependencies. Figure 4.6 provides a representation how the qualities build on and reinforce each other. In terms of a concrete implementation, the IDN design triad (Figure 4.7) enables the assessment of a given design by representing a space in which all qualities are positioned together and in relation to each other and where the interactor's experience can be mapped over time. The values for these relative measurements can be established via self-observation of the designer (as a first step) and by means of user research methods such as post-factum questionnaires (Roth & Koenitz, 2016), or stimulated recall. In this way, it is possible to see whether the qualities pass a minimum requirement, are balanced, and ideally support a kaleidoscopic experience.

Design principles

Design principles represent an intermediate level, more concrete than aesthetic qualities, but still on a higher level of abstraction than individual building blocks. They serve as an organizing abstraction for a number of building blocks, and are

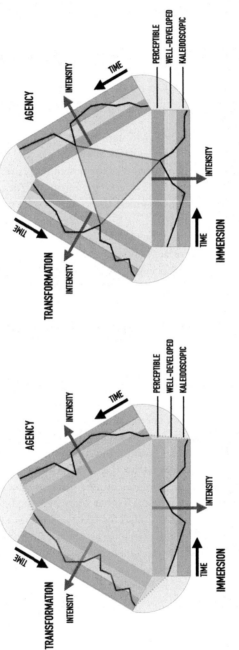

FIGURE 4.9 An entire IDN represented in the IDN design triad (shaded area on the left) and a particular moment in time (triangle on the right)

best described as an overarching goal – for example, 'scripting the interactor' as a collection for all design decisions that orient the audience in their role. The relationship between design principles and aesthetic qualities is flexible and multivariant, meaning that a design principle can serve several aesthetic qualities. For example, scripting the interactor supports *immersion*, but also facilities *agency* and enables the experience of *transformation* (Figure 4.6).

Cyberbardic or co-creative principle

The first principle is a prerequisite for IDN design. The *cyberbardic principle* marks the contrast to traditional narrative authoring. The cyberbard, a term introduced by Murray in *Hamlet on the Holodeck* (1997), is not a storyteller in the traditional sense, but a system-builder who creates a protostory – a space of narrative possibilities with opportunities to explore and experience. Instead of readers/viewers, the cyberbard has an audience of interactors whose participation and co-creation are essential elements to the work. The cyberbard says: 'I will sit back and watch with amazement what the audience will do with my creation.' On an abstract level, all IDN design follows the cyberbardic principle. Yet, on a more concrete level, building blocks that facilitate the expressive performance by interactors that enable creative solutions or full co-creation, adhere to this principle.

How to engage the interactor and keep them engaged in the "non-trivial effort" (Aarseth 1997) of interacting with IDN is the concern of the next two principles. This is a foundational aspect for IDN design, as the audience's active participation is essential. In this regard, challenge-focused video games have the advantage of clear reward structures, oriented on continued measurable improvement and winning. For IDN, creative solutions are necessary, which means there is ample room for innovation.

Curiosity principle

The *curiosity principle* puts the focus on strategies for initial engagement. The following questions concerned with narrative development create such interest:

- in a holistic sense – 'Where can I take this to?',
- in regard to particular characters – 'Who will this character turn into?' or
- in terms of particular perspectives – 'Is this the whole story?' and 'What other sides to it exist?'
- by starting from a challenge – 'how can I reach the summit?'
- by beginning with confusion – 'what happened here?', 'Is this the truth?'
- or by offering an abundance of choices – 'So many things to explore – where do I start?'

One way to create this initial curiosity is in the form of a prologue, which draws the audience in and preps them for further engagement. A particularly interesting example in this regard is the beginning of *Firewatch* (Campo Santo, 2016), which

FIGURE 4.10 *Firewatch* intro: hypertext choice above and consequence in 3D environment below

combines a hypertext fiction representing the past and a 3D environment representing the present. The interactor progresses on a hiking trail to a remote location in the latter, while learning about the reasons for being there in the former. A particular convincing moment in the prologue happens when the interactor experiences the consequences of a choice they have made in the hypertext past (how they posed for their partner) in the present time of the 3D environment in the form of a drawing found in a diary (Figure 4.10).

Continued motivation principle

The *principle of continued motivation* has to do with careful management of interactor interest by offering just enough information to interactors to keep them going without revealing so much as to make the next part of the experience seem boringly obvious (e.g., a simplistic good/evil choice that puts the interactor on a predictable trajectory without further complications). There are many examples in non-interactive forms of narrative that show how to keep this balance – for example, in the printed detective story, thriller film genre, and many episodic long-form TV series. However, the challenge for IDN is to keep the audience actively engaged – not just by reading or viewing, but by interacting.

A number of concrete building blocks motivate this kind of continuous engagement, for example, ambiguous choices, small narrative gaps that leave space for the interactor to fill, and the temporary removal of control so that the interactor values more being in control at other times. Surprises are another good strategy to keep the interactor motivated as long as they do not invalidate prior developments to such a measure that the interactor feels purposefully misled. For the same reason, confusion of the interactor should be avoided as well as design choices that make progress exceedingly hard for the interactor.

Delayed consequences are a particularly powerful building block for continued motivation. Instead of providing the immediate feedback of some video games (e.g., if you go left, you meet a deadly monster and are killed immediately, so next time you go right), delayed consequences build up over time, as a result of the interactor's continued activity. For example, in an interactive version of *Little Red Riding Hood*, the interactor starts with Red as a blank character. Depending on the interactor's choices, Red develops into a timid, aggressive, or flirtatious girl over time. The consequences of this development are revealed much later when Red is faced with an attacking wolf. The timid girl has no way to defend herself, while the aggressive girl can fight the wolf, and the flirtatious girl can talk her way out of the situation. A key aspect of this strategy is to make the interactor aware that their current choice could matter in the future, even if it may seem of minor importance in the moment. The use of the phrase "Clementine will remember that" marks a concrete implementation in *The Walking Dead* (Telltale Games, 2012), hinting at delayed consequences (Figure 4.11).[7]

Continued motivation can also be understood as oppositional to strongly guided design approaches, frequently understood as putting the interactor 'on rails.' If the motivation to continue is strong enough, rails are not needed. A good example is the blinking red light on top of the island's highest elevation in *Dear Esther* (The Chinese Room, 2008). Interactors might explore the lower parts of the island at any pace they might choose, but the motivation to reach the summit, the enticing red light (Figure 4.12), is always present and will eventually bring the interactor there.

Scripting the interactor principle

The *principle of scripting the interactor* (Murray, 1997) is a strategy which casts interactors in a specific role and provides sufficient information to perform well in it, including contextual information on how to behave. A particular compelling example of this strategy is the way Weizenbaum's *Eliza* (1966) puts the interactor

FIGURE 4.11 *The Walking Dead* notifies interactors that characters will remember actions

FIGURE 4.12 Continuous motivation of the interactor: the lure of the red blinking light in different phases of the game. Images taken from The Chinese Room's *Dear Esther* © 2008–2016 Sumo Digital Ltd. Permission granted to Routledge Books by the copyright owner

in the role of a patient consulting a therapist. *Eliza's* simulated Rogerian therapy sessions can mimic a real-life counterpart for a short while because it creates a context in which the limited abilities of the AI can be sufficient. In Rogerian therapy, the therapist restrains themselves to reacting to the patient's utterings and *Eliza's*

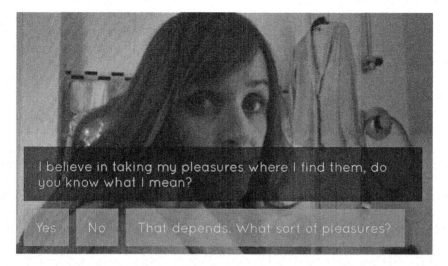

FIGURE 4.13 The initial scripted role changes over time in *Karen* by Blast Theory (2015)

replies are in line with this specific type of conversation. Scripting the interactor can therefore also be used to explain restrictions to the interactor – for example, a technical limitation could be explained as characteristic of the interactor's character or situation, or as a property of the virtual world in which an IDN takes place. A creative use of this design principle is in Blast Theory's *Karen* (Blast Theory, 2014) which scripts the interactor into the role of client seeking help from a life coach, only to subvert that role in interesting ways later on when the roles start to become reversed (Figure 4.13).

Opportunity magnitude principle

The *principle of opportunity magnitude* pertains to the amount of narrative material and opportunities for interaction. An IDN artifact should offer enough narrative material to fully cover all alternate paths offered. However, providing material for many alternate choices constitutes a challenge for tight production budgets and available time to complete a project. In general, IDN creators should therefore prioritize interactive opportunities over length of experience when they have to make a choice. Ideally, the audience should never feel that they are restricted in their choices. As I have mentioned before, this does not mean to give in to the fallacy of 'total freedom,' but instead to provide meaningful opportunities in line with character traits, situation, and context. For example, if the protagonist is on the run after having escaped a prison, they will choose actions in line with this situation and not walk back toward the prison. Similarly, the interactor can be scripted to expect a call back the next day, as for example, in *Karen* (Blast Theory, 2014), or in a few hours as in *Lifeline* (3 Minute Games, 2015) and thus will not expect any

FIGURE 4.14 *Unpacking* provides a magnitude of opportunities for interaction that match the situation of unpacking after a move. Image courtesy of Which Beam

options for interaction in the meantime. This design principle can therefore also be described as 'providing enough choices that make sense in a given situation so that the interactor does not feel restricted even if they actually are.' The craft here is in restricting the design space to the options which feel natural in a given situation, and then provide sufficient material to flesh it out. It is helpful to consider that 'fleshing out' does not mean to arrive at something where every detail is 'fully specified,' as interactors are able to fill in the blanks with their own imagination and often feel empowered when they are given the opportunity to do so. For example, in *Unpacking* (Witch Beam, 2021), the interactor encounters packed moving boxes and needs to empty them. While doing so, a narrative of the owner of these items emerges. Each chapter in this narrative-focused game is finished once all boxes have been unpacked and all items have been put in an appropriate location. This means there is a clear mapping between the situation and the magnitude of opportunities for interaction (Figure 4.14).

Believability principle

Narrative in any form is an art of reduction and emphasis. The *believability principle* in IDN design means that not every feature of the real world needs to be represented in the digital work, as the aim is not in creating a realistic depiction but a believable one. This aspect has first been described by Joseph Bates in the context of virtual characters (Bates, 1992). A good example is *Night in the Woods*[8] (Infinite Fall, 2017), where the characters are depicted as animals while they represent human issues. The

FIGURE 4.15 Protagonist Mae Borowski, depicted as a cat, is a believable character due to her struggles growing up. Image courtesy of Scott Benson

depiction of a young woman struggling with growing up as well as the backdrop of a city that has undergone economic decline are believable, even though they are not realistic (Figure 4.15). The artistic rendition enables the creators to fully focus on the important aspects of the narrative instead of putting extra effort into a realistic presentation.

Real-life equivalency principle

The *real-life equivalency principle* means to ask, whether an action required from the interactor will seem to be in line with real-life experiences for the given role and context. For example, if we want the interactor to search for truth, we can consider under what situations we would search for truth in real life. Such situations occur in a number of contexts and roles, for example, as a juror in a court case we expect to search for truth by means of evaluating conflicting testimony and pieces of evidence. Additional real-life "truth seeking" roles include detective, private investigator, and journalist. An indication that this principle has been violated is when an action 'feels wrong' as in the final scene of *A Way Out* (Hazelight Studios, 2013) where the protagonist is forced to kill their companion with no alternative offered.

It is important to be aware that this principle is context-dependent, as behaviors and experiences can differ considerably between societies and cultural settings. Creating a proper context is therefore a good method to assure *real-life equivalency*. In *Gone Home* (The Fullbright Company, 2013) the context is carefully framed for this reason. The narrative is set in a time before smartphones and even widespread use of cell phones to explain how the protagonist returning home from studying abroad cannot easily contact her family (Figure 4.16). In addition, the

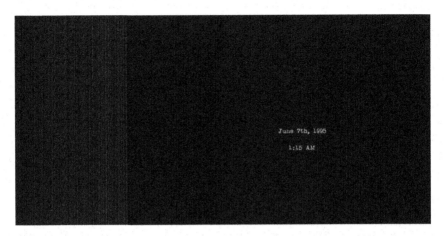

June 7th, 1995

1:15 AM

FIGURE 4.16 A call to an answering machine and a date before smartphones creates a particular context for *Gone Home*. Image courtesy of Fullbright

interactor is told that the family has moved houses, explaining how she does not know her own family's house but has to find a way in and discover the house for herself.

Relevance principle

Is an interaction necessary? If the only action available is entering a house, do we need a separate interaction concerned with opening the door to the house? And what about leaving that house? IDN design is also about stripping away unnecessary interaction. For example, entering a building might only require a single click and not a full interaction with the door handle and door. Another aspect of relevance is the problem of 'chore' – forcing the interactor to repeat tasks that do not serve the narrative progression. Once the interactor has discovered a particular path, we should not force them to repeat all the steps unless we deliberately want to make a point that requires such a potentially annoying repeat action. The issue is that discovering the path for the first time and investigating it for overlooked details a second time might be essential to the experience, but from the third time on the original purpose is lost. A solution is to use some form of interactive narrative compression, for example, by providing a map function that enables quick access to different locations, a well-established building block of IDN design that already existed in the early graphical adventure game *The Secret of Monkey Island* (Lucasfilm Games, 1990). (Figure 4.17)

Building blocks/design conventions

At the lowest and most concrete level of IDN design are building blocks or conventions that represent particular design decisions. Unlike the related effort

FIGURE 4.17 Map function in *The Secret of Monkey Island* (1990). *The Secret of Monkey Island* © & ™ Lucasfilm Ltd. All Rights Reserved

in collecting and describing design patterns (Barwood & Falstein, 2002; Björk & Holopainen, 2004), building blocks are clearly defined to be at the lowest, most granular level of the hierarchy of design elements, which means they serve the higher goals of design principles to achieve aesthetic qualities. The following form provides categories to describe IDN building blocks.

Name of the building block

Provide a name for the building block

Description

Provide a description

Image

Optional, showing example use

Primary function(s)

What is the general function of the building block?

Examples for use

Provide examples for use

Design principle(s)

Which design principle(s) are served by the building block?

Design Intention

What is the intention with the building block? What design purpose does it serve?

Production impact

What is the impact of this building block on the production of this building block? Does it require major time investments or specialized facilities?

Manifestation

e.g., Screen-based, audio, etc.

Interdependence
Does this building block depend on the presence of another type of building block?
Cultural Dependence
Is this building block dependent on a specific cultural context? For example, does it require particular cultural knowledge to be understood? Low-medium-high with optional explanation.
IDN building blocks form v. 1.0

Examples of building blocks

Scripting introductory text

An example of a building block is the use of introductory text in the beginning of an IDN to script the interactor into a certain mood and context as, for example, with the date and time in *Gone Home* (Figure 4.16). The same building block can be found in a number of additional IDN works, for example, in many narrative games by Telltale Games (*The Walking Dead* (Telltale Games, 2012), *The Wolf Among Us* (Telltale Games, 2013), and *Game of Thrones* (Telltale Games, 2014): "This game series adapts to the choices you make. The story is tailored by the way you play.") Conversely *Heavy Rain* (Quantic Dream, 2010) starts with the tagline "Make choices. Face the consequences." Similarly, *Life is Strange* (Dontnod Entertainment, 2015) scripts interactors in the following way. "Life is Strange is a story-based game that features player choice, the consequences of all your in-game actions and decisions will impact the past, present and future. Choose wisely…" *The Witcher* 3 (CD Project RED, 2015) also features this building block. "The fate of individual characters, and sometimes even entire alliances, depends on your decisions." Additionally, *The Banner Saga* (Stoic Studio, 2014) scripts the interactor to expect perspective changes. "The story in the Banner Saga changes based on the choices you make. You will occasionally switch between lead characters, witnessing the story unfold from different perspectives." *Detroit: Become Human* (Quantic Dream, 2018) sets the mood with the sentence: "Remember: this is not just a story. This is our future."

The following section describes "Scripting intro text" using the building block form.

Name of the building block

Scripting intro text
Description
A sentence or two of text in the beginning of an IDN that alerts the interactor of her ability to change to course of the narrative.
Image
Cf. Figure 4.16: A call to an answering machine and a date before smartphones creates a particular context for *Gone Home.*

Primary function(s)

Provides the context and alerts the interactor to areas of application and the extent of the interactor's agency within the narrative.

Examples for use

Heavy Rain (Quantic Dream, 2010): "Make choices. Face the consequences."

The Walking Dead (Telltale Games, 2012), *The Wolf Among Us* (Telltale Games, 2013), and *Game of Thrones* (Telltale Games, 2014): "This game series adapts to the choices you make. The story is tailored by the way you play."

Gone Home (The Fullbright Company, 2013): "June 7, 1995. 1:15 AM"

Life is Strange (Dontnod Entertainment, 2015): "Life is Strange is a story-based game that features player choice, the consequences of all your in-game actions and decisions will impact the past, presence and future. Choose wisely..."

The Witcher 3 ("The Witcher 3 [Video game]," 2015): "The fate of individual characters, and sometimes even entire alliances, depends on your decisions."

The Banner Saga (Stoic Studio, 2014) scripts the interactor to expect perspective changes: "The story in the Banner Saga changes based on the choices you make. You will occasionally switch between lead characters, witnessing the story unfold from different perspectives."

Detroit: Become Human (Quantic Dream, 2018): "Remember: this is not just a story. This is our future."

Design principle(s)

Scripting the interactor

Design Intention

Script the interactor by providing context and/or set expectations

Production impact

Minimal

Manifestation

Screen-based text

Interdependence

No

Cultural Dependence

Low

Delayed consequences hint

Delayed consequences are a means to implement the continued motivation design principle and keep interactors engaged. This means that the interactor needs to be made aware that something might happen later as the consequences of a current action – some form of a hint is necessary for this effect to happen. I already mentioned the phrase "Caroline will remember that" in *The Walking Dead* (Telltale Games, 2012), as an example for a concrete implementation. The corresponding design building block – "Delayed consequences text hint" – is described below.

Name of the building block

Delayed consequences text hint

Description

A sentence or phrase which alerts the interactor that an action will have later consequences.

Image (showing example use)

Cf. Figure 4.11: *The Walking Dead* notifies interactors that characters will remember actions.

Primary function(s)

Emphasize the importance of an action by making the interactor feel that there will be significant consequences later on.

Examples for use

The Walking Dead (Telltale Games, 2012), but also many other titles from the same studio, for example, *The Wolf Among Us* (Telltale Games, 2013) and *Game of Thrones* (Telltale Games, 2014): "X will remember that," where X is a significant character.

Design principle(s)

Continuous motivation principle

Design Intention

Convince the interactor that an action is meaningful and thus create the feeling of agency even if nothing significant happens later on.

Production impact

Minimal, easy to implement.

Manifestation

Screen-based text

Interdependence

No

Cultural Dependence

Low

Interactor character amnesia

A frequent conundrum for IDN design is the knowledge gap between the interactor and the character role they should fill. Scripting the interactor into the role as in the entry sequence in *Firewatch* (Campo Santo, 2016) is one way to address this issue. Another way is to have the interactor character experience amnesia and thus explain the absence of knowledge. The corresponding design building block "Interactor character amnesia" is described below.

Name of the building block

Interactor character amnesia
Description
The interactor character experiences amnesia
Image
N/A
Primary function(s)
The interactor, along with their character in the IDN experience, start with a clean slate in terms of knowledge about the past.
Examples for use
Harry Du Bois, the protagonist in *Disco Elysium* (ZA/UM, 2019), experiences amnesia and thus knowledge about him will be built by the interactor during the experience.
Design principle(s)
Curiosity principle (initially), continuous motivation principle (motivation to find out more about the character, real-life equivalency
Design Intention
Bring the knowledge of the interactor in line with the knowledge of the character in the IDN experience while also providing a real-life equivalent explanation for the situation. In addition, creating a malleable character that the interactor can develop in various ways.
Production impact
Minimal, easy to implement.
Manifestation
Various – can be stated in textual form in an introduction, come up in a dialogue, or as an inner monologue. Graphic representations can also be used – e.g., blurred imagery, black and white filters, etc.
Interdependence
No
Cultural Dependence
Low

Collecting IDN design building blocks

Collecting IDN design building blocks is an ongoing effort which will need a combined effort by the community (cf. Koenitz, Roth, & Dubbelman, 2018a; Koenitz, Roth, Dubbelman, & Knoller, 2018b). An initial collection and form for entry of additional building blocks can be found at the book's companion website: https://understandingIDN.com/buildingblocks/.

When is a building block a convention?

The elements on this level are all *design building blocks*. However, if particular building blocks have reached widespread understanding – they produce the same effects in audiences – we can also describe them as design conventions. The latter are generally understood to appear only after some time has passed and the understanding of a particular design building block becomes automatic and therefore conventional. However, it is difficult to assess how much time actually needs to pass for something to become conventional, as we cannot exclude the possibility of a successful design building block being adopted very rapidly and hence becoming an instant convention. There are examples in the history of art and design when a novel aspect had such an immediate and lasting impact. For example, the Dada collage, whose instant conventional nature can be seen in the fact that four different artists – Raoul Hausmann, Hannah Höch, John Heartfield, and George Grosz – claim to have invented it at the same time, but also the design of Apple's first iPhone in 2007 and its use of a multitouch screen, which profoundly influenced a whole industry immediately after its unveiling.

The IDN design process

In this section, I will describe steps for an IDN design process, with a focus on preliminary questions, the creation of paper and digital prototypes, and initial user testing. These steps are part of the IDN pre-production process, but the division is not as strict as in film production. Prototyping is likely to also happen again later in the production process, for example, to test changes or additional features. The pre-production aspect of an IDN production process will be more similar for different kinds of IDN, while later parts of the process will differ depending on the specific form (i.e., game, interactive documentary, VR/AR experience, etc.).

Overall, the IDN design process can be divided into four parts:

1. Pre-production
    1.1. Treatment
    1.2. Preliminary questions
        1.2.1. Why create an IDN and not a non-interactive form?
        1.2.2. What type of IDN?
    1.3. Paper prototype
        1.3.1. Outline and flowchart
        1.3.2. Index cards
    1.4. Digital prototype
    1.5. Prototype testing
2. Production
3. User testing and evaluation
4. Post-release maintenance

Pre-production

Treatment

The start of an IDN project is a short treatment that describes the project. One or two paragraphs are sufficient, but specific formal requirements might exist in some contexts. The treatment should describe the project, its goals, and particular aspects of the experience.

IDN design preliminary questions

The next step in the process is a catalogue of questions focused on the why and what in order to achieve clarity in relation to the purpose and scope of the experience.

Why create an IDN and not a non-interactive form?

Design is always as much about the decision what *not* to do as well as what to do. The decision for the creation of an IDN – with all its creative opportunities and practical challenges – needs to be a conscious choice. The question all creators should ask before embarking on an IDN project is: why make an IDN and not a non-interactive form? In some cases, non-interactive, traditional forms of narrative (like the novel, movie, documentary or newspaper article) might be the right format and not an IDN. There are also pragmatic considerations. In principle, the decision to create an IDN and not a non-interactive narrative form should be no different from the choice between the novel and theatrical play. Yet, what makes this choice different is the pragmatic reality that the design and production process of these earlier forms is much more established, which translates into easier access to financing, a larger body of experienced and trained professionals, and many more established workflows. I am not writing this to dissuade anyone from creating IDN works, but instead to engender a realistic understanding of the task at hand – the considerable, but also immensely rewarding creative and practical challenge involved in IDN design and production. This reality check is necessary as a basis to make the best decision possible for successfully producing IDN works under the best possible circumstances. The following eight questions are designed with this aim in mind. If the answer to any of them is "yes," then there is a good reason to create an IDN. Several positive answers are a strong indication that IDN is the way to go.

1. Do traditional forms (movie, documentary, novel, etc.) impose problematic limits for the project?
2. Should the audience have an active part in shaping the experience and/or influence the outcome?
3. Does the project require the presentation of many different perspectives or of competing narratives?
4. Should the audience be able to make decisions and see their consequences?

5. Is the ability to enable different experiences through replay crucial?
6. Does the project need to make large amounts of data accessible and comprehensible?
7. Should the audience be able to add content to the project?
8. Does the project enable a novel perspective and experience of existing material?

What type of IDN?

A next preliminary question is what type of IDN fits the project. The following categories provide a first orientation, but mixed variants and novel types are certainly possible.

Personal experience narrative

This type focuses on the personal experience of the protagonist, either in a first- or third-person perspective. Recurring themes in this type of IDN are personal trauma and ways to overcome it, often mixed with more immediate challenges and secrets to uncover. *Dear Esther* (The Chinese Room, 2008), *Gone Home* (The Fullbright Company, 2013), *Life is Strange* (Dontnod Entertainment, 2015), *Firewatch* (Campo Santo, 2016), *Night in the Woods* (Infinite Fall, 2017), *Florence* (Mountains, 2018), *Mutazione* (Die Gute Fabrik, 2019), *Neo Cab* (Chance Agency, 2019) and *Unpacking* (Witch Beam, 2021) are all examples in this regard. This type of IDN is well-suited for focused and detailed experiences that typically last several hours. A variation of this type, facilitating longer experiences, are the episodic series produced by Telltale Games, such as *The Walking Dead* (Telltale Games, 2012), *The Wolf Among Us* (Telltale Games, 2013), and *Game of Thrones* (Telltale Games, 2014).

Character development

Here, the focus is on longer-term character development, often with role-playing elements and sometimes open-world scenarios resulting in emergent narratives. Examples in this category include *The Witcher 3* (CD Project RED, 2015), *Red Dead Redemption 2* (Rockstar Studios, 2018), and *Disco Elysium* (ZA/UM, 2019). These types of IDN works require considerable resources for development and can provide expansive and long-lasting experiences, for example, in the *Mass Effect* series (Electronic Arts, 2007) where the interactor develops a character across three different titles or with the vast open world in *Red Dead Redemption 2* where the interactor can explore at will.

Parallel perspectives

In a parallel perspective IDN, two or more perspectives are presented alongside each other, often allowing the interactor to change between the conflicting narratives at pre-defined moments. A typical example is the award-winning interactive documentary *Last Hijack Interactive* (Duijn et al., 2014), in which the complex topic of piracy in Somalia is represented through parallel narrative threads of a pirate, a ship's captain, and intermediaries negotiating the release of a captured ship. This type is often used in interactive documentaries and is ideal to show alternative perspectives – another example are the two sides in the Palestinian-Israeli conflict portrait *Gaza Sderot* (Muzayyen & Elmaliah, 2009) through parallel lives in the adjacent settlements.

Stakeholder

The stakeholder perspective is similar to parallel perspectives, but applies an accumulation of perspectives from the voices of different stakeholders presented in shorter statements. An example is the interactive documentary *Fort McMoney* (Dufresne, 2013) that depicts the complex situation of the real-life Canadian town Fort McMurray, which became a boom town after massive oil sand deposits had been found there. A complex situation ensued that included environmental protection issues, massive population growth, and the resulting urban planning challenge, as well as conflicts between newcomers to the town and the existing population. *Fort McMoney* conveys these issues mostly through stakeholders, which the interactor can interview or visit and thus learn about the complex situation. This type is well suited for the exploration of a complex topic where many different opinions are involved.

Alternate or fictional realities

This type of IDN creates a fictitious setting in order to enable reflection on a complex topic without the problematic implications of recreating historical situations. A prominent example is the narrative video game *Papers, Please* (Pope, 2013) which invites reflection on complicity in an oppressive state by casting the interactor into the role of a customs officer who needs to feed their family and is faced with ever-changing regulations and difficult moral decisions leading to potentially dire consequences, for example, letting a terrorist into the country and being responsible for the ensuing murders. Similarly, *Herald* (van den Schilden, 2017) takes its audiences to an alternate 19th century reality in order to explore the effects of colonialism.

Location-based experiences

This type of IDN is particularly suited for bringing history as well as cultural and natural heritage alive (Dionisio, Nisi, Nunes, & Bala, 2016; Haahr, 2017), aided by what we might understand as the 'aura' of a historical location (Dow et al., 2005; Engberg, Bolter, Freeman, & Liestøl, 2021). Examples of location-based experiences include *Walk1916* (Cushing & Cowan, 2016), an experience focused on the women in the 1916 Easter Rising in Dublin, and *Kampen om Maden 1914–1918* (Haunted Planet Studios, 2020), an experience set in a historical fort exploring food policies in Denmark during WW1.

Sensorial immersion

Virtual reality engrosses the interactor and separates them from the outside world. This complete sensorial immersion can transport them to a different space and time. Some of the most impressive works use this opportunity to recreate claustrophobic situations, such as in a *Breathtaking Journey* (Kors, Ferri, Van der Spek, Ketel, & Schouten, 2016), which puts the interactor into the situation of a refugee being smuggled into Europe in the back of a truck with barely enough air to breath, or *6x9* (The Guardian, 2016), an experience of a solitary confinement cell in the United States. More recently, *Goliath* (ANAGRAM, 2021), depicting the inner life of a man experiencing psychosis, is testimony to the potential of IDN in a fully immersive environment. So far, however, the aspect of agency remains underdeveloped in many titles, which makes artistic sense for the kind of experiences mentioned that are designed to convey restrictions of movement and decision-making. Yet, in other titles, such as *Wolves in the Walls* (Fable Studio, 2020) or *The Book of Distance* (Okita, 2020), the interactor is placed in the mostly inconsequential role of a sidekick aiding only with narrative progression, typically asked to turn a lever, hold a torchlight, or to silently agree with the protagonist.

Sandbox

This kind of IDN work puts the interactor in the position of decision-maker in a complex situation and is modeled after real-life. Simulation games like *Sim City* (Maxis, 1989) and *The Sims* (Wright, 2000), in which the interactor controls a city's or virtual character's fates through their decisions, are examples of this category, as is *PeaceMaker* (Sweeney, Brown, & Burak, 2007), a game in which the interactor attempts to find a peaceful solution to the Arab-Israeli conflict. This type facilitates reflection on complex issues with a focus on possible solutions.

Data narrative

This type of IDN puts a narrative interface on big data and uses elements such as real-time data visualizations to make data comprehensible. An example project for this type of IDN is *The Industry* (Duijn, 2018), an award-winning work that depicts the illegal drugs industry in the Netherlands. The work contains several years' worth of data from the Dutch police on drug-related incidents and allows interactors to input their zip code and see all illegal activity in the vicinity of their homes. The work also features diagrams of relationships between "employees" of the industry as well as audio interviews with them.

Behind the scenes

This type of IDN invites reflection by offering interactors an 'inside view' of the mechanics of a complex situation. An example includes the Dutch project *The Asylum Machine* (Blankevoort & van Driel, 2015), which lets the interactor explore the inner workings of the process for asylum seekers in the Netherlands in great detail. Every step of the process is depicted and the interactor is invited to reflect on the bureaucracy and idiosyncrasies. This reflection is encouraged through built-in questions that ask the audience to propose improvements to the process.

Transmedia projects

Transmedia projects can have IDN components, for example, a narrative game as part of a larger storyworld such as the Star Wars franchise. It is important to understand that just because a project extends over several types of media, including digital representation, it does not automatically become an IDN work. The challenge for the IDN designer in such projects is not just to create a mere "interactivized" extension of non-interactive content so that the owners of the intellectual property rights can claim to have fulfilled a perceived need for an interactive version. This danger exists particularly with the 'west-coast' franchise-style of transmedia projects and to a lesser extent with the more integrated, 'east-coast' style. For the former, it is important to heed Henri Jenkin's advice (Jenkins, 2004) that interactive forms should concentrate on expressions that differ from those in other mediated representations.

What form of IDN?

The choice of form (e.g., narrative-focused video game, interactive fiction, interactive documentary, AR/VR/MR experiences, interactive film, journalistic interactive, etc.) is determined by a variety of aspects, including the personal preferences of the creators, intended target audience, pre-existing material (e.g., documentary footage). available resources, and financing opportunities.

Paper prototype

Outline and flowchart

Once the preliminary questions have been answered and an initial type of IDN has been selected, it is time for paper-based prototyping. The first step is to sketch out a general outline of events. The next step is to draw a flow diagram in order to visualize sequencing and choice points. Procedural aspects, like character traits, inventory items, societal rules, relationships with other characters, or time limits are considered and noted in the flow diagram. Alternatively, the flowchart can be created by arranging the index cards in the next step.

Index cards

The next step in this phase of the design process is the use of index cards or sticky notes. The cards can contain text as well as storyboard-style rough sketches. Each card represents a choice and is given an index number, allowing for branching and sequencing. Depending on the form of IDN chosen, the choices will be either discreet branching decisions or be determined by procedural aspects, such as state memory and rule systems or a combination of both. Many IDN use branching systems, where one choice follows the other (e.g., hypertext fiction or interactive films like *Bandersnatch* (*Bandersnatch*, 2019)). In this case, a card could contain the question 'Where do you want to go?' and then provide two choices: 'to the forest' (go to card 11) and 'go to the village' (go to card 21).

Conversely, many narrative games feature a combination of branching and procedural elements. This means the available choices are dependent on procedural elements such as a character's attributes, inventory items, prior encounters, rule systems, and so forth. Here, an index card could have a question such as 'you encounter a wolf. What do you do now?' And then offers a number of choices depending on the current status of variables: [check inventory for weapons, if found, fight wolf with *inventory item*], [check character strength, if > 90: 'fight bare handed'], [if companion present: fight wolf together], and [else 'run away']. In this case, the first three options depend on variables, which in the case of a paper prototype can be realized with the help of a special 'sequence card' that can be used to keep track of such procedural elements.

IDN works with emergent narratives are based mostly on procedural elements. This form can be prototyped using a combination of character sheets containing variables and different event cards representing situations (e.g., a problem to solve, or an encounter with other characters) happening in the course of the experience.

Prototyping with index cards can be used to define paths leading to different endings or alternatively different paths leading to the same ending. It will also help to identify imbalances in the design (e.g., more developed paths vs. less developed paths) as well as the need for additional challenges or rules in order to prevent dead ends and unintended shortcuts.

Digital prototype

The next step in the IDN design process is a digital prototype. Presentation software, such as Microsoft PowerPoint[9], Apple Keynote[10], Google Slides[11], or Open Office Impress[12] can be used in a pinch, but purpose-made rapid prototyping tools such as Adobe XD[13] or Figma[14] will offer more options. A popular tool for prototyping IDN is Twine[15]; however, the focus on hyperlinked text can be restrictive considering the multimodal nature of IDN. A digital prototype helps to check interaction and narrative pacing. At this stage, unnecessary narrative elements will be removed and missing ones added. To improve the understanding of visual aspects during this step, scans of the index cards from the prior phase or rough stand-in graphics can be used. These visualizations can be used for compiling a list of assets to be created in the production phase.

Prototype testing

Both paper and digital prototypes should be extensively play tested and adjusted when issues are encountered. Play testers should be representative of the target audience and the designer(s) themselves should playtest as well. If the intended audience is not well-defined, it is important to include both participants with prior experiences of interactive works and without them.

The following 'sanity checks' help to identify issues during this phase. They use the design principles established earlier. Ideally, an IDN work should offer a solution for each of the sanity checks.

Sanity check 1: curiosity principle
An important insight for IDN design is that interactors need to have a good reason to start engaging with an IDN artifact and put in work to progress. Consequently, there needs to be a convincing promise of narrative development, answering to any of the following perspectives:

- Holistic – Where can I take this?
- Character – Who will this character turn into?
- Perspective – Is this the whole story? What other sides to it exist?
- Challenge – Will I reach the summit?
- Resolve confusion – What happened last night?

Sanity check 2: continued motivation principle
Once an interactor has been successfully onboarded, the focus changes to keeping them interested in continuing. Here the question is to find a balance between perceived narrative progress and the lure of undiscovered aspects. Interactors will be up for a challenge as long as progress is not exceedingly hard or becomes a repetitive chore. Questions to ask are: are you making progress? Do you want to continue? Does any task feel repetitive and like a chore? Some of the following concrete strategies can be used for continued motivation:

- Ambiguous choices
- Temporary removal of control (such that control becomes more precious)
- Surprises (sparingly)
- Avoid exceedingly hard/plainly obvious paths or decisions
- Delayed consequences – make the interactor aware that their current choice could matter in the future ('Clementine will remember that.')

- Hint at future developments
- Indications of progress – make the interactor aware that previous choices led to the current situation
- Small narrative gaps for the interactor to fill in and make the experience even more their own

Sanity check 3: scripting of the interactor

Here, the question to ask is whether the interactor knows their role and understands how to act. 'Who are you?' and 'What can you do now?' are questions to ask for this sanity check.

Sanity check 4: opportunity magnitude principle

A final sanity check is with regard to the amount of narrative material and opportunities for interaction. Is there enough to do, find out, and wonder about to keep going? In order make extensive experiences possible, IDN creators should always prioritize interactive opportunities over length of experience. Questions to ask for this sanity check are:

- Do you feel restricted?
- Is there anything you wish you could do, but cannot?
- Do you feel overwhelmed?

Testing using the IDN design triad

The IDN design triad described earlier provides a way for designers to understand how well-developed the aesthetic qualities are during the experience of a particular work. As a prototype will not provide a complete experience, it is best used by the designer(s) themselves for prototype testing; by traversing the experience and providing an assessment of all three dimensions (immersion, agency, transformation) at every choice point. A seven-point scale is used to record the assessments: 0 (imperceptible), 1 (perceptible), 2 (borderline well-developed), 3 (well-developed), 4 (borderline kaleidoscopic), 5 (kaleidoscopic/highly developed), 6 (fully kaleidoscopic/ very highly developed) (Figure 4.18). This approach can be described as similar to ethnographic methods, but is openly subjective.

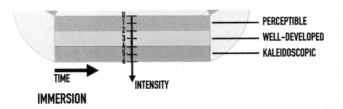

FIGURE 4.18 Assessment scale for prototype user testing, here shown only for immersion

IDN production

Once the protype phase has come to completion with the testing phase ending to the satisfaction of the creators, it is time to move to production. This phase includes the creation and integration of final assets as well as adjustments to structure and interaction. The particulars of the production phase will differ between different forms of IDN works (i.e., narrative game, interactive documentary, XR production). The specifications of many particulars of production are outside of the scope of this volume. The role of the designer during production is to make sure that the original design intention is preserved and to iteratively adjust the design if necessary (e.g., because aspects of the original design cannot be realized for technical or budgetary reasons).

IDN user testing and evaluation

User testing of an IDN at the end of the production process is necessary for a variety of reasons. First, unexpected behavior can arise from procedural combinatorics or the application of artificial intelligence (AI) (cf. Koenitz & Eladhari, 2021) and these effects might only appear late in the production process. Second, user testing will help identify areas needing attention before release. Third, by including a broad cohort of testers who are more representative of the actual audience for an IDN work, additional issues can come to light, including those of inexperienced and very well-versed members of the target group.

The IDN design triad provides a mapping for this purpose. It can also yield a more precise understanding at this point, as prototypes are limited due to a variety of factors (low fidelity of graphics impacting immersion, incomplete features and outcomes affecting perceptions of agency and transformation, etc.). User research methods supply the data for the IDN design triad's visualization using the seven-point measurement scale introduced earlier. A concrete method to use at this stage is Christian Roth's measurement toolbox (Roth, 2016), which provides a granular perspective on the IDN user experience with 14 dimensions and a way to test the qualities of immersion, agency, and transformation (cf. Roth & Koenitz, 2016 and for an application in a concrete analysis Roth, 2019). The following graphic shows how Roth's dimensions (sans the kaleidoscopic) map to the aesthetic qualities of IDN (Figure 4.19).

The result is a graphical representation that helps to visualize issues needing attention as well as particularly effective design choices (Figure 4.20).

Yet, many other methods can also be used in this capacity, for example observational methods such as think-aloud protocols (Lewis, 1982), Schønau-Fog's continuation method (Schønau-Fog, 2012), stimulated recall (Pitkänen, 2015), ethnographic methods, and focus group interviews (Eklund, 2015). In the latter cases, however, ready-made mappings to IDN design elements might not exist and thus would need to be constructed as part of the evaluation process. In order to do so, the description earlier in this part of the aesthetic qualities provides a starting

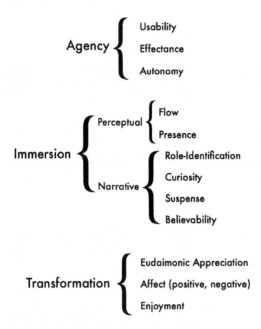

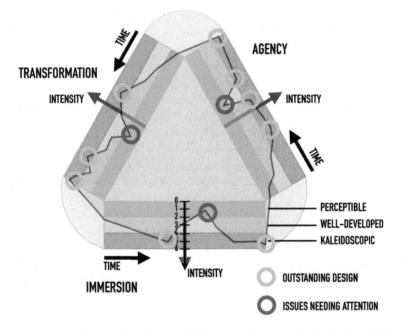

FIGURE 4.19 Roth's 14 dimension mapped to the qualities of immersion, agency, and transformation (Roth & Koenitz, 2016)

FIGURE 4.20 Outstanding design and issues needing attention in design triad mapping

point. Roth's mapping (Figure 4.19) as well as the particular type, form, and goals are important considerations in constructing hypotheses and questions for user testing and evaluation of IDN.

A particular warning applies in terms of evaluation frameworks designed for non-interactive narratives. At best, they provide limited insights when it comes to IDN. In the worst case, they will portray IDN more negatively than necessary and appropriate due to assumptions no longer correct with IDN, such as authorial control or the type of coherence only possible in the absence of agency.

Examples of good IDN design

I want to end this part with a list of works (in alphabetical order) showing best practices in IDN design in a variety of ways. I highly recommend IDN designers to familiarize themselves with these titles. In addition, these works can be used to introduce design clients to IDN. This section illustrates that the experiential aesthetic qualities of immersion, agency, and transformation as well as the kaleidoscopic can be evoked with different means using design principles in a flexible manner. For each of the titles, I point out particular interesting or well-designed features, some of which I have already mentioned in this part. This list is subjective and many other great titles exist. I would love to hear about reader's favorites – please contact me on the book's companion website (http://understandingIDN.com).

Spoiler Alert: the following descriptions contain spoilers – if you prefer to experience any of the following titles without prior knowledge, please skip the respective subsection for now and come back after the experience.

Brothers. A Tale of Two Sons *(Starbreeze Studios, 2013)*

For: the physical experience of loss.

In this narrative video game, two brothers are sent to fetch medicine for their sick father from a remote location. In order to get there, they need to traverse difficult terrain, which requires them to work together. For example, the younger brother cannot swim and can cross a river only on the back of his older sibling, while the younger brother can be lifted up onto a rock in order to help the older brother up. In order to facilitate this mutual interchange, the game features unique mechanics with which the interactor controls both brothers at the same time, using both hands on a multitouch device or game controller. Immersion thus happens via the engagement with the overall task of fetching the medicine and by learning the unusual mechanics. Agency is experienced via the accomplishment of mastering the mechanics and progressing toward the goal. In the course of the journey, the relationship between the brothers transforms as the younger brother slowly grows up. The turning point in the narrative comes when the older brother dies midway during the experience. By that time, the interactor has gotten used to the companionship of the two brothers, both emotionally and in terms of using both hands to control them. The death is therefore not only an emotional shock, but also felt physically, as one hand all of a sudden becomes useless. This creates a particular kaleidoscopic moment in the realization of loss and the inevitable ending of life. This design choice makes for a profound experience that affects many interactors deeply. What is at work here is the design principle of scripting the interactor into a particular role, which is then abruptly changed. Yet, the experience does not stop here, as the mission is not over and the ailing father still needs his remedy. The lone sibling has to return and, on that journey, there is another kaleidoscopic moment when the little brother has to overcome his fear of swimming. The way to cross is by using the dormant other hand, which becomes available again in this moment, signaling that the little brother is growing up by integrating his older sibling's abilities.

Dear Esther *(The Chinese Room, 2008)*

For: atmosphere, freedom of movement without losing the narrative thread and a surprising, but consequential ending.

A great example of a personal experience narrative (PEN) in which the bleak landscape of an abandoned island mirrors the protagonist's inner condition. Also, for the lure of the destination, which I have already mentioned as a great example of the continuous motivation principle implemented through the seemingly simple device of the blinking red light at the end of a tall antenna mast (Figure 4.12).

While moving across the island, the interactor triggers voiceovers in different locations in which an unknown man reads parts of a letter to the interactor character's deceased wife. In addition, there are also hallucinations of prior experiences. The narrative which emerges is about the terrible loss of Esther due to a car crash involving a drunk driver. As the experience progresses, the mental and physical state of the protagonist deteriorates, and the narrative vignettes become increasingly desperate and hopeless. The experience ends when the interactor's character has reached the top of the island and climbs the mast, finally jumping to end his misery. This is an ending which, while foreshadowed earlier, is still a shock when it happens, but it also a relief given the protagonist's dire situation.

Immersion is created through the beautifully rendered landscape and the compelling voiceovers of the pieces of the letters to Esther. Agency exists in the freedom to explore the barren island while transformation happens in the interactor's understanding of the protagonist's situation, supported by the changes in the immersive environment and the deteriorating mental and physical health of the protagonist. The ending is a kaleidoscopic moment, evoking reflections on loss, suffering, and death.

Detroit: Become Human *(Quantic Dream, 2018)*

For: the representation of several characters in parallel. Also great for the integrating of the options map into the experience.

This narrative video game is set in a future Detroit where androids with artificial intelligence are commonplace as servants to humans. The work explores the question of what happens when artificial beings reach consciousness and thus 'become human.' The interactor controls several characters each in a different stage of 'becoming human', providing an immersive experience. The quality of agency is experienced through choices with far-reaching consequences for every character, transforming them in the process (e.g., from a collaborator with humans to a "deviant" fighting for the android's rights). Along with transformation of characters, the narrative changes and leads to various outcomes. The high level of agency can also lead to a character's death at different points in the narrative, providing kaleidoscopic moments of reflection and lingering transformation as the game continues with the other characters. Finally, the progression maps, which are presented after each part, are a great example for kaleidoscopic design by showing how the narrative system works and how the parts fit together (Figure 4.5). In terms of design principles, this IDN work provides continued motivation through its expansive set of characters controlled by the interactor. In line with the opportunity magnitude principle, many interesting choices are available. In addition, the available choices and the overall narrative is oriented on the believability principle, fitting within the chosen fictional future setting (notwithstanding stereotypical depictions, especially of forms of abuse).

Disco Elysium *(ZA/UM, 2019)*

For: character development, compelling ethical decisions, the design of a complex society, and an interesting cast of characters make this IDN work an outstanding experience.

This role-playing video game is focused on narrative and character development and does not feature traditional combat. The interactor acts in the role of a downtrodden detective with amnesia and thus tries to find out facts about himself as much as about the dead body he is assigned to investigate. There is a rich environment and cast of characters for immersion, meaningful choices creating agency in the approach toward the investigation and the environment in general and transformation of the character through these choices. Leading to kaleidoscopic insights into the psychological composition of the protagonist and the rich world he exists in. This work implements its IDN design principles successfully, creating curiosity in the main character, environment, and character development right from the start. The work scripts the interactor into the role by having them build the character up themselves. It keeps interactors motivated through continuous developments and by always providing additional opportunities for interaction. The environment and society it depicts is believable and makes sense in terms of real-life equivalency. The relevance principle is the only one which is less well implemented since travel can be a chore and the map function for fast travel needs be obtained as an item and is limited in functionality.

Florence *(Mountains, 2018)*

For: the non-verbal, interactive representation of a relationship.

Florence manages to be testimony to the wonder of falling in love, but also to the difficulties of maintaining a relationship and the horror of a breakup without resorting to extensive textual descriptions or long cinematics. Instead, the designers of this experience have found many graphical and interactive ways to depict a relationship, for example, making room in a cupboard for the partner to move in (Figure 4.1) or speech bubbles that fit together like puzzle pieces depicting how in sync the couple is during the heyday of their relationship. The work's immersion comes from the many fitting graphical metaphors and associated interactions. Agency in this piece is local and does not affect the overall outcome. Transformation happens in the relationship going from the first meeting to the breakup and a new beginning for the protagonist. The motivation to continue comes from a combination of the age-old topic of love and the novel way of experiencing it. What makes this IDN work easy to traverse is the use of real-life equivalent depictions and known design conventions (e.g., speech bubbles) whenever possible.

Fort McMoney *(Dufresne, 2013)*

For: the representation of a complex, multidimensional situation and connection between narrative information and a live online discussion forum that rewards interactors' efforts. Unfortunately, this title is no longer directly accessible due to the obsolescence of Flash. However, a good description can be found at the MIT docubase[16]. *Fort McMoney* depicts the real-life city Fort McMurray in Canada, a small town transformed by the finding and subsequent mining of oil sand deposits. I have already described the overall premise of this work in the 'stakeholder' category of IDN types. As an IDN form, this work belongs in a category of its own as "interactive documentary + live discussion form." In the interactive documentary, the interactor can traverse the city of Fort McMurray and learn about its situation by observation and also by conversations with stakeholders representing different population groups – from newcomers intending to make money quickly to long-established inhabitants trying to preserve as much of old times as possible. In the discussion forum, interactors can ask questions pertinent to the complex situation described by aspects such as urban planning issues, negative environmental impact, and newcomers vs. old-timers. Immersion comes from the depiction of complex situations, the engagement with actual stakeholders, and the high production quality. Agency is in the choice of who to talk to, but even more so as a participant of the discussion forum. Transformation happens through the continuously growing understanding of the complex situation, and kaleidoscopic insights are enabled through the engagement with other opinions in the discussion forum.

In terms of design principles, the discussion forum acts as a particular continuous motivation to explore the world of *Fort McMoney*. The principles of real-life equivalency and believability are fulfilled in this interactive documentary.

Kentucky Route Zero *(Cardboard Computer, 2013–2020)*

For: an IDN experience inspired by magic realism using a unique visual language[17], featuring compelling characters (including a dog), magic devices and hidden worlds embedded in an imagined Kentucky.

This long-form IDN video game spans several distinct chapters and is conveyed through stylized and surreal environments as well as extensive dialogues between characters. Immersion comes from the fascination of discovering and exploring a hidden world underneath the surface, but equally from the believable and varied anti-hero characters. The journey explores the 'underworld' or the 'unseen' in more than one sense, featuring low-income workers and displaced people.

The experience of agency comes from having control over several characters as well as the many dialogue choices. Agency reaches a peak in co-creative moments that are also transformative – the interactor will compose poems and a song during the course of experience. Further transformation is of the characters through the interactor's choices. The premise of the work can be seen as kaleidoscopic as it shows a different configuration of reality and focuses on a segment of society which is often overlooked. This means kaleidoscopic experiences are frequent whenever the interactor explores passages that are in contrast to reality and invite reflection.

In terms of design principles, the work catches the audience's attention by using the very first scene to reveal an underworld beneath the surface. The work is believable within its own setting of magic realism. Continuous motivation is provided by the many fascinating and frequently surreal environments, but also the ongoing character development and the change of interactor character in different chapters. The intermissions between chapters also serve an important role in continuing motivation as they provide moments of reflection and facilitate a change in pace and focus.

Last Hijack Interactive *(Duijn et al., 2014)*

For: this is a rare example of a successful conversion of non-interactive material to IDN, by careful design and by adding graphics to the videos. This is a great example of making a complex topic (piracy in Somalia) accessible and showing 'the other side.'

In this IDN work, the interactor is in control of the perspective and can change, for example, between those of the hijacker, the captain of a hijacked ship, the captain's wife at home, and a security expert (Figure 4.21) – and thus experiences agency. In addition, infographic timelines on topics, such as money flow and the history of Somalia, provide additional information. Every change of perspective and piece of information transforms the current traversal of the work and can be seen as another turn of the metaphorical kaleidoscope providing a different perspective. Through replay, the kaleidoscopic understanding of the subject increases further. The additional graphics are believable and fit well with the documentary material. The design with multiple parallel timelines propels the narrative forward,

FIGURE 4.21 The interactive documentary *Last Hijack Interactive* features multiple parallel timelines and augments videos with graphics, as shown here. Image courtesy of Producer: Submarine Channel and Directors: Femke Wolting & Tommy Pallotta

reducing the need for continued motivation, but adhering to the opportunity magnitude principle by allowing to switch to other perspectives and additional information.

Lifeline *(3 Minute Games, 2015)*

For: the masterful use of a text-only experience by scripting the interactor as a part of a long-distance conversation with an astronaut, where text is the only viable means of communication.

The design of this text-based IDN work is an excellent example of the design principles of scripting the interactor and believability. The interactor is scripted into accepting that the long-distance conversation is only possible via text. Believability is further enhanced by the clever use of time to create well-motivated narrative gaps – the astronaut will sign off regularly in order to report back when he has reached a destination after a march of several hours, or to sleep. This design choice also serves additional purposes: it invites the interactor's fantasy to fill the time gaps and stretches out the material to create a multi-day experience. Immersion is created by orchestrating the experience as a conversation in which the interactors are frequently asked to make decisions for the astronaut, providing agency over the course of the narrative. Transformation happens to both the narrative and the interactor's perception through reports that describe what the decisions have led to.

Mutazione *(Die Gute Fabrik, 2019)*

For: the cast of compelling characters and gardening as a central metaphor of care and growth; also a thought-provoking depiction of old age.

In this IDN work, the interactor's character (15-year-old Kai) is sent by her mother to an island populated by mutants, including her grandfather Nonno who is in bad health and supposedly dying. Surrounding Nonno is a community of characters who all have their own issues, including unrequited love and deep trauma. This situation creates immersion and many opportunities for interaction with the other characters and environment. The initial encounter with Nonno is difficult but also hints at Kai's special abilities that she still needs to develop, providing continued motivation.

The experience of agency comes from multiple sources, including exploring of the island, conducting conversations with other characters and by honing Kai's skill in cultivating gardens (Figure 4.22), which requires finding seedlings, matching plants that grow together, and regular maintenance. The gardens transform the ecosystem of the island along with the grandfather's health. Additionally, the island society transforms through Kai's conversations and influence, which brings to light the many unsolved conflicts in the community. The characters, their issues, and the conversations with them are believable and enable kaleidoscopic insights into human relationships.

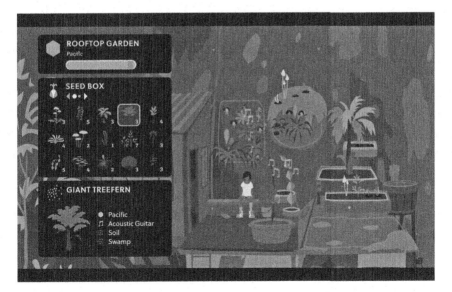

FIGURE 4.22 Gardening is an important activity in *Mutazione*. Image courtesy of Die Gute Fabrik

Papers, Please *(Pope, 2013)*

For: the depiction of the multitudes of different kinds of pressure members of societies face under totalitarian rule.

Papers, Please excels because the design avoids simplistic binary good/bad perspectives and instead manages to have the interactor experience the complexity of living under a totalitarian regime. The interactor is scripted into an assigned (not chosen) role of customs officer who has to decide who may enter their home country. There is considerable pressure in the role – including performing well under constantly changing rules in order to earn income for a family, protecting the country from terrorist attacks, accepting or resisting bribes, assisting a resistance group, and looking out for themselves and their family. New travelers are constantly arriving to cross the border and there is little time to check the documents according to ever-changing rules. Violating the rules results in monetary punishment, which affects the interactor's family. Letting the wrong people into the country can lead to deadly terrorist attacks. In a sense, there are no good options, just a struggle to make the least bad decisions and survive. In the best cases, the interactor's character will be cleared in an investigation and will survive or they will manage to emigrate to another country. In the worst cases, the experience ends with the death of all family members caused by the interactor's inability to provide for them, or by the deaths of innocent bystanders.

Save the Date *(Cornell, 2013)*

For: cross-session memory and meta-narrative.

The premise of this narrative-focused game is deceptively simple: go on a date and make sure your romantic interest survives. Yet, things are not so easy, as the date keeps dying from various causes, including an allergy-induced shock and an attack by ninjas. Every death forces a restart but the experience is unlike the endless repeating loop of the movie *Groundhog Day* (1993) – with every death, additional options for the interactor appear. For example, if the date died from an anaphylactic shock caused by inadvertently eating a dish with peanuts at a Thai restaurant, the interactor can warn her about this dish the next time around. Cross-session memory is the defining feature of this IDN title, but having this additional knowledge does comes with its own issues. If the interactor does not carefully manage their knowledge, they will appear as a stalker and the date will not even happen. Yet, even with additional knowledge, and seeming progress in leaving the dangerous city, the date keeps dying, leading to a meta-narrative dialogue in which the interactor will discuss her role as a character in a video game with the date. The work draws interactors in quickly through its familiar real-life equivalent premise of a date, and then provides an immersive narrative in which they experience agency by making decisions and transformation by gaining additional options in each playthrough. The challenge of keeping the date alive provides continuous motivation, while there is yet another option to try for a considerable time, testimony to a well-implemented opportunity magnitude principle. A kaleidoscopic level comes in through the meta-narrative conversation with the character and the resulting reflection on what has been going on, leading to a suggestion by the date how the experience can be ended without her dying. The one 'successful ending' built into the game – not going on a date right at the beginning – also provides a moment of kaleidoscopic insight as this option conflicts with the normalized perspective on 'winning' in a video game after considerable effort.

Unpacking *(Witch Beam, 2021)*

For: using very few words, this IDN title conveys a narrative of growing up.

In this calm and almost meditative experience, the interactor unpacks the narrative of a female character growing up. The design of this IDN work relies on a situation most of us are familiar with – unpacking after moving by opening moving boxes and placing items in dressers, cupboards, and on other types of furniture (Figure 4.10), thus making use of the real-life equivalence principle. Consequently, only minimal scripting of the interactor is required. Immersion is created from the combination of curiosity ('what will I find next?') and the evocative spaces which are to be filled with the unpacked belongings. Agency is experienced in the activity of finding a space to put the items. This process transforms the space and, in turn, creates a narrative of the item's owner, transforming the interactor's understanding of her. Each new level represents a new apartment and thus a different stage in her life – as a small girl, a teenager, a college student, and so forth. This situation piques our curiosity and provides continued motivation as there is always something new to unpack, which translates into ample opportunities for interaction, but also for reflection by noticing what was left behind, adding new mosaic pieces to the narrative. Restrictions in terms of placement exist only for items of particular emotional significance – in line with the relevance principle – which act as narrative vectors and help the interactor to understand the character's transforming interests and values.

Summary: IDN design

In this part of the book, I discuss IDN design, concentrating on the practical elements after the theoretical focus of part three. I started with the specific opportunities and challenges of IDN design. Two fundamental aspects are the changed role of the audience-as-interactors and creators-as-designers of dynamic systems. In terms of challenges, I discussed a range of frequent misunderstandings before concentrating on IDN design and its elements. The following sections described aesthetic categories (immersion, agency, transformation, and the kaleidoscopic), design principles, and building blocks. I introduced the IDN design triad as a way to visualize and evaluate the experience of an IDN over time and finally described an IDN design process from treatment to evaluation of the finished product. The part ended with a discussion of examples showing best practices.

Notes

1 In line with my usage of IDN design, I take IDN designer as an umbrella term to mean job titles related to the creation of IDN, including 'narrative designer', 'game writer', 'narrative system architect' etc.
2 The minor in "Interactive Narrative Design" at HKU, created with my involvement, might be the exception, but is not a full academic program.
3 Released in five chapters over the course of seven years.
4 Notwithstanding this particular title's shortcomings in terms of reinforcing patriarchic gender roles as pointed out by Mahli-Ann Butt (2018).
5 See the discussion of these terms in the introduction. As in the previous parts, I will use interactivity throughout to mean interactivity 2.
6 The most positive experience of *Train* might be for spectators observing the interactors.
7 My point here is to give an example how delayed consequences can be *communicated* to the interactor. I am aware that *The Walking Dead* works mostly with an illusion of delayed consequences.
8 I am aware that the lead designer of this work has been accused of physical and emotional abuse by Zoë Quinn, and subsequently died. Quinn was the initial target of "Gamer Gate," a vicious, misogynistic campaign against women in games. I denounce this behavior and recommend to read Zoe Quinn's account of the events (Quinn, 2017)
9 www.microsoft.com/en-us/microsoft-365/
10 www.apple.com/keynote/
11 www.google.com/slides/about/
12 www.openoffice.org/product/impress.html
13 www.adobe.com/products/xd.html
14 www.figma.com
15 https://twinery.org
16 https://docubase.mit.edu/project/fort-mcmoney/
17 I would have loved to reproduced screenshots from this work. Unfortunately, permission to use screenshots from *Kentucky Route Zero* was not given.

References

3 Minute Games. (2015). Lifeline. Big Fish Games.

Aarseth, E. J. (1997). *Cybertext*. JHU Press.

ANAGRAM. (2021). Goliath.

Ascott, R. (1964). The Construction of Change. *Cambridge Opinion*.

Aylett, R. (1999). Narrative in Virtual Environments – Towards Emergent Narrative. Presented at the Proceedings of AAAI Symposium on Narrative Intelligence.

Baker, C. (2012, July 23). Will Wright Wants to Make a Game Out of Life Itself. Retrieved June 20, 2022, from https://web.archive.org/web/20141229200435/ www.wired.com/2012/07/mf_iconswright/all

Bardzell, S., Bardzell, J., Forlizzi, J., Zimmerman, J., & Antanitis, J. (2012). Critical Design and Critical Theory: The Challenge of Designing for Provocation (pp. 288–297). Presented at the Proceedings of the Designing Interactive Systems Conference, ACM. http://doi.org/10.1145/2317956.2318001

Bateman, C. (Ed.). (2007). *Game Writing: Narrative Skills for Videogames*. Boston, MA: Charles River Media.

Bates, J. (1992). *The Nature of Characters in Interactive Worlds and the Oz Project* (No. CMU-CS-92-200). Carnegie Maellon University.

Barwood, H., & Falstein, N. (2002). The 400 Project. Retrieved June 30, 2017, from www.theinspiracy.com/the-400-project.html

Bioware. (2009). *Dragon Age: Origins.* Electronic Arts.

Björgvinsson, E., Ehn, P., & Hillgren, P. A. (2010). Participatory Design and "Democratizing Innovation" (pp. 41–50). Proceedings of the 11th Biennial Participatory Design Conference. http://doi.org/10.1145/1900441.1900448

Björk, S., & Holopainen, J. (2004). *Patterns in Game Design (Game Development Series).* Charles River Media.

Blankevoort, E., & van Driel, E. (2015). *The Asylum Machine.* The Hague. Retrieved from http://asielzoekmachine.nl

Blast Theory. (2014). Karen [Video game]. iTunes. Retrieved from https://itunes.apple.com/us/app/karen-by-blast-theory/id945629374?mt=8

Brathwaite, B. (2009). The Mechanic is the Message. Retrieved April 2, 2020, from https://mechanicmessage.wordpress.com

Butt, M.-A. (2018, March 15). "We Need to Talk About 'Florence' and Emotional Labour." Retrieved February 22, 2021, from www.theliftedbrow.com/liftedbrow/2018/3/14/we-need-to-talk-about-iflorencei-and-emotional-labour-by-mahli-ann-butt

Calleja, G. (2013). Narrative Involvement in Digital Games. Presented at the Foundations of Digital Games.

Campo Santo. (2016). Firewatch. Portland, OR: Panic.

Cardboard Computer. (2013-2020). Kentucky Route Zero. West Hollywood, CA: Annapurna Interactive.

CD Project RED. (2015). The Witcher 3. Warsaw: CD Project.

Chance Agency. (2019). Neo Cab. Fellow Traveller.

Coleridge, S. T. (1894). *Biographia Literaria; Or, Biographical Sketches of My Literary Life and Opinions; and Two Lay Sermons.* London: George Bell and Sons.

Cornell, C. (2013). Save the Date. Paper Dino Software.

Cushing, A. L., & Cowan, B. R. (2016). Walk1916: Exploring How a Mobile Walking Tour App Can Provide Value for LAMs. *Proceedings of the Association for Information Science and Technology,* 53(1), 1–5. http://doi.org/10.1002/pra2.2016.14505301147

Die Gute Fabrik. (2019). Mutazione. Steam.

Dionisio, M., Nisi, V., Nunes, N., & Bala, P. (2016). Transmedia Storytelling for Exposing Natural Capital and Promoting Ecotourism. In *Technologies for Interactive Digital Storytelling and Entertainment* (Vol. 10045, pp. 351–362). Cham: Springer International Publishing. http://doi.org/10.1007/978-3-319-48279-8_31

Dontnod Entertainment. (2015). Life is Strange. Dontnod Entertainment.

Dow, S., Lee, J., Oezbek, C., MacIntyre, B., Bolter, J. D., & Gandy, M. (2005). Exploring Spatial Narratives and Mixed Reality Experiences in Oakland Cemetery (pp. 51–60). Presented at the Proceedings of the 2005 ACM SIGCHI International Conference on Advances in Computer Entertainment Technology. http://doi.org/https://doi.org/10.1145/1178477.1178484

Dubbelman, T. (2016). Narrative Game Mechanics. In F. Nack & A. S. Gordon (Eds.), *Interactive Storytelling 9th International Conference on Interactive Digital Storytelling, ICIDS 2016* (pp. 39–50). Springer International Publishing. http://doi.org/10.1007/978-3-319-48279-8_4

Dufresne, D. (2013). Fort McMoney. National Filmboard of Canada & Arte. Retrieved from www.fortmcmoney.com

Duijn, M., Interactive Director, Wolting, F., Co-Director Documentary, & Pallotta, T., Co-Director Documentary. (2014). Last Hijack Interactive. Amsterdam: Submarine Channel.

Duijn, M., Interactive Director. (2018). The Industry. Amsterdam: Submarine Channel. Retrieved from https://theindustryinteractive.com/

Eklund, L. (2015). Focus Group Interviews as a Way to Evaluate and Understand Game Play Experiences. In P. Lankoski & S. Björk (Eds.), *Game Research Methods: An Overview*. Lulu. com.

Electronic Arts. (2007). Mass Effect [Video game]. Edmonton: Electronic Arts.

Engberg, M., Bolter, J. D., Freeman, C., & Liestøl, G. (2021). The Acropolis on the Immersive Web. *The Journal of Media Innovations*. http://doi.org/ https://doi.org/10.5617/jomi.8794

Fable Studio. (2020). Wolves In The Walls. Meta Quest.

Freebird Games. (2011). To the Moon. Freebird Games.

Fullerton, T., Swain, C., & Hoffman, S. S. (2008). *Game Design Workshop* (2nd ed.). Burlington, MA: Morgan Kaufmann.

GDC Podcast Ep. 25. (2021, October 21). Player Agency, Politics, And Narrative Design In Disco Elysium. Retrieved March 21, 2022, from https://gdconf.com/news/player-agency-politics-and-narrative-design-disco-elysium-gdc-podcast-ep-25

Haahr, M. (2017). Creating Location-Based Augmented-Reality Games for Cultural Heritage. In *Technologies for Interactive Digital Storytelling and Entertainment* (Vol. 10622, pp. 313–318). Cham: Springer International Publishing. http://doi.org/10.1007/978-3-319-70111-0_29

Harrell, D. F., & Zhu, J. (2009). Agency Play: Dimensions of Agency for Interactive Narrative Design. Presented at the AAAI Spring Symposium: Intelligent Narrative ....

Haunted Planet Studios. (2016). Walk 1916: Women of the Rising. Haunted Planet Studios.

Haunted Planet Studios. (2020). Kampen om Maden. Dublin: Haunted Planet Studios.

Hazelight Studios. (2013). A Way Out. Redwood City, CA: Electronic Arts.

Hocking, C. (2007). Ludonarrative Dissonance in Bioshock: The Problem of What Game is About. http://clicknothing.typepad.com/click_nothing/2007/10/ludonarrative-d.html

Infinite Fall. (2017). Night in the Woods. Finji.

Jenkins, H. (2004). Game Design as Narrative Architecture. In N. Wardrip-Fruin & P. Harrigan (Eds.), *First Person: New Media as Story, Performance, and Game*. Cambridge, MA: MIT Press. Retrieved from www.electronicbookreview.com/thread/firstperson/lazzi-fair

Juul, J. (2005). *Half-Real*. Cambridge, MA: MIT Press.

Koenitz, H., & Eladhari, M. P. (2021). The Paradigm of Game System Building. *Transactions of the Digital Games Research Association*, 5(3).

Koenitz, H., Roth, C., & Dubbelman, T. (2018a). Engaging the Community in Collecting Interactive Narrative Design Conventions. *ChiPlay 2018*. http://doi.org/https://doi.org/10.1145/3270316.3271533

Koenitz, H., Roth, C., Dubbelman, T., & Knoller, N. (2018b). Interactive Narrative Design beyond the Secret Art Status: A Method to Verify Design Conventions for Interactive Narrative. *Materialities of Literature*, 6(1), 107–119.

Koenitz, H., Roth, C., Knoller, N., & Dubbelman, T. (2018c). "Clementine Will Remember That" – Methods to Establish Design Conventions for Video Game Narrative. Presented at the Proceedings of the 2018 DiGRA International Conference The Game is the Message, Torino, Italy. Retrieved from www.digra.org/wp-content/uploads/digital-library/DIGRA_2018_paper_290.pdf

Kors, M. J. L., Ferri, G., Van der Spek, E. D., Ketel, C., & Schouten, B. A. M. (2016). A Breathtaking Journey. On the Design of an Empathy-Arousing Mixed-Reality Game. (2nd ed., pp. 91–104). Presented at the ChiPlay 2018, New York, NY, USA: ACM. http://doi.org/10.1145/2967934.2968110

Lewis, C. H. (1982). *Using the "Thinking Aloud" Method In Cognitive Interface Design*. IBM.

Lucasfilm Games. (1990). The Secret of Monkey Island. San Francisco, CA: Lucasfilm Games.

Mateas, M., & Stern, A. (2005). Structuring Content in the Façade Interactive Drama Architecture (pp. 93–98). Presented at the Proceedings of the First AAAI Conference on Artificial Intelligence and Interactive Digital Entertainment, Marina del Rey, California: AAAI Press.

Maxis. (1989). Sim City. Redwood Shores, CA: Maxis.

Mountains. (2018). Florence. Annapurna Interactive.

Murray, J. H. (1997). *Hamlet on the Holodeck: the Future of Narrative in Cyberspace.* New York: Free Press.

Murray, J. (2005). Did It Make You Cry? Creating Dramatic Agency in Immersive Environments. Presented at the Virtual Storytelling 2005, Strasbourg France.

Murray, J. H. (2011*). Inventing the Medium: Principles of Interaction Design as a Cultural Practice.* Cambridge, MA: MIT Press.

Murray, J. H. (2016) (2nd edition). *Hamlet on the Holodeck* (pp. 1–558). New York: The Free Press.

Murray, J. H. (2018). Research into Interactive Digital Narrative: A Kaleidoscopic View. In R. Rouse, H. Koenitz, & M. Haahr (Eds.), *Interactive Storytelling: 11th International Conference for Interactive Digital Storytelling, ICIDS 2018* (Vol. 11318, pp. 3–17). Cham: Springer Berlin Heidelberg. http://doi.org/10.1007/978-3-030-04028-4_1

Muzayyen, al, K., & Elmaliah, R. (2009). *Gaza/Sderot.* Strasbourg: Arte. Retrieved from http://gaza-sderot.arte.tv/

Naughty Dog. (2014). The Last of Us [Video game]. Tokyo: Sony Computer Entertainment.

Naughty Dog. (2016). Unchartered 4: A Thief's End. Tokyo: Sony Computer Entertainment.

Naughty Dog. (2020). The Last of Us 2. Tokyo: Sony Entertainment.

Netflix (2019). Bandersnatch.

Newheiser, M. (2009, April 7). Michael Samyn, Auriea Harvey Tale of Tales. Retrieved July 14, 2022, from www.adventureclassicgaming.com/index.php/site/interviews/473/

Night School Studio. (2016). Oxenfree. Glendale, CA: Night School Studio.

Okita, R. (2020). The Book of Distance. National Film Board of Canada.

Pearce, C. (2004). Towards a Game Theory of Game. In N. Wardrip-Fruin & P. Harrigan (Eds.), *First Person: New Media as Story, Performance, and Game.* Cambridge, MA: MIT Press. Retrieved from www.electronicbookreview.com/thread/firstperson/tamagotchi

Pitkänen, J. (2015). Studying Thoughts: Stimulated Recall as a Game Research Method. In P. Lankoski & S. Björk (Eds.), *Game Research Methods: An Overview.* Lulu.com.

Pope, L. (2013). Papers, Please. 3909 LLC.

Quantic Dream. (2010). Heavy Rain. [PlayStation 3] Sony Computer Entertainment.

Quantic Dream. (2018). Detroit: Become Human. San Mateo, CA: Sony Interactive Entertainment.

Quinn, Z. (2017). *Crash Override: How Gamergate (Nearly) Destroyed My Life, and How We Can Win the Fight Against Online Hate.* Public Affairs.

Rockstar Studios. (2018). Red Dead Redemption 2. Rockstar Games.

Roth, C. (2016). *Experiencing Interactive Storytelling.* Vrije Universiteit Amsterdam. Retrieved from https://research.vu.nl/en/publications/experiencing-interactive-storytelling

Roth, C. (2019). The "Angstfabriek" Experience: Factoring Fear into Transformative Interactive Narrative Design. In *Interactive Storytelling* (pp. 101–114). Springer, Cham. http://doi.org/10.1007/978-3-030-33894-7_11

Roth, C., & Koenitz, H. (2016). Evaluating the User Experience of Interactive Digital Narrative (pp. 31–36). Presented at the 1st International Workshop, New York, New York, USA: ACM Press. http://doi.org/10.1145/2983298.2983302

Roth, C., & Vermeulen, I. (2012). Real Story Interaction: The Role of Global Agency in Interactive Storytelling. In *Technologies for Interactive Digital Storytelling and Entertainment* (Vol. 7522, pp. 425–428). Berlin, Heidelberg: Springer Berlin Heidelberg. http://doi.org/10.1007/978-3-642-33542-6_44

Ryan, J. (2017). Grimes' Fairy Tales: A 1960s Story Generator. In N. Nunes, I. Oakley, & V. Nisi (Eds.), (Vol. 10690, pp. 89–103). Cham: Springer International Publishing. http:// doi.org/10.1007/978-3-319-71027-3_8

Schell, J. (2008). *The Art of Game Design: a Book of Lenses*. Amsterdam; Boston: Elsevier/ Morgan Kaufmann.

Schønau-Fog, H. (2012). "Sure, I Would Like to Continue." *Bulletin of Science, Technology & Society*, *32*(5), 405–412. http://doi.org/10.1177/0270467612469068

Sengers, P., Boehner, K., David, S., & Kaye, J. (2005). Reflective Design (pp. 49–58). Presented at the Proceedings of the 4th Decennial Conference on Critical Computing: Between Sense and Sensibility, ACM. http://doi.org/10.1145/1094562.1094569

Starbreeze Studios. (2013). Brothers: A Tale of Two Sons. 505 Game.

Stern, A. (2008). Embracing the Combinatorial Explosion: A Brief Prescription for Interactive Story R&D. In *Interactive Storytelling: First Joint International Conference on Interactive Digital Storytelling, ICIDS 2008 Erfurt, Germany, November 26–29, 2008, Proceedings* (Vol. 5334, pp. 1–5). Berlin, Heidelberg: Springer Science & Business Media. http://doi.org/ 10.1007/978-3-540-89454-4_1

Stoic (2014). The Banner Saga [Video game].

Sweeney, T., Brown, E., & Burak, A. (2007). PeaceMaker. ImpactGames. Retrieved from http://peacemakergame.com

Søndergaard, M. (2020). Troubling Design: A Design Program for Designing with Women's Health. *ACM Transactions on Computer-Human Interaction*, *27*. http://doi.org/10.1145/ 3397199

Tale of Tales. (2009). The Path. Ghent: Tale of Tales.

Telltale Games. (2012). The Walking Dead [Video game]. San Rafael: Telltale Games.

Telltale Games. (2013). The Wolf Among Us. Telltale Games.

Telltale Games. (2014). Game of Thrones. San Rafael: Telltale.

Tale of Tales. (2015). Sunset. Ghent: Tale of Tales.

The Chinese Room. (2008). Dear Esther. Portsmouth, UK: The Chinese Room.

The Fullbright Company. (2013). Gone Home. Portland, OR: The Fullbright Company.

The Guardian. (2016). 6x9. London, UK: The Guardian. Retrieved from www.theguard ian.com/world/ng-interactive/2016/apr/27/6x9-a-virtual-experience-of-solitary-conf inement

van den Schilden, R. (2017). Herald: An Interactive Period Drama. Utrecht: Wispfire.

Walk, W. (2018, May 14). The Myth of the Monomyth. Retrieved May 31, 2018, from www. gamasutra.com/blogs/WolfgangWalk/20180514/318014/The_Myth_of_the_Monom yth.php

Weizenbaum, J. (1966). Eliza — a Computer Program for the Study of Natural Language Communication Between Man and Machine. *Communications of the ACM*, *9*(1), 36–45. http://doi.org/10.1145/365153.365168

Witch Beam. (2021). Unpacking. Humble Games.

Wright, W. (2000). The Sims [Video game]. Redwood City, CA: Electronic Arts.

ZA/UM (2019). Disco Elysium. Tallinn: ZA/UM.

Part 5

WHERE TO GO FROM HERE

Advocacy, opportunities, and future work

Interactive digital narrative is a reality – an ever-growing practice in its many variants and a creative frontier for continuous innovation and invention. In this final part of the book, I will consider the current status of IDN, as well as opportunities for the application of IDN and strategies on how to increase the knowledge about, and use of, IDN. As I will show, opportunities exist aplenty, yet knowledge about IDN is limited, especially outside specialist circles of academics and creatives concerned with the topic. This realization does not diminish the considerable achievements in the form of the many excellent works that have been created. Yet, when we step back and look at the wider contemporary media landscape, we see that long-established forms of narrative – books, films, documentaries and TV series – are highly successful with audiences and critics. Examples in this regard include the *Harry Potter* books and subsequent movies, the *Lord of the Rings* cinematic adaptations, and the *Star Wars* movies reboot. Another recent development is the success of *Game of Thornes* and other episodic TV dramas that turned Netflix, Amazon, Hulu and others into streaming TV powerhouses. The wide availability of broadband internet has changed the media landscape. On-demand availability, 'binge watching,' streaming of video gameplay on platforms like Twitch, and the success of low-budget productions on YouTube are the current reality. However, these examples show how the digital medium is used as a delivery mechanism only and not for its specific expressive qualities. It is traditional non-interactive narrative – in updated formats – that still clearly dominates the public (and much of the professional) perception of narrative. And for good reason: everybody knows what a movie or novel is, while someone working on interactive digital narrative has much explaining to do. What is it? Where can I see one? So, it is a video game? Some are? Is it like the 'Choose your own Adventure' books? More than that? But it has a story arc? Maybe? How can you call it narrative then? Questions like these point to one uncomfortable truth about IDN – there is still much to do to

DOI: 10.4324/9781003106425-5

achieve wider recognition of interactive forms of narration. The emphasis on a cross-cutting specific perspective in this volume is therefore also a strategic choice, grounded in the observation that more than half a century of fragmented practice and piecemeal efforts have not created the recognition and general awareness IDN deserves.

This condition is particularly unfortunate as there is a clear need for IDN right now, especially when it comes to non-fiction content, for which the above assessment in regard to the continued dominance of non-interactive forms is equally valid. Humanity is in a situation of multiple simultaneous crises described by issues such as global warming, migration, aging populations, pandemics, and global injustice that challenge established systems of government, education, economic production, and trade. These problems are a concern on the global scale as well as for individuals. What all of these issues share is a high level of complexity – for example, there is no simple solution when we want to transform existing economies for sustainability while keeping jobs and preventing price hikes for energy and goods. The model of old-style democratic discourse, carried out by educated readers of static newspaper articles, as described by Habermas (Habermas, Lennox & Lennox, 1974), is no longer adequate in our contemporary condition of complex, intertwined issues and challenges. Indeed, the very idea of a static representation might be incompatible on a fundamental level with the dynamic nature of the complex problems we are facing. And yet, a considerable number of people seemingly want to hear – and believe in – simple, fixed narratives. Recent years have provided ample opportunities to observe where simplistic non-interactive narrative can lead to, for example, Brexit, the storming of the US Capitol, the scapegoating of migrants for job losses in changing economic conditions, the partisan framing of the non-partisan health issue of mask-wearing during the COVID-19 pandemic, as well as numerous conspiracy theories around vaccination. These issues constitute evidence why new narratives are necessary to represent our complex reality, organize the discourse, and help us find solutions to monumental challenges. What we need are representations of complexity that foster systemic thinking by facilitating an understanding of multiplicity, interconnectedness, and long-term effects. IDN works have the potential to fulfill this role and provide an essential toolset for understanding and communication in the 21st century, but further efforts are required to realize this potential. This entails finding strategies for raising the general awareness of IDN and foster IDN literacy. At the same time, it also means to identify opportunities for the application of IDN and realize them.

Raising awareness of IDN

A better understanding of IDN as a theoretical concept and as a specific design discipline – the topics of earlier parts of this volume – are important steps toward realizing the full potential of this expression. However, the question remains how to raise the awareness about IDN and its potential in general audiences, media producers, educators, and policy makers? There is no simple quick-fix to solve this problem, and the best possible answer in this situation is a multi-pronged strategy consisting of advocacy, education, research, and creative production, while combining short-term and longer-term goals.

In order to develop such a strategy, it is necessary to reconsider the challenges IDN faces, but this time decidedly with a perspective concerning society at large. I have already talked about the dominance of non-interactive forms of narrative and how these forms become normalized in public discourse and the school system. There are a number of ways in which this hegemony can be addressed in the short term – through *IDN advocacy* by means of public speaking, awards, workshops, and high-profile critique in established media outlets pointing out the advantages of IDN in representing many contemporary issues. More widespread *IDN literacy* is a long-term effect which will come from the integration of IDN works in pre-school and school curricula, but also from teaching about IDN as an expressive form. Getting IDN into school curricula is an important step forward for IDN also for another reason. Something that is on a publicly sanctioned K-12 (kindergarten to 12th grade) curriculum is considered by many members of the public to be of cultural value and something which is not, much less so. As soon as IDN is taught alongside literature in schools, these disadvantages in terms of public recognition and perception will disappear. A university-level discipline of *IDN study and design* will assure continued research and professional training. In addition, it is necessary to consider production and financing aspects, the ethics of IDN, and the important issue of archiving. In the following sections, I will first describe aspects of short-term *IDN advocacy* before turning to the longer-term strategy of *IDN literacy*.

IDN advocacy

The distinction between short- and long-term strategies is based on how quickly they can affect any kind of change. Overall, all strategies aimed at raising awareness of IDN need to be seen a bundle of measures that work in concert. For example, the integration of IDN in general childhood education (kindergarten and school) might be the single-most important step forward for IDN, both in terms of literacy and recognition. This strategy is a future-oriented one by being focused on generations who are growing up. Yet, to make this change happen in the education system, it is necessary to focus on whoever makes decisions now. The people that need to be convinced in order to put IDN on school curricula are adults – elected officials, education administrators, school board members and so forth. In this context, a focus on education has to go hand-in-hand with advocacy, as many people in key positions first have to be convinced to give IDN a chance, before any actual education regarding IDN can happen. Many decision-makers might have never heard of interactive digital narrative, although there is a good chance they are aware of concerns regarding the effects of violent video games on children and teenagers. These concerns, even though shown to be mostly without merit after a significant research effort (for a good overview see the meta-studies by Ferguson et al. (2015; 2020)), still reappear in public debates. In principle, disentangling interactive digital narratives from violent video games could therefore provide a rhetorical strategy for IDN to overcome these concerns. However, such a broad categorial distinction is problematic from an academic perspective and would also run into practical issues, as the understanding of what constitutes violence can vary between different cultural contexts and is also dependent on the respective framing of a given work.

Instead, a more promising and sustainable approach is in emphasizing the specific advantages of IDN at any given opportunity. The following aspects can be used as a backbone for IDN advocacy, for example, in public talks, critique, and workshops.

- *Multiperspectivity*: the ability of a IDN to represent different perspectives in one artifact and allow interactors to switch between them on their own account.
- *Participation*: the empowerment of the audience as interactors who make their own decisions.
- *Decisions and consequences:* interactors can make decisions and see the consequences of their actions in IDN. These consequences can be the aggregated result of several decisions.
- *Replay:* in an IDN, interactors can restart the experience, revisit prior decisions, and try out different paths.
- *Integration of user-generated content:* in principle, interactors can make permanent changes to IDN by using built-in means (i.e., building a house in a sandbox-type IDN) or by uploading their own material (i.e., pictures from their smart phone).
- *Up-to-date*: content can be kept current through the integration of live data.

Besides these foundational advantages, compelling works are essential for IDN advocacy. The creative opportunity of IDN needs to be communicated to creative professionals at every opportune moment in order for more seminal works to be conceived. At the same time, existing award-winning IDN and positive use cases backed by academic studies are crucial elements for a positive message about IDN.

Award-winning IDN works

Awards are public recognitions of excellent work and thus provide ammunition for advocacy. There are many excellent IDN works and I have mentioned some throughout this volume. To enter as many IDN works as possible in general-purpose competitions is a concrete strategy by itself to improve the knowledge about IDN and raise its profile. Another part of this strategy is to mention these awards as often as possible.

The most valuable awards for IDN advocacy are general purpose ones. What I mean here are awards not specifically tailored toward IDN, but for general media products. A "best narrative design" distinction from a games competition will be less valuable for IDN advocacy than the international Emmy award and the Prix d'Europe for *The Last Highjack Interactive* (Duijn, Wolting, & Pallotta, 2014) or the Peabody award for *The Industry* (Duijn, 2018). At the same time, more than 60 game of the year awards for *The Walking Dead* (Telltale Games, 2012) also show the considerable success of narrative-focused approaches in the space of games. Another great example in this category is the Hugo award in 2021 for the video game *Hades* (Kasavin, 2020), as the first IDN work to win the main prize for science fiction that was previously reserved for literary works.

Positive use cases

Positive use cases – especially if they are evaluated and supported by user studies – provide potent arguments for IDN. A current example is the use of IDN in citizenship education by Erik Blokland et al. (Blokland et al., 2021) in collaboration with Dutch NGO Critical Mass. An earlier example is the study by Scott Parrot et al. (Parrott, Carpentier, & Northup, 2017) which provides evidence for the positive effects of an IDN to combat prejudices against migrants. More work on studies investigating the prosocial effects of IDN are needed, using established academic evaluation frameworks. In particular, Christian Roth's specific framework (Roth, 2016; Roth, Klimmt, Vermeulen, & Vorderer, 2011; Roth, Vorderer, Klimmt, & Vermeulen, 2010) can be used in this capacity. However, it is important to carefully consider which effects and parameters to evaluate, as the warnings by Steinemann et al. (Steinemann et al., 2017) and van t Riet et al., (van t Riet, Meeuwes, van der Voorden, & Jansz, 2018) suggest, both of which show that interactivity alone does not automatically improve the experience or create the desired results. For any concrete IDN work, the design choices need to be carefully considered in line with the desired outcome, In particular, empathy is a problematic category when it comes to intended prosocial effects, as for example Rebecca Rouse has pointed out (2021), extending earlier work by Bloom (2018).

Public speaking about IDN

Giving talks and lectures is another important aspect of IDN advocacy. The more we talk about IDN, the better. In this capacity, all of the aforementioned aspects – specific advantages, award-winning IDN, positive use cases – can be used. A basic rundown of a talk about IDN could be the following:

1. Prepare the audience for novel narrative forms. As non-interactive, Eurocentric forms of narration are perceived as a norm in many settings, it is a good practice to expand their horizon first.
2. Present IDN as a novel narrative form with specific characteristics.
3. Explain basic concepts of IDN such as *interactivity 1+2*, dynamic artifact, and the changed roles of audiences and creators (cf. the introduction of this book).
4. Provide an area of potential application (e.g., representing a complex topics).

5. Show examples from the chosen domain of application.
6. Mention the capacity for further developments and additional types of IDN.
7. Wrap up.

The first point might simultaneously be the most important and least obvious one. Yet, from what I have learned in my own practice, this first step is essential as without it, the message will most likely not get across since narrative fundamentalism is widespread. Concretely, this can be done, for example, by talking about Kishōtenketsu and various other non-western narrative forms from different geographic regions of the world (cf. Koenitz, Di Pastena, Jansen, de Lint, & Moss, 2018). Once the point has been made that narrative can be quite different from the Eurocentric way in which the subject is still presented in many school systems, it is much easier for the audience to accept that narrative can also be interactive. Another important aspect is to explain the basic concepts that distinguish IDN from non-interactive forms of narration, such as *interactivity 2* of planning and execution and the dynamic artifact.

High-profile IDN critique

High-profile critique of IDN in established media outlets is both a short-term and a long-term strategy. Short-term in the sense that it can be established quickly and long-term in the sense that it is an important element of IDN literacy by a wider audience. What I mean here are reflections and recommendations by critics in mainstream media outlets including broadsheet newspapers such as the New York Times, radio programs such as NPR, and cultural magazines in TV networks such as the BBC, ARTE, ARD, SVT, and so forth. Such high-profile critique is well-established for books, TV, and films, but IDN is lacking these kinds of cultural ambassadors who tell their audiences with authority what to read and see and thus command a considerable influence on overall taste and buying/viewing decisions. The question is therefore how to change this situation and usher in an era of IDN critics, a new type of Roger Ebert[1] for IDN.

Ebert is an interesting case for other reasons, too – his opinionated article pronouncing that "video games can never be art," (Ebert, 2010) alerts us to another obstacle IDN is facing in terms of full recognition. What Ebert cannot see when he relegates video games to a place far below art is that he compares an interactive form to non-interactive forms. Ebert is trained in seeing and interpreting, but not in interacting. He writes about what he sees, and not about what he has done or could have done. What Ebert does not understand is that interactive forms such as video games and IDN are in principle incomplete and only become realized once we start engaging with them. Many things in an interactive work might seem mundane for an observer, but they surely feel different once we are part of the action – doing something yourself is very different from observing the same action by someone else. Ebert looks from the outside as a highly skilled observer, but he fails to understand how it is to be 'inside the action.' Indeed, it feels as if mainstream critique has yet to understand Roy Ascott's fundamental insight regarding cyber-netic art from 1968:

> I make structures in which the relationships of parts are not fixed and may be changed by the intervention of a spectator. [...] the participant becomes responsible for the extension of the artwork's meaning.
>
> *Ascott, 1968*

IDN works are not art in the same way Ebert is considering art – fixed works in which every stroke of paint, every word, and every part of the visible frame has been placed with the outmost care in the knowledge they will never change afterwards. In contrast, the outmost care of the interactive artist creating a dynamic system is placed elsewhere – on making space for participation and creating opportun-ities for interaction. Of this artistic endeavor, mainstream critique knows too little and this is what we have to change. A possible strategy in this regard could be to gather critiques written by authors knowledgeable in IDN and targeted toward the general populace with the aim to become a syndicated service. This IDN critics service could be a shared project, for example, between a journalism school and ARDIN (Association for Research in Digital Interactive Narratives). In the longer run, becoming an IDN critic should be seen as a possible career path for students studying IDN research and practice, but also for graduates of related fields such as games studies and media studies.

IDN literacy

Widespread IDN literacy is a longer-term goal. So far, most people learn about IDN only by accident during their teenage years, most likely in the form of narrative-focused video games. And most have never discussed interactive digital narrative in school or learned to use any related critical vocabulary as they do for print literature (at least on a basic level). Also, most have never tried to make IDN works themselves. It is these elements that literacy of mediated forms comes from – own experience through exposure, guided reflection of existing works using critical vocabulary, and guided creation and reflection of own works. Much of kindergarten all the way to the final grade of high school is filled with these types of activities for print literature and almost no time is spent on interactive forms of narration, digital or otherwise. In other words, what is missing is IDN literacy.

This kind of literacy is long overdue – in the 21st century, we are surrounded by the digital medium, from the news app on our smart phone to engrossing XR (extended reality) experiences. Yet, technical and expressive potential by itself, without critical reflection, rarely results in usage scenarios that best fit societal needs. It is important to make informed and ethical decisions on how to best use digital technology in general and specially IDN in a given scenario. IDN literacy is a crucial prerequisite for making such decisions. Yet, the corresponding training to achieve digital literacy – let alone IDN literacy – is either entirely missing in many school systems or is considerably lacking in depth and quality. As a result, many digital natives are 'digital naïves' when it comes to a deeper understanding of the inner workings of the digital medium. To change this situation, we need to do for the digital medium and IDN what we have done for the Guttenberg age of the written word – make basic training in comprehension, evaluation, and creation a foundational aspect of our school education.

More concretely, to achieve IDN literacy means to cover all three aspects of experience, reflection, and creation. It is not enough to use IDN as part of a topical curriculum (e.g., an IDN about competing perspectives in a history class). Critical reflection about IDN as a mediated expression – for example, in contrast with a description in a history book, is equally important. Experiments in building interactive digital narratives is the final crucial element. All three aspects can happen on several levels – for example, in kindergarten we can start by experiencing simple branching stories for exposure. Then we can continue with choice-based scenarios aimed at reflection that show how different outcomes are possible. The following questions can serve as the starting points for such activities. If Amali does not agree with Omar, what will they do and what can be the consequences? If Jaimee sees Tom and Ali fight, what can happen when he interferes? If an adult tells you to do something, do you always have to do it? What is a reasonable punishment if a child does something wrong? Creation at this level can happen, for example, as a playful experience for younger kids exploring a purpose-made authoring tool with pre-made components, such as the Mobeybou system that teaches children about different cultures (Sylla & Gil, 2020).

In elementary school through to high school, students can be exposed to ever-more complex IDN representations – for example, using *The Sims* (Wright, 2000) to explore the economic pressures of grown-up lives or *Papers, Please* (Pope, 2013) to consider the pressures of living under a totalitarian regime. Further examples can be found in the next section under the heading "Educating with IDN."

For critical reflection, IDN experiences can be compared to print literature and movies about the same topics. On the side of creation, the pedagogical experiments Collette Daiute and Robert Duncan have developed in exploring the communication between IDN designers and audiences in a classroom setting (Daiute & Duncan, 2017; Daiute, Duncan, & Marchenko, 2018; Daiute, Cox, & Murray, 2021) are promising examples on a more advanced level. And while Daiute et al.'s work presently targets university undergrads, they could certainly be adapted for high-school level and introduced in a school curriculum.

It is crucial for the further development of our democracies that we achieve IDN literacy, for several reasons. I will point out three of the most important ones. First, to raise awareness of systemic thinking and multiplicity of perspectives as a basic skill applicable to many situations. Future generations should no longer accept simple truths, but should ask 'what are the other perspectives? What are the alternatives to this plan? What could go wrong if we do this?' Second, to provide a concrete approach for communicating and discussing multiple perspectives and complex topics in the form of IDN that can be applied on a basic level by many, thanks to mandatory training in kindergarten and school. Third, to assure that the expressive potential of IDN is widely understood and critically reflected, as otherwise there is the danger that the potential of IDN will become an instrument of the digital elite, and, in some cases, even used for negative societal goals.

In this context, it is instructive to consider the 'early days of the internet' – the period of the nascent world wide web in the early 1990s before the ban on commercial use was lifted in 1995 – which is sometimes described as a vibrant, helpful, and commercial-free space for communication and expression. Commercialization was, however, not the only reason for the end of this participatory era. The early world wide web thrived, in part, because a much larger percentage of its users were also tech-savvy creators (most were computer scientists) who understood the intricacies of the underlying technology and how to use it for their own expressive purposes. When the general use of the WWW started to rise ca. 1993/1994, the balance between creators and users changed drastically toward the latter, and the consumer-oriented turn followed as a consequence. This is a development we need to counter with IDN education.

Opportunities for the application of IDN

There are opportunities for IDN whenever its specific advantages can be applied. This is true in particular when more than one perspective on a given topic exists or several outcomes are possible. Many aspects of our current reality – including topics such as global warming, personal psychological issues, or political decision-making – fit this description. At the same time, IDN can be a tool to make oppressed voices heard without simply replacing the oppressive narratives and thus endangering the important long-term memory of injustice. Used in this way, IDN can be a tool for decolonialization and for restoring justice. IDN can be applied in both fictional and non-fictional treatments of such topics. Conversely, given the specific characteristics of IDN, there is an opportunity to create *speculative IDN* – works which allow interactors to explore plausible future scenarios, connecting non-fiction and fictional aspects, while taking cues from speculative design (Auger, 2013; Dunne & Raby, 2013) and design fictions (Tanenbaum, Tanenbaum, & Wakkary, 2012).

I have already mentioned education as an important application area for IDN. The following sections describe example applications of IDN in areas of education, personal health, representations of history and cultural heritage, as well as democratic participation. These descriptions are meant to illustrate the potential for IDN and are by no means exhaustive – many more applications are possible.

Educating with IDN

Education is an important area of application for IDN, as narrative is a crucial part of education on all levels – from simple kindergarten-level tales to non-fiction narratives in subjects such as geography, politics, and history in high school, college, and post-graduate education. Wherever static narratives have been used so far, IDN provides opportunities for a more inclusive and complete representations in the same subjects.

For historical topics, Eurocentric, patriarchic accounts can be contrasted with perspectives that so far have been oppressed or neglected – for example, the narrative of the white colonial "settlement" of the US vs. native American perspectives or the crusades described also from a Muslim point of view. Another specific opportunity is in presenting changing perspectives on historical events which were suppressed and misrepresented such as the 'Tulsa race massacre,' a 1921 incident in which a white mob destroyed an affluent black neighborhood in Tulsa, Oklahoma. Similarly, the many contributions of women to society could be contrasted to the long-dominant male-only view and used to expose the oppression of women in the public sphere. Conversely, the same overarching mechanic of multiperspectivity can also be used to depict topics where several valid perspectives exist – for example, different interpretations of the same phenomena by different parties in democratic countries, or various hypotheses about the use of prehistoric structures such as the Hypogenum in Malta. A concrete example for the use of IDN in education is in citizenship training (Blokland et al., 2021), mentioned in the section of positive use cases. Other examples of IDN that can used in educational settings include the already mentioned internationally award-winning interactive documentaries *Last Highjack Interactive* (Duijn et al., 2014) and *The Industry* (Duijn, 2018).

The ability of IDN to present its audiences with decisions and show their consequences – even aggregated and delayed ones – has an application in teaching politics, in particular when it comes to political decision-making, where the challenge often lies in understanding the complex immediate and long-term effects of policies. Good examples of IDN which enable such experiences come from NewsGamer (www.newsgamer.com), a media company specialized in producing political decision-making IDN. *Collapsus,* focused on future energy security from Amsterdam-based media production house Submarine Channel (https://submarinechannel.com/game/collapsus-energy-risk-conspiracy/), is another example in this regard, as is *Survive the Century* (https://survivethecent ury.net) which is concerned with climate change and was produced by a team from the US and South Africa. Further examples are included in the collection of Journalism Games (http://journalismgames.com) compiled by Lindsay Grace and his team at the University of Miami. Additionally, IDN with a more satirical perspective on current issues can help spur discussions in the classroom – for example, the works by Paolo Pedercini under his Molleindustria label (www. molleindustria.org/) or by Ian Bogost (http://bogost.com/games/). Narrative-focused games can provide the experience of specific political/historical situations, for example, being part of a resistance group in WW2 as in *Attentat 1942* (Charles Games, 2017) or a judge during the French revolution as in *We, The Revolution* (Polyslash, 2019).

This list only scratches the surface, as many more suitable examples of IDN for use in educational settings exist. This application of IDN can be classified as education *using* IDN in contrast to teaching *about* IDN. As I mentioned before, to achieve IDN literacy, it is important to also put reflection about IDN as a mediated expression as well as IDN creation on the curriculum.

IDN for mental health

Narrative therapy is an established approach in the treatment of psychological issues (Angus & Hardtke, 1994; C. Brown & Augusta-Scott, 2006; Madigan, 2019) and interactive board games have been used with therapeutic purpose (Eladhari, 2018). IDN for therapeutic use is therefore a logical next step. While earlier approaches where more experimental (e.g., Davis, Nehaniv, & Powell, 2004), current approaches aim at producing solutions ready for actual deployment, supported by recent news that a first video game (EndeavorRX) has been approved by the FDA agency in the US as a prescription medication to treat ADHD in children 8–12[2]. A concrete example in this regard is *betwixt*[3] (Harmon, Gale, & Dermendzhiyska, 2021), a mobile app focused on improving mental well-being and resilience, which is set to undergo clinical trials for therapeutic use in the near future. Another promising approach is a tool in development by University of Florida PhD student Sarah Brown that enables college students to reflect on and change their own narratives in order to improve their mental health (S.A. Brown & Chu, 2021). Yet another application of IDN for therapeutic use is described by Nele Kadastik and Luis Emilo Bruni in the context of hearing-related pediatric care (Kadastik & Bruni, 2021). Here, interactive narratives are used to facilitate and stimulate conversations between children, parents, and healthcare providers and to make sure that the children's voice is heard.

Representation of history and cultural heritage

While I mentioned that several potential and realized examples of IDN for the representation of history have already made an impact in the context of education, it is worth pointing out additional applications as an indication of further opportunities. A particularly relevant aspect is the preservation of testimonies from eyewitnesses. Traum et al., describe such as system where recorded testimony by a holocaust survivor is transformed into an interactive narrative system that applies artificial intelligence to enable spoken conversations with the digitally preserved survivor about his experiences (Traum et al., 2015). Similar systems could be deployed to preserve important public testimony of other historical events, as well as interactive memories of loved ones in a more private capacity. A conversation with grandparents and other deceased relatives could be realized in this way and might provide a level of solace for the survivors.

Augmented reality provides another opportunity for the representation of history and cultural heritage through IDN, strengthened through the element of embodiment, the awareness of the aura of the actual place. Some examples include applications that connect cultural heritage with tourism (Dionisio, Nisi, Nunes, & Bala, 2016; Haahr, 2017; Nisi, Wood, Davenport, & Oakley, 2004; Silva, Prandi, Ferreira, Nisi, & Nunes, 2019). I have also previously described some of these opportunities, which include the recreation of historical events in the location where they happened, but also the use of alternate history IDN as a defamiliarization device to provoke reflection (Koenitz, 2021).

Narrative interfaces to (big) data

'Big data' has been a buzzword for years, describing large amounts of collected data which can be used to learn trends, patterns, identify connections, and predict future developments, mostly concerned with human behavior – for example, as consumers or as citizens acting in a pandemic. The interpretation of big data is normally left to specialists, as data is difficult to interpret. To make big data accessible and comprehensible, IDN can be applied as a narrative interface. An example for this type of IDN is Mirka Duijn's previously mentioned work *The Industry*, which depicts the illegal drugs industry in the Netherlands. The work allows interactors to input their zip code and see all illegal drug-related activity in the vicinity of their homes using data from the Dutch police. This kind of an interactive narrative layer could be applied to facilitate insights about many other types of big data, including population movements, building activities, flow of goods, and voting behavior.

Democratic participation

The effects of political decisions could be explored by means of IDN in order to facilitate informed discourse and to create opportunities for democratic engagement – for example when it comes to the effects of new national legislation or of local infrastructure measures, such as the construction of a wind energy park, a new city quarter or the planning of an urban renewal project. IDN can combine information with participation, for example, by assuring that decisions can be made only after information about a certain subject has been taken in and understood by the audience. The level of understanding can be improved and verified through integrated measures such as discussion forums, AI-powered chat bots or multiple-choice tests. An early example in this regard is the interactive documentary *Fort McMoney* (Dufresne, 2013). Depicting the real-life city of Fort McMurray in Alberta, Canada, this IDN provides information about a small settlement-turned-boomtown by the discovery of oil sand deposits and the manifold challenges it faces as a consequence, from environmental concerns to urban planning issues and societal conflicts. What makes *Fort McMoney* an exemplar work is the integration of a discussion forum, in which participants can discuss the depicted topics. A particular built-in mechanic rewards interactors who have explored more of the piece and thus taken in more information with higher ranking and more influence in the discussion forum. These kinds of measures aimed at enhanced reflection and participation should be developed further to make IDN an even better tool for facilitating public discourse and democratic participation. One concrete strategy in this regard would be to empower citizens to contribute additional perspectives and make these visible to affected communities and decision-makers. Such purposed-made IDN for democratic participation would improve upon established forms of democratic participation, such as national polls, or 'town halls', in regard to informed decision-making by citizens.

Areas for future work: an infrastructure for IDN

For IDN to thrive, a functioning infrastructure needs to be in place. These include an academic discipline to assure continued research as well as training of future professionals, as I have described in the first section of this volume. ARDIN, the Association for Research in Digital Interactive Narratives plays a significant role in this regard. To complement the academic efforts on the professional side, there should be an industry association to represent creatives and producers. The following areas for future work are opportunities for collaboration between industry and academia.

Production and financing models for IDN

On the production side, traditional narrative forms are supported by well-established workflows and financing models. These two areas need further attention from the research and professional communities with the aim to establish IDN production workflows and create financing models for the creation of IDN. The former means to consider whether and how IDN production could, for example, be integrated into the existing workflow of a newspaper, or a TV news report. The latter is concerned with possible financing models for IDN productions. So far IDN – with the exception of commercially successful narrative-focused games – have not found a sustainable financing model. Interactive documentaries rely on one-off financing support from public and private organizations and therefore pronouncements of a golden age (Ursu et al., 2009) have been premature. Similarly, journalistic interactives and newsgames (Bogost, Ferrari, & Schweizer, 2010) are seen by many news organizations as expensive experiments which have not yielded the expected financial return by themselves and are now mostly used to drive traffic to a newspaper website which means IDN serve as 'bait' to lure subscribers. Both of these examples are testimony to the 'add-on conundrum' – IDN are neither documentaries plus interactivity nor are they newspaper articles plus interactivity. This is the reason why the Netflix entry into IDN production with *Bandersnatch* is significant, because a streaming service is not wedded to traditional rules of marketing and production. The fundamental shift that needs to happen is for producers and audiences to see IDN as a product category of its own and not as a by-product of traditional book, newspaper, film, or TV production. IDN production currently means to create more content than necessary for more traditional forms in order to support opportunities for interaction via alternative paths and multiple perspectives.

Consequently, the respective financing models for non-interactive media do not fit and new ones – for example, as a public service paid by taxes or supporters – need to be established.

IDN ethics

Similar to the products of the printed press, IDN are powerful and can be created with both good and bad intentions. Ethical considerations are therefore a requirement if we want to assure that IDN are used as a recognized force for good. In traditional journalism, the importance of ethics is widely recognized and many journalistic organizations have created extensive ethical codes of conduct for their staff, for example. the New York Times' publication *Ethical Journalism – A Handbook of Values and Practices for the News and Editorial Departments* (The New York Times, n.d.).

At the same time, ethics guidelines cannot be defined as absolutes, as they need to be adjusted to changing technology and societal circumstances. For this reason, the Center for Journalism Ethics at the University of Wisconsin-Madison, defines ethics as a "dynamic, evolving activity of applying, balancing, and modifying principles in light of new facts, new technology, new social attitudes and changing economic and political conditions" (Ward & et al, n.d.).

A crucial prerequisite to all discussions of ethical concerns in IDN design and usage is an understanding of its specific qualities in contrast to fixed narratives forms. IDN as a dynamic, systemic form is principally open to unexpected consequences and unintended uses and this central aspect shifts a part of the ethical responsibility to the audience as interactors. Certainly, the IDN designer should take all reasonable measures to keep the interactor focused on the intended understanding and prevent experiences that contradict the intended aim. However, we need to be aware that unintended transgressions can happen, just as Will Wright, the lead designer of *The Sims* never intended for his creation to be used for trapping virtual characters in a cellar to torture them in. Consequently, there is a limit to the designer's responsibility with highly procedural systems.

With this central aspect as the basis, we can then start to discuss ethical implications of IDN production and use. Together with Agnes Bakk and Jonathan Barbara I have developed a first framework for IDN ethics in the form of the following catalogue of guidelines for creators. They are intended as a starting point for further discussion in the IDN community. In the future, IDN creators might need to develop and adopt guidelines similar in scope to the New York Times' ethics handbook (The New York Times, n.d.).

1. Creators and interactors share the responsibility for the effects of IDN systems, provided that:

    a. Creators are responsible for all effects of an IDN system that can reasonably be foreseen.

    b. Creators are responsible for taking reasonable measures to inform interactors of their role within an IDN experience as well as what opportunities they have for interaction.

    c. Interactors are responsible for their actions when experiencing IDN, as long as they understand their role and how they can interact.

2. Creators should not deceive interactors about their role or opportunities for interaction; exceptions require specific artistic or educational purposes.
3. Creators need to inform interactors about potential health risks.
4. Accessibility needs to be assured in IDN design. IDN need to accommodate interactors with different levels of abilities and prior experience with interactive artifacts.
5. Creators need to be transparent about their perspective-taking.
6. IDN representations need to responsibly represent intersectional regimes of oppression, including those based on gender and fixed gender roles, sexual orientation, origin, appearance, and neurodiversity. IDN provide specific opportunities to expose such regimes of oppression.
7. IDN featuring multiple perspectives should assure that each perspective is treated fairly and responsibly.
8. A given work should take advantage of the multifaceted representation capabilities of IDN and should portrait complex situations accordingly. Undue simplification and trivialization of complex situations should be avoided.
9. Creators need to take the context a work is placed in, the surrounding society and available infrastructure, into consideration.
10. Creators should accommodate interactors with different levels of prior knowledge in regard to the topic of the respective work.
11. An IDN needs to scaffold the experience for the interactor so that they arrive at an understanding of how their actions have resulted in the outcome.
12. When content is represented which includes 'insider knowledge' (e.g., 'cultural insiders', specific societal groups or national customs), IDN creators need to provide a reasonable amount of context so that the content can also be understood as best as possible by an audience of 'outsiders' (Koenitz, Barbara, & Bakk, 2023).

Modular and extensible authoring tools

Currently, there are no standard authoring tools for IDN. This situation compares unfavorably to game design, where Unity[4] and Unreal Engine[5] have achieved a combined status of market saturation and it makes sense to use either of these platforms in training for designers in the workplace. The free tool Twine[6] is widely used but its focus on text-based hyperfiction (images and sounds can be added, but the default is text only) is a considerable restriction in terms of harnessing the expressive multimodal potential of narrative in the interactive digital medium. This problem still persists, even if Twine is used only as a prototyping tool, as this phase of the design already structures the designers' creative process and has considerable influence on the final work. There are good reasons that the pre-production materials for film include both the textual script and a visual storyboard.

Ironically, as Yotam Shibolet has detailed (Shibolet et al. 2018), there are more than 300 IDN authoring tools, yet many of these are dormant and closed to further development and collaboration, a wasteful practice Mirjam Eladhari and myself have described as "Sisyphean tool production" (Koenitz & Eladhari, 2019).

The way forward here is threefold – low threshold of entry, author-orientation, and modularity. The first aspect means to make a tool easily accessible also for beginners and affordable, either as a free open-source software a la Twine or with free versions for students and smaller projects in the way Unity and Unreal Engine provide them. Author-orientation requires increased research in understanding what IDN creators want and need in order to build better tools. A starting point in this regard are the criteria for comparing authoring tools Shibolet has introduced (Shibolet et al. 2018) and further developed in the INDCOR project (Shibolet & Lombardo, 2022). Modularity means to create a technical standard which would allow different developers to contribute their best efforts to an overarching goal, without being weighted down by the need to produce a complete application. A proposal for an open exchange format exists (Nicolas Szilas et al. 2011), yet there are several ways in which a more open, modular approach can be achieved – for example, through published APIs or plugin-interfaces in the way offered by Unity or Unreal Engine.

The burning issue of archiving

When it comes to the preservation of digital artifacts, including IDN, the house is burning. We need a much stronger emphasis on digital archiving to prevent the loss of significant parts of our digital cultural heritage. In a recent conversation, Stella Wisdom, Digital Curator at the British Library put it succinctly:

> Nothing much is going to happen with the remnants of Roman walls near my home in St Albans, if we do not do anything with them in the next ten years, but digital artifacts will disappear and become inaccessible at an accelerating pace if we do not act immediately
>
> *personal conversation 2021*

Every day, digital works are lost forever because they exist on CD ROMs or floppy disks that become unreadable or on hard drives that no longer function. If you are old enough to remember 'burning' your own CD ROMs, you might remember the good feeling of just having made a long-lasting backup. However, it turns out that the longevity of these and other storage media have been considerably overstated. And even if the data is preserved, the question remains whether the works are still playable. Flash, Director, early versions of Java, Classic MacOS programs or those for DOS and early Windows versions can only be made to run with significant effort. I know this from my own experience, as one of my projects as a PhD student at Georgia Tech was to make an older work of Janet Murray's lab playable again, which required emulator software and while I got it running, the only longer-term solution seemed to be a screen recording, as there was no guarantee that the emulator would still be supported within several years in the future. When it comes to archiving, analog works are superior so far. The color in some older photographs might have faded, but we can still look at them. Paintings and printed books– properly stored – can last for centuries. We take for granted that we can read *Don Quixote* half a millennium later, but if we do not act now and make digital preservation a priority, many of the works of our digital age will not survive even a full decade. To improve the longevity of IDN, we need to make sustainability an important consideration of IDN creation. At the same time, we need to support digital archiving in libraries and other institutions. Proper documentation, open-source code, and modularity whenever possible are steps in the right direction. By modularity I mean the separation of document format, authoring tool, and playback engine which allows the development of new engines to read and play back old formats – for example, the SCUMM engine of the early LucasArt adventure games.

The procedures laid out by the Electronic Literature Organization in their report on "Born-Again Bits – A Framework for Migrating Electronic Literature" (Liu et al., 2005) provide a description of possible measures and different approaches, and are concretely implemented at the electronic literature archives[7]. These efforts can serve as an example for preservation of digital artifacts, but more work on this subject is urgently needed.

IDN – a narrative expression for the 21st century

Narrative is a fundamental aspect of human existence. We communicate, remember, and form our identities (Ricoeur, 1991) through narratives. Conversely, concrete manifestations – narrative forms – are in constant flux, driven by technical and artistic innovation. Interactive digital narrative is a big evolutionary step which brings fundamental changes to creators, artifacts, and audiences, while requiring corresponding development in both theory and practice. Accordingly, this volume offers specific approaches in the form of the SPP model and in the framework for IDN design. Both are meant as a foundation for an academic field and for a specific design discipline by offering a clear departure from legacy perspectives. They are extending earlier work by pioneering scholars such as Brenda Laurel, Pamela Jennings, Celia Pearce and Janet Murray and would not have been possible without the many contributions of the research and design communities over the past 30 years. "It is a waste of energy and resources to make applications that merely imitate media that exist in other forms, such as print, television, and film." (Jennings, 1996) – Pamela Jennings' fundamental insight is still as true today as it was years ago. IDN works are not merely extending earlier forms – they are a narrative expression with multiple manifestations, from journalistic interactives to narrative-focused games to interactive documentaries and many more. IDN are simultaneously post-literature, post-film, post-documentary and post-newspaper.

The fallacy of narrative fundamentalism, of denying the possibility for new narrative expressions like IDN, is in taking a specific point in the evolution of narrative forms as the definitive end point of an ongoing development. Yet, this imagined point in time does not exist. Rather, new developments happen while existing forms transform, but rarely disappear. IDN does not mean the end of earlier narrative forms. We will read books and see movies for a very long time in the future. They are fantastic expressive forms with considerable potential for innovation. However, IDN extends the range of narrative expression in ways not available to these earlier forms with dynamic, multilinear, multi-perspective, generative, participatory, and co-creative works.

Beyond the expressive and conceptual aspects, IDN is significant as a societal, prosocial project. We live in a time where a newspaper-based society of educated citizens is no longer a reliable foundation for democracy. Instead, we face a reality where considerable parts of democratic societies do not read newspapers on a regular basis. Conversely, a plethora of unvetted, but easily available information surrounds us. This information entropy provides a fertile ground for extremist messages in social media, online videos, and websites which sometimes feature production quality that rival established news outlets. In addition, the complexity of many current issues exceeds the capacity for representative of fixed, immutable narrative forms. IDN have clear advantages in this case, in terms of breadth of presented material as well as depth of audience engagement and opportunities for learning. Consequently, IDN can be applied for understanding complex issues and to support and enhance democratic participation. On a more personal level, IDN can help us with decision-making by letting us try out different paths and experience different outcomes. Furthermore, IDN can increase well-being by applying and further developing insights from narrative therapy.

We are only just starting to use the expressive potential of IDN and therefore the example application areas mentioned above are just the beginning. It is this potential that makes IDN a narrative expression for the 21st century and I cannot wait to see what else will be created by applying it.

Notes

1 Roger Ebert (1942–2013) was an influential US film critic for the Chicago Sun-Times. He won a Pulitzer Prize for his critiques and is commemorated with a star on the Hollywood walk of fame.
2 www.cnbc.com/2020/06/17/video-endeavorrx-is-first-video-game-approved-by-fda-to-treat-adhd.html
3 www.betwixt.life
4 https://unity.com/de
5 www.unrealengine.com/
6 https://twinery.orgf
7 https://eliterature.org/electronic-literature-archives/

References

Angus, L., & Hardtke, K. (1994). Narrative Processes in Psychotherapy. *Canadian Psychology/ Psychologie Canadienne, 35*(2), 190.

Ascott, R. (1968). The Cybernetic Stance: My Process and Purpose. *Leonardo, 1*(2), 105. http://doi.org/10.2307/1571947

Auger, J. (2013). Speculative Design: Crafting the Speculation. *Digital Creativity, 24*(1), 11–35. http://doi.org/10.1080/14626268.2013.767276

Blokland, E., Cullinan, C., Mulder, D., Overman, W., Visscher, M., Zaidi, A., et al. (2021). Exploring Multiple Perspectives in Citizenship Education with a Serious Game. In A. Mitchell & M. Vosmeer (Eds.), *Interactive Storytelling 14th International Conference on Interactive Digital Storytelling, ICIDS 2021* (pp. 1–14). Springer International Publishing. http://doi.org/10.1007/978-3-030-92300-6_28

Bloom, P. (2018). *Against Empathy.* Vintage.

Bogost, I., Ferrari, S., & Schweizer, B. (2010). Newsgames. *Journalism at Play.*

Brown, C., & Augusta-Scott, T. (2006). *Narrative Therapy.* SAGE.

Brown, S. A., & Chu, S. L. (2021). "You Write Your Own Story": Design Implications for an Interactive Narrative Authoring Tool to Support Reflection for Mental Health in College Students. In A. Mitchell & M. Vosmeer (Eds.), *Interactive Storytelling 14th International Conference on Interactive Digital Storytelling, ICIDS 2021* (pp. 312–321). Cham: Springer. http://doi.org/10.1007/978-3-030-92300-6_30

Charles Games. (2017). Attentat 1942. Prague: Charles Games.

Daiute, C., & Duncan, R. O. (2017). Interactive Imagining in Interactive Digital Narrative. In N. Nunes, I. Oakley, & V. Nisi (Eds.), (pp. 282–285). Cham: Springer International Publishing.

Daiute, C., Cox, D., & Murray, J. T. (2021). Imagining the Other for Interactive Digital Narrative Design Learning in Real Time in Sherlock. In *Vosmeer* (pp. 1–8). Springer International Publishing. http://doi.org/10.1007/978-3-030-92300-6_46

Daiute, C., Duncan, R. O., & Marchenko, F. (2018). Meta-communication Between Designers and Players of Interactive Digital Narratives. In R. Rouse, H. Koenitz, & M. Haahr (Eds.), *Interactive Storytelling: 11th International Conference for Interactive Digital Storytelling, ICIDS 2018.* Cham: Springer Berlin Heidelberg.

Davis, M., Nehaniv, C., & Powell, S. (2004). Towards an Interactive System Facilitating Therapeutic Narrative Elicitation in Autism, 1–11.

Dionisio, M., Nisi, V., Nunes, N., & Bala, P. (2016). Transmedia Storytelling for Exposing Natural Capital and Promoting Ecotourism. In *Technologies for Interactive Digital Storytelling and Entertainment* (Vol. 10045, pp. 351–362). Cham: Springer International Publishing. http://doi.org/10.1007/978-3-319-48279-8_31

Dufresne, D. (2013). Fort McMoney. National Filmboard of Canada & Arte. Retrieved from www.fortmcmoney.com

Duijn, M. (2018). The Industry. Amsterdam: Submarine Channel. Retrieved from https://theindustryinteractive.com/

Duijn, M., Wolting, F., Co-Director Documentary, & Pallotta, T., Co-Director Documentary. (2014). Last Hijack Interactive. Amsterdam: Submarine Channel.

Dunne, A., & Raby, F. (2013). *Speculative Everything: Design, Fiction, and Social Dreaming.* Cambridge, MA: The MIT Press.

Ebert, R. (2010, April 16). Video Games can Never be Art. Retrieved November 19, 2021, from www.rogerebert.com/roger-ebert/video-games-can-never-be-art

Eladhari, M. P. (2018). Bleed in, Bleed Out – A Design Case in Board Game Therapy. Presented at the DiGRA '18 - Proceedings of the 2018 DiGRA International Conference: The Game is the Message, Turin, Italy.

Ferguson, C. J. (2015). Do Angry Birds Make for Angry Children? A Meta-Analysis of Video Game Influences on Children's and Adolescents' Aggression, Mental Health, Prosocial

Behavior, and Academic Performance. *Perspectives on Psychological Science, 10*(5), 646–666. http://doi.org/10.1177/1745691615592234

Ferguson, C. J., Copenhaver, A., & Markey, P. (2020). Reexamining the Findings of the American Psychological Association's 2015 Task Force on Violent Media: A Meta-Analysis. *Perspectives on Psychological Science, 15*(6), 1423–1443. http://doi.org/10.1177/1745691620927666

Haahr, M. (2017). Creating Location-Based Augmented-Reality Games for Cultural Heritage. In *Technologies for Interactive Digital Storytelling and Entertainment* (Vol. 10622, pp. 313–318). Cham: Springer International Publishing. http://doi.org/10.1007/978-3-319-70111-0_29

Habermas, J., Lennox, S., & Lennox, F. (1974). The Public Sphere: An Encyclopedia Article (1964). *New German Critique*, (3), 49–55.

Harmon, S., Gale, H., & Dermendzhiyska, E. (2021). The Magic of the In-Between: Mental Resilience Through Interactive Narrative. In A. Mitchell & M. Vosmeer (Eds.), *Interactive Storytelling 14th International Conference on Interactive Digital Storytelling, ICIDS 2021* (pp. 1–5). Cham: Springer. http://doi.org/10.1007/978-3-030-92300-6_35

Jennings, P. (1996). Narrative Structures for New Media. *Leonardo, 29*(5), 345–350.

Kadastik, N., & Bruni, L. E. (2021). A Transmedia Narrative Framework for Pediatric Hearing Counseling. In A. Mitchell & M. Vosmeer (Eds.), *Interactive Storytelling 14th International Conference on Interactive Digital Storytelling, ICIDS 2021* (pp. 1–14). Cham: Springer. http://doi.org/10.1007/978-3-030-92300-6_36

Kasavin, G. (2020). Hades. San Francisco: Supergiant Games.

Koenitz, H. (2021). Reflecting in Space on Time: Augmented Reality Interactive Digital Narratives to Explore Complex Histories. In J. A. Fisher (Ed.), *Augmented and Mixed Reality for Communities* (pp. 183–198). Boca Raton, FL: CRC Press.

Koenitz, H., Barbara, J., & Bakk, A. (2023). An Ethics Framework for Interactive Digital Narrative Authoring. In C. Hargood, D. Millard, A. Mitchell, & U. Spierling (Eds.), *The Authoring Problem*. Cham: Springer.

Koenitz, H., Di Pastena, A., Jansen, D., de Lint, B., & Moss, A. (2018). The Myth of "Universal" Narrative Models. In R. Rouse, H. Koenitz, & M. Haahr (Eds.), *Interactive Storytelling: 11th International Conference for Interactive Digital Storytelling, ICIDS 2018* (pp. 107–120). Cham: The 3rd International Conference for Interactive Digital Storytelling. Retrieved from https://doi.org/10.1007/978-3-030-04028-4_8

Koenitz, H., & Eladhari, M. P. (2019). Challenges of IDN Research and Teaching. In R. E. Cardona-Rivera, A. Sullivan, & R. M. Young (Eds.), *Interactive Storytelling: 12th International Conference on Interactive Digital Storytelling, ICIDS 2019* (Vol. 11869, pp. 26–39). Cham: Springer Nature. http://doi.org/10.1007/978-3-030-33894-7_4

Liu, A., Durand, D., Montfort, N., Proffitt, M., Quin, L. R. E., Réty, J.-H., & Wardrip-Fruin, N. (2005). Born Again Bits. Retrieved December 5, 2021, from www.eliterature.org/pad/bab.html

Madigan, S. (2019). Narrative Therapy. Theories of Psychotherapy Seri.

Nisi, V., Wood, A., Davenport, G., & Oakley, I. (2004). Hopstory: An Interactive, Location-Based Narrative Distributed in Space and Time. In *Technologies for Interactive Digital Storytelling and Entertainment* (Vol. 3105, pp. 132–141). Berlin, Heidelberg: Springer Berlin Heidelberg. http://doi.org/10.1007/978-3-540-27797-2_18

Parrott, S., Carpentier, F. R. D., & Northup, C. T. (2017). A Test of Interactive Narrative as a Tool Against Prejudice. *Howard Journal of Communications, 0*(0), 1–16. http://doi.org/10.1080/10646175.2017.1300965

Polyslash. (2019). We. The Revolution. Warsaw: Klabater.

Pope, L. (2013). Papers, Please. 3909 LLC.

Ricoeur, P. (1991). Narrative Identity. *Philosophy Today*, *35*(1), 73–81. http://doi.org/10.5840/philtoday199135136

Roth, C. (2016). *Experiencing Interactive Storytelling.* Vrije Universiteit Amsterdam. Retrieved from https://research.vu.nl/en/publications/experiencing-interactive-storytelling

Roth, C., Klimmt, C., Vermeulen, I. E., & Vorderer, P. (2011). The Experience of Interactive Storytelling: Comparing "Fahrenheit" with 'Façade'. In *Technologies for Interactive Digital Storytelling and Entertainment* (Vol. 6972, pp. 13–21). Berlin, Heidelberg: Springer Berlin Heidelberg. http://doi.org/10.1007/978-3-642-24500-8_2

Roth, C., Vorderer, P., Klimmt, C., & Vermeulen, I. (2010). Measuring the User Experience in Narrative-Rich Games: Towards a Concept-Based Assessment for Interactive Stories. *Entertainment Interfaces*.

Rouse, R. (2021). Against the Instrumentalization of Empathy: Immersive Technologies and Social Change. In J. A. Fisher (Ed.), *Augmented and Mixed Reality for Communities* (pp. 3–19). Boca Raton, FL.

Shibolet, Y., & Lombardo, V. (2022). Resources for Comparative Analysis of IDN Authoring Tools. In M. Vosmeer & L. Holloway-Attaway (Eds.), *Interactive Storytelling* (pp. 513–528). Springer International Publishing.

Silva, C., Prandi, C., Ferreira, M., Nisi, V., & Nunes, N. J. (2019). Towards Locative Systems for, and by, Children - A Cognitive Map Study of Children's Perceptions and Design Suggestions. *Creativity & Cognition*.

Steinemann, S. T., Iten, G. H., Opwis, K., Forde, S. F., Frasseck, L., & Mekler, E. D. (2017). Interactive Narratives Affecting Social Change. *Journal of Media Psychology*, *29*(1), 54–66. http://doi.org/10.1027/1864-1105/a000211

Sylla, C., & Gil, M. (2020). The Procedural Nature of Interactive Digital Narratives and Early Literacy. In *Interactive Storytelling* (pp. 258–270). Springer, Cham. http://doi.org/10.1007/978-3-030-62516-0_23

Tanenbaum, T., Tanenbaum, K., & Wakkary, R. (2012). Design Fictions (pp. 347–350). Presented at the Proceedings of the Sixth International Conference on Tangible, Embedded and Embodied Interaction, ACM. http://doi.org/10.1145/2148131.2148214

Telltale Games. (2012). The Walking Dead [Video game]. San Rafael: Telltale Games.

The New York Times. (n.d.). Ethical Journalism. Retrieved May 12, 2022, from www.nytimes.com/editorial-standards/ethical-journalism.html

Traum, D., Jones, A., Hays, K., Maio, H., Alexander, O., Artstein, R., et al. (2015). New Dimensions in Testimony: Digitally Preserving a Holocaust Survivor's Interactive Storytelling. In H. Schoenau-Fog, L. E. Bruni, S. Louchart, & S. Baceviciute (Eds.), *Interactive Storytelling 8th International Conference on Interactive Digital Storytelling, ICIDS 2015* (pp. 269–281). Cham: Springer. http://doi.org/https://doi.org/10.1007/978-3-319-27036-4_26

Ursu, M. F., Zsombori, V., Wyver, J., Conrad, L., Kegel, I., & Williams, D. (2009). Interactive Documentaries: A Golden Age. *Computers in Entertainment (CIE)*, 7(3).

van t Riet, J., Meeuwes, A. C., van der Voorden, L., & Jansz, J. (2018). Investigating the Effects of a Persuasive Digital Game on Immersion, Identification, and Willingness to Help. *Basic and Applied Social Psychology*, *40*(4), 180–194.

Ward, S. J. A., & et al. (n.d.). Ethics in a Nutshell. Retrieved November 21, 2021, from https://ethics.journalism.wisc.edu/resources/ethics-in-a-nutshell/

INDEX